CONFLICT AND DECISION MAKING
An Introduction to Political Science

Conflict
&
Decision Making
An
Introduction to
Political Science

by Paul H. Conn
Michigan State University

Harper & Row, Publishers
New York Evanston San Francisco London

CONFLICT & DECISION MAKING: An Introduction to Political Science

Copyright © 1971 by Paul H. Conn.

Standard Book Number: 06-041352-2

LIBRARY OF CONGRESS CATALOG CARD NUMBER: 70-151333

FOR MY PARENTS

Contents

Preface

Presumably, everyone knows what politics is. Everyone deduces that political science is the study of politics. Why, therefore, have political scientists had so much trouble defining their basic concerns both to themselves and to students? Why do students enroll in political science courses with expectations concerning subject matter and mode of presentation that often are at great odds with the manner in which the course is presented?

In order to understand what an introduction to political science should do, it is necessary to define goals. The questions a student should ask of a political science book or course include: How does this information enable me to think more intelligently about current problems? What kind of order does it give to my understanding of the confusing, contradictory, and often frustrating day-to-day political events?

The political scientist therefore is trying to develop a theory or set of theories that helps to interpret existing phenomena. This does not mean that he sees things the average person cannot see. Rather, he is trained to look for specific things that allow him to make sense out of events.

Perhaps the political scientist's role can be understood best through analogy. At the most elementary level we all note differences among various substances, yet we do not know what it is that makes these substances different from each other. Nor, if we are given a variety of different substances, can we be sure which among them are most similar. The chemist does not see anything that we cannot see: but he has been trained to look for specific things. Although the chemist may have sophisticated instruments to help guide his inquiry, we can still

assert that without training the general public could not use such instruments to interpret phenomena in a coherent way. The chemist
knows that differences in substances can be explained by variations in
atomic structure and the way in which the component molecules hold
together to form a structure. Consequently, he knows what to look for.
He can discuss similarities or differences between substances in terms
of molecular structure, and he can make certain predictions about the
behavior of substances under different conditions. The chemist has
learned to look for certain clues, to seek the most important factors so
that he can analyze his problem and suggest some explanations or
predictions. Indeed, this is the purpose of training in any kind of aca-
demic discipline: to show students what to look for so that they can sort
through events and know how to distinguish important from unimportant
aspects.

If a discipline trains people in analysis, then an introduction to a discipline should acquaint people with the particular theory or theories
that prevail in the discipline and the modes of analysis that are peculiar
to it. This statement applies to political science as well as to chemistry
or physics. Although the level of sophistication in political science is not
equivalent to that of physics or chemistry, the principle of **trained and
ordered analysis guided by theory** is crucial to all three disciplines.

What then is the meaning and use of theory? In general terms, a
theory is an economical way of perceiving and ordering reality.
Theories act as guides to research. They stipulate what the most important variables are, and what the observer should look for. They
allow the researcher to sift through the endless varieties of observations,
to focus his attention on a limited set of data, and to make observations
from that limited data about the larger universe with which he is concerned. Theories, therefore, are economical in that they filter out su-
perfluous data, but there is nothing mystical or incomprehensible about
them. Given a wide range of material or events to analyze, a theory
focuses your attention on the most important data, gives you some idea
of how to make sense of that data, and suggests reasonable expectations concerning what you are likely to find. All sciences work from
theories. Some theories turn out to be invalid or inadequate, but they
are all important to the extent to which they determine what the observer will look at and what he will ignore. Here again we are talking
about a training activity. The purpose of political science books is to
enable us to make sense out of events, to see if there is a pattern underlying series of behavior, and, if there is a pattern, to make educated
guesses about the likely consequences of maintaining or altering such
a pattern.

Perhaps this last factor explains the differing sets of expectations
mentioned in the beginning. Students often demand relevance in their
courses, particularly in political science. They want the instructor to talk
about current events—about what is happening now. This request is

reasonable but can be fulfilled honestly only if the student is taught his instructor's frame of reference and mode of analysis. The purpose or goal of an introductory course is to acquaint the student with the way political scientists think about problems, which is not so interesting initially as discussing current events. But it is far more relevant in that it helps the student develop his critical capacities and bring them to bear on the important problems challenging our society.

Hence, refinement of the critical capacities is what we attempt to achieve in this textbook. We shall discuss the political scientist's means of analysis and focus our attention on the world in a particular way. It would be gratifying to say that this book represents a total and integrated theory of politics. Such is not the case. The present state of knowledge in political science would make such an enterprise no less than foolhardy. Instead we shall use a particular concept—conflict—as a unifying focus for our analysis. Certainly, conflict is not the only organizing concept one could use. Several approaches can be applied. Any one of them will, of necessity, concentrate on some aspects of politics and pay little attention to others. I make no claim that a conflict model will allow us to exhaust all of the aspects that affect the operation of political systems. However, I feel that conflict is an appropriate focus for an introductory text because it concentrates our attention on the most visible and stressful aspects of political action. As we shall see, conflict is a pervasive and continuous phenomenon. It permeates the life of any society and is particularly evident in highly developed, complex societies such as the United States. We shall maintain that societies develop the various governmental and political structures as the means for adjudicating conflict. Political systems differ from one setting to another, but all seek to resolve conflict. When they fail to do so, either through accommodation, negotiation, and judicial procedure, or through the use of coercion, the institutions of those societies tend to die and to be replaced by institutions and methods that can successfully resolve conflict.

In this book we shall discuss the nature of conflict. Although many of our examples and extended discussions will be based on the American experience, examples will be drawn from foreign countries as well. If analytic concepts have value, they should be useful in more than one setting. It is important, therefore, to note cases outside the United States. Analogy can be a dangerous method of instruction. The analogy may represent a simplification of reality, but if it helps the student, by using examples with which he is familiar, to understand a particular concept or idea, the risk is worth taking. In discussing conflict, we shall be concerned with the ways in which conflicts arise, the resources necessary to engage in conflict, and the dynamics of conflict situations. We shall be concerned with the way in which legal and institutional structures condition the manner in which political systems respond to conflict—that is how they make decisions, the costs of various institutional structures for decision making, and the means that can be employed for resolving conflict. The student should thus become aware of the political process as a continuous, ongoing activity. This is the real excitement and relevance an introduction to political science can provide: an awakening to the fascinatingly complex and dynamic nature of political systems.

ACKNOWLEDGMENTS

In the preparation of this manuscript the help and stimulation of my colleagues, students, department, and university were abundant. In this sense the book represents a collective effort. Therefore there are numerous individuals whom I would like to thank publicly. This book was developed from the introductory course in political science at Michigan State University. Many thanks are owed my undergraduate students, who were amazingly tolerant toward me as I tried to develop a relatively new style of introductory course. Their comments and criticisms were most helpful in designing this book, and its approach is in part a reflection of their effort and suggestions. I would also like to thank the graduate students who assisted me in that course and made suggestions for this book, particularly Mark Hyde and Terry Smith.

I owe a particular debt of thanks to Charles Press, Chairman of the Political Science Department at Michigan State University, for his encouragement and constant support. I would also like to thank my colleagues Joseph Schlesinger, David Bell, and Edward Azar for their many helpful suggestions and comments, and David Meltz for his careful reading of many sections of this manuscript, which strengthened it considerably. I would also like to thank Ruth Curtiss, who typed the original draft, and Sandra Meltz, who typed the final manuscript.

I owe thanks to my editors at Harper & Row, Walter Lippincott and Sally Cerny. Particular thanks go to Sally, whose help was indispensable and who sensibly arranged to have her child born immediately after she had completed all work on this manuscript. Such loyalty from an editor must be unusual. Finally, but certainly not least, there is the traditional thanks an author is supposed to give to his wife. In this case, the thanks is not perfunctory but strongly felt. My wife Carol was a constant source of help and encouragement and was remarkably adept at appearing and disappearing at exactly the right strategic moments.

According to time-honored custom, I give credit for all that is good in the book to those who have helped and begrudgingly accept all blame for any errors or flaws.

Paul H. Conn

CONFLICT AND DECISION MAKING
An Introduction to Political Science

Chapter 1

The Nature of Conflict

The use of the term **conflict** with reference to political systems often brings to mind physical violence, coercion, rioting, and other forms of destructive or negative behavior. It implies a collision: a battle between individuals or groups with different standards, norms, or goals. Yet conflict may be violent and nonviolent. Arguments, disagreements, and elections all can be considered forms of conflict even though there may not be violence associated with them. In fact, conflict and the presentation of conflicting demands have been the mechanisms by which change has been introduced into societies and by which man has progressed. Conflict is a part of everyday social as well as political life. It arises from such mundane ideas as a better way to produce certain goods as well as from such spiritual questions as the most proper way to assure mankind's ultimate salvation. Both pragmatists and unabashed ideologues live in a setting of almost perpetual conflict. Governmental activity is supposed to moderate this conflict so that citizens can pursue their individual goals without being enmeshed in a setting of perpetual warfare.

We sometimes mistakenly think that modern times are peculiarly prone to conflict or confrontation. Often yearnings are expressed for some golden era when life was simpler and quieter. Perhaps in the past life was simpler, but it is unlikely that it was quieter or free of conflict. Relatively speaking, the conflicts of the past may not seem as pressing as those of the present, but surely to the men living in those times their conflicts were as violent and pervasive as ours appear to us today.

CONFLICT AS A FACT OF LIFE

If we accept the premise that conflict is a natural consequence of man's existence, what corollaries can we find? The most obvious one is that the development of civilization has been accompanied by a striving to create political institutions that allow a society to cope with its problems and to settle its conflicts. Some theorists maintain that man is inherently good and that the basis for his conflicts arises from this artificial creation called society. Whether or not this theory is true is inconsequential, since we cannot return to the state of the noble savage. Men live and will live in communities. Consequently, they must establish laws and institutions which enable them to function together.

Nonpolitical Conflicts

We have indicated that conflict is a pervasive aspect of human life and that political activity centers around the resolution of conflict. Yet obviously not all conflicts are political in their implications. A disagreement between two persons usually is not resolved through political means. However, if the dispute becomes heated enough or if the participants think that the stakes are high enough, they may very well turn to political institutions (courts or legislatures) to seek a resolution. Similarly, marital disagreements usually are not subject to political resolution, yet when the conflict becomes deep or basic enough, final recourse is made to legal institutions which again interpret the laws or statutes (made by the legislature) that pertain to the particular dispute. Labor-management disagreements normally are handled outside the realm of political institutions, but when the national interest is at stake, either governmental mediators are brought in or the government uses its power of injunction to try to reach a settlement of the conflict as quickly as possible. All these instances of conflict are essentially nonpolitical in nature but ultimately the participants have recourse to political institutions for their resolution. The character of political institutions is such that as long as they are effective they are the ultimate or authoritative agents for the resolution of conflict. That is, ultimately all conflicts which cannot be settled by the parties to the dispute will be subject to the jurisdiction or arbitration of some kind of governmental body, be it a court, a legislature, or an executive agency.

Conflict in Newly Independent Nations

One can probably differentiate among political systems in terms of their capacity to resolve conflicts or to maintain conflict within certain bounds which do not threaten the overthrow of the regime. Regimes which cannot successfully handle the conflicts most salient within their societies are often unstable political systems characterized by rapid succession and turnover, both in the personnel and in the method of government.

For example, some of the newly independent, formerly colonial societies are plagued with the instability resulting from inadequate resolution of conflict. Coups have been frequent and executive and legislative institutions have not achieved widespread acceptance. The conclusion of World War II marked the end of the colonial empires. Former possessions demanded and in the next two decades gradually won their independence. But independence has not proved a panacea for their problems. Most have had a history of great political instability. In part this instability results from the fact that colonial regimes suppressed the kinds of conflict which were present in the society. The various independence movements in these countries provided a temporary unity against a common enemy. Yet once that common enemy (the former colonial power) was gone, the basis for unity broke down and the society was forced to come to grips with its basic problems. The ingredients of conflict were there and had been there for years; thus the societies were forced to create political institutions which were capable of meeting these conflicts and could be accepted by the population as legitimate. Unfortunately, devising these institutions is not an easy process, particularly under the pressures to change the society from a traditional to a modern culture. It is the strain of trying to resolve their conflicts quickly, often without sufficient experience for dealing with them, that results in a failure to limit the scope of conflict and causes instability.

Yet such critical conflicts are not solely restricted to newly independent states, even though they may be clearly illustrated there. As any present-day observer can easily note, developed societies also are beset by conflicts which threaten to destroy the legitimacy and capability of long-existing political institutions.

What we have indicated is that the management, limitation, or resolution of conflict is a task common to all political regimes and provides the basis for the stability or lack of stability in political systems. Having said this, however, it is important to define more precisely the nature of conflict so that we can understand it better.

Conflict as the Product of Change

Conflict in a society is most often the product of **change.** When circumstances change in a society or community, the existing pattern of social and economic relations is altered. Change often advantages some groups while disadvantaging others, or at least sets the stage for the presentation of demands by groups and individuals who find that such changes have altered their status or environment. For example, it was the rise of trade and a merchant class, the growth of towns, and later the advent of industrialization which contributed to the end of feudalism in Western civilization. The changing circumstances led to conflicts between various groups, to the rise of an urban and eventually middle class, and to a redistribution of rewards within the society. The growth in power of the British House of Commons can be traced largely to the breakdown of the feudal system and the demands of a rising middle class for political institutions which more closely approximated the change in circumstances that the end of feudalism had brought about.

Thus, if we can for a moment forget the pejorative association of conflict with violence, we can see that conflicts are intimately bound up with change. This is not to imply that conflict exclusively or even primarily arises from changing economic conditions. For example, the much-talked-about "generation gap" is not a new phenomenon. Conflict between parents and adolescents or young adults is a universal phenomenon. What it represents is an uneasy period when relationships change. When children move into adulthood, they often find that it requires conflict for both themselves and their parents to perceive the changing circumstances of their relationships.

Out of these changing circumstances and conflicts new means of coping with problems emerge. Societies, when constantly faced with certain sets of conflict, develop regular channels to handle them. As circumstances and the nature of the specific conflicts change, the political system, if it is viable, develops new techniques for response. And since conflict is closely linked with change, someone or some group of people must respond to changing conditions and make the necessary accommodations. In this sense, conflict is a useful force, prodding societies to grow and to adapt their structures. Whether such change will be beneficial or not is, of course, unknown at the time and depends on the perspective of the individual who is evaluating such change.

TYPES OF CONFLICT

How, then, can we differentiate among types of conflict? Surely there are instances of conflict which most persons would not think of as being useful; conflict can be detrimental to society. Of course, a judgment as to whether conflict is performing useful or harmful purposes by its nature must be subjective. For example, if you live in a society where you strongly favor the existing political and social structures and where the great majority of the population also seems to favor them, then conflict is useful or at least not harmful when it is capable of being handled through the existing institutional structure and does not represent a threat to that structure. From the perspective of the person who desires changes but also wants to keep the existing political or socioeconomic institutions, the demands for change will most often be phrased in a way which does not challenge or threaten existing institutions. Conflict which does challenge such institutions would be regarded by such a person as "bad."

On the other hand, in the judgment of those persons who regard the institutions of their society as corrupt, decadent, or unjust, conflict which is maintained or resolved within the framework of existing institutions is bad because it will not help solve the underlying problems within the society. Conflict which challenges the existing institutional structure (the "establishment") is perceived by these persons as "good." The designation of conflict as good or bad is based upon the perceptions of the individuals engaged in the conflict. For example, some unions, like the International Typographical Union, have institutionalized a system of two-party competition for leadership positions. This type of electoral conflict is viewed by them as healthy conflict. However, one could suggest that conflict which threatened the integrity of the union, its ability to provide benefits for its members, would be regarded by such members as bad conflict.[1]

Similarly, societies can be differentiated in terms of the probable dimensions of conflict. Within stable societies conflict which attacks the existing structures may be perceived by a majority of the population as bad; in other countries similar attacks may be so common as to evoke sustained discussions of the appropriateness or legitimacy of existing structures and action designed to change such institutions.

In societies where there is wide consensus as to the desirability of the institutional structures, the range of conflict will be limited and will tend to take place through existing channels. On the other hand, as consensus on either existing institutions or the prevailing ideology breaks down, conflict may take on broader dimensions, eventually challenging the existing institutions and/or values. We can differentiate societies on the basis of the range of conflict which is present and make statements about the relative stability of one society as opposed to another. Where consensus is fairly widespread and conflict is narrow, we would expect a society to be stable. Where there is little consensus, we would expect conflict to be broad in scope and consequently to pose great problems for stability.

Conflict in Stable Societies

One of the factors which determines whether a society or a political system will achieve a measure of stability or acceptance by the population is the capacity of that political system to resolve its conflicts. Obviously, where conflict builds up and is incapable of being resolved, adherence or loyalty to existing political institutions breaks

---

[1] The International Typographical Union is one of the few unions which has developed a meaningful two-party competitive system. In most other unions institutionalized competition is absent and often has been perceived as detrimental to the cause of unionism and the need to present a united front to the employer. For an excellent study of the ITU, see Seymour Martin Lipset, Martin Trow, and James Coleman, **Union Democracy,** New York: Free Press, 1956.

down. Where the range of conflict is very wide, where it encompasses many important issues, the problems which political institutions face in handling these situations are great.

Stable political systems are those systems that have been capable of managing their conflicts either through a systematic use of coercion or by persuasion, accommodation, and bargaining. Such societies may be said to have established a normal pattern of politics; that is, they have developed and institutionalized a particular and habitual response to various situations of conflict. These normal patterns vary from one society to another, but the characteristic of a society with a normal pattern of politics is the relative stability over time of the political institutions. This development of a normal pattern of politics or conflict resolution is important because it allows the citizens of a society to pattern their behavior with some degree of probability as to the consequences of that behavior. Only in a relatively stable society can people interact with each other in a regularized manner and with predictable results. For the political system, as we indicated earlier, is the ultimate arbiter of all conflicts; and only if people can make some predictions as to the reactions of the political system can they work with each other with assurance as to the outcome of their arrangements.

One example of the range of conflict and its implications for various societies can be seen in the role of political parties in different societies. In democratic societies political parties represent a form of institutionalized conflict.

If we look at the Republican and Democratic parties in the United States, we see that both parties are fairly similar. Both grant legitimacy and approval to the existing institutional structures, and both do not seek any comprehensive changes in the socioeconomic structure of the society. The bases of differences between the two parties are differences of policy orientations. Between the parties conflicts tend to be specific and confined. Neither party perceives its policy preferences as incapable of being resolved within the framework of the existing political system. This confinement of conflict has been characteristic throughout most of the history of the United States: Conflict has been specific and has tended not to threaten existing institutions. The one major exception to this, of course, was the Civil War. In the Civil War the conflict extended even to the question of what political system would exist in this country, and indeed, whether the United States would continue as one nation.

Effects of Unsuccessful Conflict Resolution

FRANCE.   Contrast, however, the general stability of the political system of the United States to the instability which has arisen from the major conflicts that have been prevalent throughout the history of modern France. In France there have been conflicts over the nature of the social and economic structures and a lack of consensus concerning basic political structures. Perhaps the single most traumatic event in French history which conditioned this conflict concerning political institutions was the Revolution. The French Revolution was a violent one dividing the population into those who desired change at any cost and those who, frightened by the spectacle of revolutionary violence, felt the need for more orderly change through a strong executive-type government. In part, this explains France's vacillation between regimes characterized by strong executive powers and regimes dominated by the legislative body and an almost impotent executive authority. From the Revolution on, republics alternated with monarchic restorations or, as in the case of the two Napoleans, empires. From the close of the nineteenth century to the present, France has had three different republics. If the question of the restoration of the monarchy is now closed, the question of the balance between executive and legislative power persists. From the turn of the century until the fall of France in 1940, France lived under the constitutional arrangements of the Third Republic. The German occupation, the collaboration of Pétain, and the Vichy government brought the Third Republic into great disrepute. The rapid collapse of the French Army in 1940 was seen as the result of a weak government.[2] It was replaced at the conclusion of the war by the Fourth French Republic. However, the establishment of the Fourth Republic was not welcomed by many segments of the society. De Gaulle's supporters opposed the republic because it allowed the weaknesses of the previous government to continue. The Communists opposed it because the other parties excluded them from participation in the government. Although the French were jubilant and united at the close of the war, by 1946 the bitter divisions and conflicts about the age-old question of the nature of the French political system had again surfaced.

The replacement of the Fourth Republic with the Fifth Republic

---

[2] William L. Shirer, **The Collapse of the Third Republic,** New York: Simon & Schuster, 1969, chap. 27, "La Drôle de Guerre."

resulted from the inability of the French institutions to handle their most pressing problem: Algeria. Again the French people exchanged their government, this time opting for a strong executive-type system and Charles de Gaulle. With de Gaulle's departure in 1968, it remains to be seen whether the French have indeed settled the conflicts over their political institutions.

In many respects France is a society characterized by a continuing conflict about the nature of its political institutions. Because the bounds of conflict are broad, there are, on the one hand, groups within the population who are advocating a complete change of institutions, and, on the other hand, groups to whom programs or specific policies are far more significant than changing or undermining the existing political structure. The nature of conflict in such a society is likely to be far more severe and violent than in a society where there is widespread satisfaction with political institutions.

ITALY.   Italy represents another case of a society in which the base of conflict is broad and directed at the very institutions of the country. Italy was unified as a nation in the late 1800s in the face of determined opposition from the Papacy. The Catholic Church was strongly opposed to unification, for it meant the loss of the papal states to the new secular state. The papal states were territories under the temporal rule of the Pope, and by 1870 were basically concentrated in and around Rome. Rome was taken by the forces behind Italian unification in 1870. Pius IX, the Pope at the time, refused to recognize the loss of the states. The conflict between the Papacy and the Italian state was not resolved until the 1929 Lateran Treaty which created Vatican City. In such an overwhelmingly Catholic country this of course had great repercussions. It tended to set those who supported the Church against those who supported the idea of a unified Italian nation. The question of the relationship of the Church to the State, despite the Lateran Treaty, was never adequately resolved and remains in large measure unresolved to this date. This struggle can be seen in the comments of prominent Italians who feel that the ties of the dominant party, the Christian Democrats, to the Papacy are so strong that this has prevented basic reform from being undertaken within the society.[3]

---

[3] Giovanni Sartori, "European Political Parties: The Case of Polarized Pluralism," in Joseph LaPalombara and Myron Weiner (eds.), **Poltical Parties and Political Development,** Princeton, N.J.: Princeton University Press, 1966, p. 143.

The Fascist legacy also left its impact in terms of conflicts over the question of executive versus legislative leadership. For the Neo-Fascists the notion of a republic is repugnant. There also exist in Italy those who still favor the restoration of the monarchy. In addition there are those on the left, Socialists and Communists, who maintain that the present political system is so tied to the Church that it is unable to engage in the kind of meaningful reform which is politically, socially, and economically necessary. This range of conflict is wide and there is little agreement about what are truly desirable political structures. It is represented in the political party structure of the country. Political parties which can be characterized as "pro-system" (willing to work within the existing institutional structures of the Italian Republic) have only some 65 percent of the seats in the Italian Chamber of Deputies (the lower house of the Italian Parliament). The rest of the seats are occupied by those opposed to the existing system or only lukewarm supporters of the republic. Among these parties are the Monarchist party, the Neo-Fascists who seek to restore a Mussolini-style government, the Socialists, the Communists, and the PSIUP, which is an extreme Socialist party. The election of so many "anti-system" representatives testifies to the depth of the conflicts within that society. And, indeed, even among the pro-system parties there are great divisions and schisms which are very difficult to breach.[4]

PRE-CIVIL WAR AMERCA. Instability in a society takes place either because a normal pattern of politics has failed or because circumstances have so changed that the normal pattern of conflict resolution is no longer applicable. For example, a pattern of politics based on bargaining and accommodation breaks down when sides to a dispute become rigid and the society becomes polarized into antagonistic and noncommunicative groups. This is what happened prior to the American Civil War. During this period the traditional pattern of bargaining and accommodation which had been applied to the question of slavery and states' rights from the very drafting of the Constitution began to break down.

From the very formation of the United States the problem of slavery had been a significant one. It was a matter of grave concern during the Constitutional Convention. There were delegates who wanted an

---

[4] Ibid., pp. 148 ff; see also John C. Adams and Paolo Barile, **The Government of Republican Italy,** Boston: Houghton Mifflin, 1962, for a discussion of Italian legislative politics.

outright prohibition on the continued importation of slaves placed in the Constitution. Those opposed pointed out that the importing of slaves was dying out in the South anyway (Virginia and Maryland had already banned further importation) and there was no need to provoke a crisis or endanger ratification over this issue. The compromise which was achieved stated that Congress could make no law banning the importation of slaves until 1808. Congress subsequently banned continued importation and the ban became effective in 1808.[5] The opening up of the western territories, the Louisiana Purchase, and the great westward expansion all raised the problem of the balance between slave and free states in the Union. The slave states wanted slavery within these territories while the free states demanded that slavery be forbidden. The final disposition of the question was postponed by a series of artful compromises. The first, the Missouri Compromise of 1820, simply drew a line through the Louisiana Purchase territories at the parallel 36° 30' declaring that every state north of the line was to be admitted to the union as a free state and every state south of the line could be admitted as a slave state.

By the 1840s the balance between slave and free states was again threatened by westward expansion and the opening up of the Pacific region to large settlements. The Compromise of 1850 attempted to resolve this problem through bargaining and persuasion. According to that compromise California was admitted as a free state, the slave trade was abolished in the District of Columbia, a stringent fugitive slave law was to be enacted, and no interference with the slave trade among the slave states was allowed. Further, it provided for Utah and New Mexico to enter the Union as slave states. But one finds that in this period there was increasingly less room for bargaining. The slavery issue became broadened to an issue of the rights of the states versus the rights of the federal government, and the country began to polarize around these basic issues.

The Kansas-Nebraska Act of 1854 represented the last time that both sides were able to reach some kind of compromise on these basic questions. The act was in part passed because of the demands for a transcontinental railway. The South held the power to veto such a project. To secure passage of the railroad a compromise with the

---

[5] Saul K. Padover, **To Secure These Blessings,** New York: Washington Square Press, 1962, pp. 224–231; also Catherine Drinker Bowen, **Miracle at Philadelphia,** Boston: Atlantic-Little, Brown, 1966, pp. 200–204.

South on the slavery question was necessary. The Kansas-Nebraska Act, in effect, repealed the Missouri Compromise and provided that Kansas and Nebraska were to be admitted to the Union on the basis of popular sovereignty; that is, the majority of the inhabitants at the time of statehood could vote whether to permit or disallow slavery. Feelings were so bitter by that point, however, that Stephen Douglas, the author of the act, probably destroyed his chances of becoming President by his association with it. After 1854 the pattern of accommodation and compromise which had been so prevalent in the past was practically useless. The conflict had become too broad and had polarized the society into two unalterably opposed camps. It finally led to armed conflict. Thus the pattern broke down, and the conflict had to be resolved through violence. Civil war in any society marks the ultimate failure of regular and peaceful procedures. No matter which side survives, there is a need to pick up the pieces and re-establish a new pattern of conflict resolution.

RUSSIA.   A breakdown of the normal pattern of conflict resolution in a different context can be seen in Czarist Russia. The normal pattern of conflict resolution under the czars was autocratic and centralized. Most conflict resolution was achieved through the bureaucracy. The absence of a spirit of innovation at the top tended to rigidify the system and its methods of conflict resolution. As the nineteenth century drew to a close, the conflicts in that society became more exacerbated, the machinery of repression more inept, and the normal government pattern increasingly more difficult to maintain. The Czarist structure first broke down in 1905 during the revolt. The revolt shattered the traditional loyalty of the people for the Czar. Neither the Russian ruler nor the bureaucracy seemed able to reassert the traditional pattern of rule or to develop an alternative pattern. The revolutions of 1917 merely struck the final blows on an already dying political system.

Both of these examples indicate something of the nature of conflict and conflict resolution. We could say that all societies face stresses and strains, and in some of them these pressures often become heightened as new circumstances arise. When the problems of conflict are allowed to build and to polarize a society, they tend to damage if not to destroy it altogether.

In the next chapter we shall briefly analyze the bases of conflict. We shall try to analyze the conditions and sources from which this ubiquitous thing, conflict, arises.

SUGGESTED READINGS

Coleman, James S., **Community Conflict,** New York: Free Press, 1957, chap. 1.

Coser, Lewis, **Continuities in the Study of Social Conflict,** New York: Free Press, 1967.

Coser, Lewis, **The Functions of Social Conflict,** New York: Free Press, 1956.

Dahrendorf, Ralf, **Class and Class Conflict in Industrial Society,** Stanford, Calif.: Stanford University Press, 1959.

Eckstein, Harry (ed.), **Internal War,** New York: Free Press, 1964.

Chapter 2

Structure of Conflict

If conflict is an inescapable phenomenon which permeates all societies, we must ask ourselves what the bases for such conflict are and whether there are categories of conflict. What conditions bring conflict about and what conditions are likely to add to or limit the intensity of conflict?

Conflicts can be divided into two broad categories: (1) those which are zero-sum and (2) those which are nonzero-sum. The basis of the conflicts in either case may be specific, with reference to such things as governmental policies, religion, or sports; or the conflicts may be very general, relating to ideologies or philosophic systems. On the whole, however, we can assume that most conflicts do fall into one of the two categories and, as a result, differ from each other not only in the structure of conflict but also in the dynamics of the conflict and the modes of resolution to which they are susceptible.

ZERO-SUM CONFLICT

Zero-sum conflict is a specific term which has been developed by game theorists and refers to the strategic situation between various protagonists. We shall not expand the theory in depth here; rather we shall discuss the general outlines of this category of conflict.

Zero-sum situations are strictly competitive ones in which the protagonists have exactly contrary preferences. Every gain for one contestant yields a corresponding loss for the other contestant. For example, a football game can be considered a zero-sum game. Team A wants to win and defeat team B, while team B's goals are the opposite. The football game is a structured event in which, barring ties, only one team can win. While we may not think of sporting events as conflicts, they really can be considered as such. In football, rather elaborate rules are developed which determine the way in which conflict is to take place. These rules allow certain types of behavior and prohibit others. The field judge, umpire, or referee is empowered to interpret the rules, make sure they are followed, and designate the winner in the contest. Although this may be a very dry description of a football game, it nevertheless does reveal its essence: two combatants competing for victory under certain rules and restrictions. The rules and restrictions are designed to keep the conflict in bounds—in the case of sporting events, to prevent serious injury which might arise if the conflict were allowed to become a free-for-all. This is why unsupervised athletics often result in more serious injuries than supervised ones.

The same observations concerning football can be made of other sports. Thus baseball, boxing, and tennis are all examples of ritualized conflict which is strictly competitive in nature. The strictly competitive nature of football can be seen in the fact that offensive and defensive squads face each other during the course of the game. For every offensive strategy that can be adopted there is a corresponding defensive strategy designed to nullify the offense. Such a situation is common to many games. For example, in the children's game of tic-tac-toe there is an effective move which can block the move of one's opponent. This is always true and perhaps explains why adults don't play that game, for it soon becomes obvious that there are perfect opposing strategies which the players can pursue and therefore no one can win. What makes football or any sporting event so interesting is that the competing or blocking strategies do not, of course, always work, and therefore people do win and the winning is a function of the degree of skill which is applied to certain strategic options.

We can note that the defining characteristic of the zero-sum game is that cooperative strategies are impossible. A conflict is zero-sum in nature when the outcomes preferred by one protagonist are precisely those which are not preferred by the other. An additional characteristic is that by the definition of a strictly competitive game, the gains of one player equal the losses of the other.[1]

Civil War

The state of civil war in a country may be analyzed as a zero-sum conflict. Civil war occurs when the set of protagonists have reached a point where the satisfaction of one combatant's preferences prohibits the satisfaction of his opponent's preferences. Secession and civil war occur when remaining united as a single country prevents the achievement of other values and, therefore, the satisfaction of those other preferences cannot be achieved through any mutually acceptable cooperative strategy.

The Civil War in the United States occurred when the North and South no longer found it plausible to pursue cooperative strategies to secure their preferences. It was fought in part over different ways of life and, as a result, differing goals as to the appropriate political structures of the society. The North and South each had mutually exclusive preferences concerning the nature of the federal Union and different ideas as to the desirability of slavery and its extension within the territories of the United States. Those in the South felt that they could achieve their goals and maintain their way of life only if the nature of the federal Union were fundamentally altered. This meant either that certain powers had to be taken away from the federal government or that the individual states had to be given some veto over federal action. On the other hand, those in the North felt that their values could not be secured if such changes in the federal Union were permitted. The conflict was set because any change in the structure of the Union would mean that the South would benefit and the North would be less able to secure its preferences, and that maintenance of the status quo political arrangements would jeopardize the position

---

[1] R. Duncan Luce and Howard Raiffa, **Games and Decisions,** New York: Wiley, 1957, pp. 59 ff.

of the South. Because it was impossible for one side to achieve its goal without blocking the other side from attaining its goal the conflict became inevitable. Because the stakes of conflict were great for both protagonists the conflict became violent and intense.

Church Versus State

Similarly, certain religious conflicts can also be usefully analyzed as zero-sum situations. Such conflicts have often been intertwined with political and economic factors as well. The Reformation was as much a political and economic movement as a religious one. The violent conflicts which took place during that period involved not merely disputes between Catholics and the so-called heretical sects, but conflicts between different views of the social and political order.

During the Middle Ages the Catholic Church occupied a unique position. After the collapse of the Roman Empire, European unity was smashed. Lacking a source of common authority and loyalty the various tribes drifted apart, engaging in almost continual fighting over territorial boundaries. The Church, however, remained a significant unifying force during this period. It maintained that its teachings and dogma knew no temporal boundaries. Its authority was to be supreme throughout Europe. Because of the uniformity of education in the Church and the common denominator of the Latin language, the Church had great strength in its claims to universality. The break with Rome took many forms. In England it was led by Henry VIII with predominantly political overtones, while in Germany it was led by Martin Luther with an emphasis on religious disagreements. In England Henry had defied papal excommunication and established the Church of England with himself as supreme head of the Church. After so doing, Henry had the Church grant him the divorce which the Pope had been unwilling to grant. As a result of the break with Rome, Henry was excommunicated. Henry made his appeal to the British population on perhaps one of the oldest of propaganda ploys. He challenged the **foreign** influence of Rome and the power of a Pope residing in Italy to dictate to the English people. England was but one example of the many countries where the forces of nationalism and separatism combined with dissatisfied religious leaders to assert independence from Roman rule.

The forces unleashed by the Reformation provided an opportunity for national leaders to assert their independence. The Church and the national leaders had different preferences and the satisfaction of one set of preferences blocked the other side from securing its desired alternatives. The Church had pursued the strategy of universality to maintain a cohesiveness to a widely disparate population of believers. Its universalist claims were designed to place the Church above the temporal ruler as the ultimate object of the citizen's loyalty. To the extent that the Church held the ultimate loyalty of the individual, the national leader's power would be limited. In any conflict between the two the Church could call upon the citizens to follow their higher duty of obeying the teachings and commands of the Church which was God's instrument on earth. The Church held the power of excommunication and had often used it against national leaders who challenged the Papacy. Excommunication condemned an individual to eternal damnation, prevented his receiving the sacraments, and placed in jeopardy the immortal soul of all who associated with the excommunicant. The threat of excommunication could challenge the leader's claim to legitimacy and often forced a prince to reach an accommodation with Rome. For those who wished to establish the supremacy of the monarchy and of the temporal state there was the need to replace the Church with the State as the ultimate object of the individual's loyalty. Prior to the Reformation both sides had adopted a more or less cooperative strategy. The costs of either side pushing too hard for its own position were greater than the benefits to be derived from maintaining the status quo.

The Reformation, however, unleashed forces which were dramatic in scope and introduced into the situation a zero-sum element. Feelings of disaffection toward the Church among the populace diminished the costs for the temporal leaders to openly compete with the Church for the ultimate loyalty of the individual. The theological and ritualistic challenge of the Reformation was so great that the leaders of the Church felt it necessary to emphatically reinforce the supremacy of the Roman Church. The nature of the conflict and the costs involved precluded cooperative strategies. The results were, of course, that Europe was plunged into a series of religious wars which continued for more than a hundred years.

NONZERO-SUM CONFLICT

Nonzero-sum conflict is much more common in the political sphere. Such conflicts are not strictly competitive, in the sense that there is at least one outcome for which the preferences of the players are not strictly opposed. This does not mean that the compatible outcomes are the most preferred for either side. Rather the nonzero-sum nature of the game permits limited cooperation between protagonists. But whether they will engage in such cooperation depends upon such factors as the peculiar character of the particular conflict, the psychological make-up of the players, and whether the nature of the conflict they are engaged in allows them to freely exchange information with each other and reach binding agreements. In the game theory literature, nonzero-sum games are classified as either cooperative or noncooperative games in terms of whether the situation allows complete freedom to exchange information and to pursue cooperative strategies. The basic distinction between the zero-sum and nonzero-sum situation is that "in strictly competitive games it is impossible for the players to achieve mutual benefit by any form of cooperation; however, in non-strictly competitive games such mutual gain is always a possibility."[2]

An example of the nonzero-sum conflict can be seen in the following case. A group of friends are sharing an apartment and they have to make a decision about what they are going to do for entertainment that evening. One wants to go to a movie, a second wants to play bridge, a third wants to bowl, and a fourth wants to go to the ball game. If each were willing to pursue his preference separately there would be no conflict. However, while each member of the group prefers his form of entertainment, each member has an even higher preference for spending the evening with the other members of the group. One possible solution is of course for each to go his own way. That solution, however, violates the higher preference which all have of spending the evening together. We can assume that this conflict will be resolved in favor of finding some form of entertainment mutually acceptable to all members of the group. Since all members can exchange information about their preferences with each other and can cooperate, it would make sense for them to resolve the situation in such a way which satisfies their highest preference of spending the evening together.

Legislative behavior is a specific political example of a situation in which members must reconcile their different preferences on the various

---

[2] Ibid., p. 89.

parts of a particular bill in order to bring about any legislation. Legislative behavior is in many ways an institutionalized means for the raising and resolution of conflict. For example, several years ago the United States Congress debated as to whether the government should be involved in the financing and administration of a system of medical care for the elderly. Much of the conflict was concerned with not only whether government should provide the medical care but also whether such a medical program for the aged should be tied to social security or should be a voluntary health insurance program. Debates over comprehensive medical care programs by the government have been persistent in the United States since the close of World War II. Eventually the supporters of medical care for the elderly and poor were successful in 1965 when Medicare legislation tied to the social security system was passed into law. We know that on the issue of medical care there were, among the supporters of the medical program, those in favor of tying the program to social security and those who wished to see the program set up separately on a voluntary basis. Each group preferred to see a medical care program established but each preferred that it be established in a certain way. A legislature is a situation which allows bargaining and exchange of information among the participants. Therefore, we can say that there exists an outcome of the legislative conflict which is acceptable to these two groups of individuals, namely passage of some kind of medical insurance program. If each is unable to secure enough votes for the most preferred form of the program, it is possible for them to pursue a cooperative strategy which allows them to achieve some form of medical program.

Because nonzero-sum situations, by definition, contain the possibility of mutually advantageous outcomes we can say that it is likely that conflicts which are zero-sum or are perceived by the contestants as being zero-sum will be more intense than nonzero-sum games, assuming that the stakes of both conflicts are equal. However, whether nonzero-sum games will resolve themselves in the adoption of mutually acceptable strategies depends upon the awareness of the players of the existence of a cooperative strategy and their willingness to defer high-risk gains, which would mean satisfaction of their preferences, to accept moderate gains, which would mean some compromise in their preferences. We can say that the difference in the nature of conflicts is affected by whether the conflict is zero or nonzero-sum.

STAKES AND THE INTENSITY OF CONFLICT

It is obvious that not all cases of conflict, either zero-sum or nonzero-sum, result in violence. There must be additional factors which condition whether a conflict will be intense and violent or relatively unimportant to the contestants. The factor we shall consider is the question of the stakes involved in the conflict and their importance to the participants.

Stakes and the Zero-Sum Situation

A poker game is a zero-sum or strictly competitive game. The rules of the game forbid collusion among the players and purposely limit information so that bluffing is a possible strategy. Information is limited because in any form of poker certain information is concealed by the players from each other in the form of closed cards. The stakes of the game are set in advance and the payoffs are constant, limited by the amount of money each of the players is willing to risk during the course of the play. Any wins by one or two players must come at the expense of the other players. We know that most poker games do not end in violence or with players exhibiting high levels of intensity and hostility. This is so because in the majority of poker games the stakes are not high enough for the participants to get unduly concerned over their losses. We do know, however, that gambling losses in such games of chance as poker do occasionally lead to violence, often when the stakes become very high and the loser is unwilling to face the consequences of losing or cannot afford to lose. In such high-stake games, tension often mounts and accusations of cheating and fraud may be made. These accusations often lead to intense conflict.

Obviously in the case of the poker game, the point at which the stakes become high enough for the players to become intensely competitive and hostile toward each other will vary from situation to situation. Not all people will think of the same stakes as being high. This, of course, depends upon the individual's utility for money. The individual in the poker game who is exceedingly wealthy and has a low utility for additional money will obviously not be particularly affected by high stakes. The individual, however, who gets involved in a poker game and watches the stakes rise and who finds that he is committing more money to the game than he can really afford may become very tense and hostile as the course of the game progresses.

If the intensity of games or conflicts is a function of the stakes, then we can say that conflicts will become intense as the utility of winning increases for the contestants. The more important it is to win and the less acceptable it is to lose, the greater the degree of intensity which will be associated with the conflict.

Stakes and the Nonzero-Sum Situation

We have so far examined the way in which changes in stakes affect or may affect the play of the game in zero-sum situations. There are similar ways in which the stakes and the size of the payoffs affect the play of nonzero-sum games or conflicts. We have defined nonzero-sum games as those situations in which there is at least one outcome which is not opposed by either of the players. Whether such an outcome will be chosen is a function of the stakes involved in the game and the risks in choosing a noncooperative strategy. We can look at the following illustration.

After the defeat of his first nominee to fill the vacancy on the Supreme Court caused by the resignation of Abe Fortas, President Nixon and his opponents in the Senate were faced with the following situation and possible sets of outcomes. The President wanted to appoint a southern conservative to the Court. The stakes involved in losing a second time were great. Rarely, if ever, in this century has a President failed twice in securing a judicial appointment for the Court. There was a high risk to the President's prestige in losing. He could adopt a high-risk strategy and try to get the most conservative justice appointed. This would be the high-gain outcome for the President. He would be able to change or shift the balance of power on the Court and reward his southern supporters. The high risk involved in such a situation was that if the President nominated a conservative southerner who was tainted with the accusation of racial bias, he might lose in the Senate again, thus risking grave damage to his prestige and placing his supporters in the Senate in a very awkward position. He could nominate a more moderate southern justice and secure some benefits, but he could be less sure of the probable behavior of the justice once he got on the Court. By maximizing his chances of getting the nomination through the Senate he might reduce the payoffs to himself of having that particular judge on the Supreme Court.

For the President's opponents the situation was similarly structured. Their high gain would be the defeat of any conservative justice the

President could nominate. In this way the opponents could hope to ensure a liberal majority on the Court. However, the risk involved in such an enterprise was that continued rejection of Court nominees might provoke a constitutional crisis between the Senate and the President and might arouse a great deal of public opposition. The more limited payoff would be to force the President to nominate a more moderate justice. Since there was little likelihood the President would appoint an outspoken liberal to the court, the opponents could settle for the less conservative justice.

President Nixon adopted a high-risk strategy which aroused his opponents when he nominated G. Harrold Carswell for the Supreme Court. The nomination of a little known federal court judge who, upon investigation, seemed to have made some questionable rulings in civil rights cases was sufficient to galvanize the President's opponents and allow them to form a coalition which was successful in blocking his second nominee. Eventually, on the third round the President chose a strategy which provided both him and his opponents a mutually acceptable although minimal payoff.

In this case the stakes were considered high enough so that both sides pursued high-risk strategies in two repeated plays of the same situation. Only on the third round were they willing to accept the outcome of the game which provided minimum gains for both sides. In this sense the game was nonzero-sum in that there was an outcome which was mutually beneficial to both sides.

SCARCITY OF RESOURCES

The possibility of payoffs in any game or real-life conflict situation depends upon the existence of resources which individuals are willing to commit to the conflict and the amount of resources which exist within the society. All resources are limited. Land is a very basic resource in any society. The amount of land determines the amount of food which can be produced, and the amount of food in some measure sets an upper limit on the size of the population which can be supported on this limited resource called land. In some societies where land seems plentiful with relation to population, the perception of land as a scarce resource is less common than in a society which has enormous population pressures and feels the scarcity of land as a means of supporting its population. The population density of India is such that it creates huge pressures on the existing supply of land to provide adequate or survival levels of food for the population as well as the need to provide housing for that population. The scarcity of food and adequate housing in that country often give rise to violent conflicts. Food riots and riots born of desperation have not been uncommon there. Where population growth is very high, the strain on limited resources to provide even minimal or subsistence standards of living to the population becomes very severe. In some of these societies the inhabitants have almost taken a fatalistic view of life in which starvation and violent conflicts over the distribution of resources seem inevitable. They see the resources of the country as constant while the threat of increased population keeps growing. The resources resemble a constant pie which must be increasingly divided among more and more individuals.[3] The threats of overpopulation are particularly explosive in countries such as India or Malaysia.

Limited Versus Constant Resources

Of course, there is a distinction which should be drawn between limited and constant resources. While it is true that all resources are in some manner limited, the sum of resources at any given time may not be constant. Even the amount of land may not be a constant figure. The example of Holland, where a system of dikes and a program of reclamation have increased the amount of usable land in that country is a case in which resources can be expanded. Even if we assume that land is a constant resource, the amount of food which can be produced on a constant sum of land can be increased. This is in effect the same as expanding the amount of land. Intensive cultivation and the use of fertilizers and other elements of modern scientific agriculture can yield a very high return from very limited amounts of land. The wealth of a society is a limited resource which is distributed in some manner among the population. However, wealth may be limited but it is not necessarily or even usually a constant sum. The increase each year of the gross national product in a country indicates that the amount of wealth has increased. In some countries wealth may be increasing at

---

[3] James C. Scott, **Political Ideology in Malaysia,** New Haven, Conn.: Yale University Press, 1968, chap. 5, "Man and Nature: The Struggle for Slices of a Constant Pie." There is little reason to doubt that the opinions of Malay administrators about the scarcity of resources and their generally pessimistic outlook on life are not relatively common in other developing areas.

a faster rate than the growth in population, in which case the maintenance of the existing system of wealth distribution is likely to leave all members of the society better off in absolute terms than they were the year before. However, where economic growth is not keeping pace with population growth, individuals will be worse off during the present year than they were the year before. When an economy is healthy and prospering, it provides a means for distribution which at least makes no one worse off than he was before.

Expanding Available Resources

Government expenditures represent the disbursement of funds for programs which benefit various segments of the society. In a society in which the amount of resources which the government can spend remains constant, the increased demands from various groups within the society for better or larger portions of governmental services or programs creates a zero-sum situation where the increased expenditure of money for one program means a decreased expenditure of funds for other programs. However, if the economy is healthy and growing, it is possible that in any given year, without raising taxes, the amount of money which the government is able to spend on various programs is greater than the previous year. Therefore, while the resources are still limited, they have been expanded.

Where the economic resources of a society are being expanded, expenditures for social welfare programs designed to aid the poor do not represent a zero-sum threat to those who are wealthy. It is possible for them to maintain their wealth and even expand their wealth while at the same time supporting, through their taxes, programs which aid the poor. If you have a society where the total output, and therefore wealth, is increasing at a faster rate than the population, it is possible in absolute terms to raise the standard of living of everyone. There is no reason why, under such a situation, it is not possible to guarantee all citizens a decent standard of living while making no citizens worse off than they had been. While it may be true that in relative terms the amount of the nation's wealth which you may hold may have declined, your absolute standard of living may remain the same or even increase. If the increase in resources is sufficiently large, the percentage may be smaller but the absolute amount of wealth which you receive will increase.

Despite the possibility of expanding the amount of resources available, many people regard as threatening **all** programs or policies which are aimed at changing the economic structures of the society. People often tend to view resources as constant and any gains for others as made at their own expense. Therefore, they are often resentful of programs that offer more than token help to those economically less fortunate.

For example, the concept of **black power** often has been frightening to white Americans. The demands of black people have been perceived as structuring a zero-sum situation where black gains must be made at the expense of whites. This often occurs because the perceptions which people have are those of constant resources. This may or may not be an accurate description of the situation. A survey was made in the Detroit area after the disastrous riots and disturbances which took place there in the summer of 1967. One of the questions put to both black and white respondents was, "What does **black power** mean?" The great majority of black Americans who were interviewed felt that black power meant getting a fair deal, getting a fair share of the resources and wealth of the country. The responses further indicated a recognition of common interests among blacks and a desire to use their power as a group in much the same way other minority groups have used their ethnic power in the past.[4]

Among the white respondents, the great majority perceived black power as "they want to take everything over." Black power was a frightening concept to these people because resources were perceived as being constant and all black gains would therefore have to come at the expense of whites. Where resources are perceived as constant and the stakes represented in the conflict seem great, intensity will rise often leading to violence. Although perceptions may not be objectively correct, so long as a participant believes them to be true, he will act accordingly.

The intensity of conflict is as much a function of attitudes and beliefs as it is a function of objective reality. To illustrate this, we may look at an example of the impact the distributions of opinion may have on society.

---

[4] Joel D. Aberbach and Jack L. Walker, "The Meanings of Black Power: A Comparison of White and Black Interpretations of a Political System," **American Political Science Review**, LXIV (June, 1970), 367–388. We have simplified Aberbach and Walker's findings. The responses they got in their interviews indicate that there is a wide variety of meanings which indviduals have placed on the term "black power."

CONFLICT AND THE DISTRIBUTION OF ATTITUDES

Assuming that it was probably true that prior to the Civil War in this country, opinions on the question of slavery resembled the bell-shaped curve in Figure 2-1.

FIGURE 2-1
PRESUMED DISTRIBUTION OF ATTITUDES ON SLAVERY IN THE UNITED STATES PRIOR TO THE CIVIL WAR

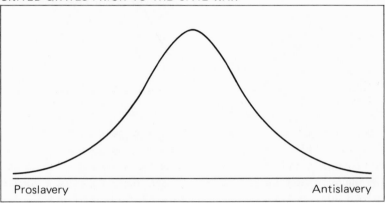

Proslavery   Antislavery

This curve indicates that there were extreme views on either end of the spectrum but that the great bulk of the population held attitudes which were not very strong in either direction. Most people had a preference or opinion in one direction or the other but they were not intensely held preferences. When opinion is distributed in this way on any issue, there is room for compromise and accommodation. The preponderance of "middle-ground" people provides a basis for resolving conflict. As long as a solution can be found satisfactory to the majority occupying this middle position, those advocating extreme solutions will find it difficult to elicit support. Figure 2-1 was probably an accurate reflection of U.S. public opinion regarding slavery up to the 1820s.

By the 1850s, however, the question of slavery had become intertwined with the question of the nature of the federal Union. As these questions and the corollary questions concerning the opening of the western territories became more interconnected and the stakes of the conflict became higher, the original distributions of opinion probably changed to resemble something like the distribution depicted in Figure 2-2. Thus, as the question of slavery became connected with other

FIGURE 2-2
PRESUMED DISTRIBUTION OF ATTITUDES ON SLAVERY IN THE UNITED STATES AT THE OUTBREAK OF THE CIVIL WAR

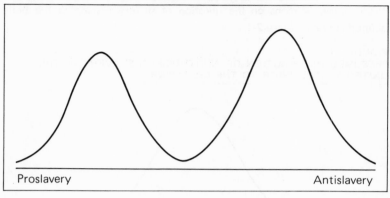

Proslavery   Antislavery

issues, most of the people who would have originally fallen into the indifferent middle were forced to take sides. We can see that the middle had collapsed, and in this new distribution the two extremes are large. The situation had become polarized, and the people were forced to take sides—to leave the comfort of the middle ground and become parties to the dispute. Thus the basis for intense conflict increases in direct proportion to the degree to which members of the society place themselves firmly on one side or the other of an issue.

INTERACTION

There is one additional basic element which is necessary for conflict to take place. The parties to conflict will engage in conflict only if there is a necessity for them to interact with each other or if both the contestants are subject to the same common authority.[5] For example, if the North and the South had originally been two separate nations, the fight over slavery would not have been necessary. While the two societies still would have had contradictory value systems, it would not have been necessary for them to make common decisions regarding this difference in values and, therefore, the basis for the conflict might have been removed (although it is probable that even if the North and South had originally been two separate nations, they would have been

---

[5] James G. March and Herbert A. Simon, **Organizations,** New York: Wiley, 1958, p. 121.

in conflict over the western territories). Unless there is a need to reach common decisions or for people to interact with each other, the existence of differing values or desires may not be a source of conflict between them.

Many people have urged the establishment of a supranational government or the strengthening of the United Nations so that it could perform this role. Yet it is important to note that several possibly undesirable consequences might result from such an organization. Many of the potential conflicts among nations exist in terms of different customs, goals, practices, ideologies, and so forth. That these differences do not always result in conflict is in part due to the fact that these nations are not subject to a common authority and, therefore, do not necessarily have to reconcile their differences. A supranational organization might impose great costs in terms of conflict. Many of these potential conflicts might very well become real because of the formation of a powerful international government which would force the various nations to conform to a single pattern of political authority, moral code, and social structure enacted by this international government.

CULTURAL CONFLICTS

An example of conflict which has been brought about because of differing cultures or life-styles subject to a common authority can be seen in the case of Belgium. Belgium is a country which is linguistically and culturally divided between the Flemings and the Walloons. The Flemings are of Dutch-German background and speak a dialect of those languages, while the Walloons are French-speaking and share the French cultural heritage. The position of Belgium astride Germany and France has meant that it has been invaded several times as these two countries have been at war. It has also meant that there have been forces within the country which strain relations between these two cultural groups, part of the legacy of hundreds of years of Franco-German hostility. The two groups are geographically separated within Belgium and historically the Walloon area has enjoyed economic and political supremacy in the country. It is only in recent years that the Flemish areas have become economically better off than the Walloon section. The two groups have vied with each other for supremacy on linguistic, cultural, economic, and political grounds. The boundaries of Belgium make the communities interact with each other in order to achieve common solutions and, therefore, the distinctions between the two cultures are a source of continuing friction.[6]

A similar situation can, of course, be noted in Canada in terms of the conflict between French Canadians and English-speaking Canadians. While the French are essentially clustered in the province of Quebec, they are a significant minority in Canada and have demanded linguistic parity between French and English and an increased emphasis on the French tradition, culture, and contributions to Canadian life. This problem has increased in significance during the last few years as the demands of the French have become more outspoken.

Most Canadians still desire a solution to the conflict within the structure of the Canadian federation. The demands of the Separatists, however, are for resolving the problem by removing the need for common interaction; that is, by declaring Quebec independent of the rest of Canada. Whether it would be economically possible for Quebec to remove itself from the Confederation remains in doubt. Nevertheless, the conflict illustrates that in this case, one of the demands being made is to remove the basis of conflict by removing the need for interaction.

It has often been noted that many of the newly independent countries, such as Nigeria or the Congo, have faced great conflicts because their boundaries were drawn as a result of the competition for empire among the European nations without any regard for tribal or ethnic boundaries. Such a demarcation of boundaries tends to create severe problems by placing antagonistic groups with different customs, norms, and beliefs in proximity to each other and forcing them to subject themselves to a common authority.

Yet this arbitrary character of boundaries is not unique to Africa or Asia. As we indicated in the case of Belgium, many European boundaries bear little regard for ethnic or linguistic differences. Switzerland maintains a delicate balance between its German-, Italian-, and French-speaking sections. Generally, whenever a country contains a highly heterogeneous population, the basis for conflict is there. In some

---

[6] Val Lorwin, "Belgium: Religion, Class, and Language in National Politics," in Robert Dahl (ed.), **Political Opposition in Western Democracies,** New Haven, Conn.: Yale University Press, 1966; Val Lorwin, "Conflict and Compromise in Belgian Politics," paper presented at the Annual Meeting of the American Political Science Association, Washington, D.C., September 1965, mimeo.

cases, such as Belgium, the conflict is relatively intense; in others, such as Switzerland, the conflict is of less importance.

CONCLUSION

What we have established, then, is that the basis of conflict lies in individuals or groups interacting with each other in situations which are either zero-sum or nonzero-sum in nature. The intensity of the conflict will be determined in part by the stakes of the game. Where the stakes are high, that is, where the cost of losing is great, the likelihood is that conflict will be intense. A significant factor conditioning whether participants will perceive the stakes as being high is the scarcity of the resources involved in the conflict and the utility of such resources to the participants. It remains now to ask what are the motives which impel people to engage in conflicting behavior. What do they hope to gain? What do they hope to defend?

SUGGESTED READINGS

Axelrod, Robert, **Conflict of Interest,** Chicago: Markham, 1970.

Luce, R. Duncan, and Howard Raiffa, **Games and Decisions,** New York: Wiley, 1957.

March, James G., and Herbert A. Simon, **Organizations,** New York: Wiley, 1958, chap. 5.

Rapoport, Anatol, **Fights, Games and Debates,** Ann Arbor: University of Michigan Press, 1960.

Shubik, Martin (ed.), **Game Theory and Related Approaches to Social Behavior,** New York: Wiley, 1964.

Chapter 3

Motivation

We have examined the structure of conflict situations and are now ready to focus on the goals and attitudes which motivate human behavior and induce people to engage in conflict. The two basic motivations for conflict can best be described as (1) **gain** and (2) **preservation,** or defense. These are large categories under which we can subsume most of the more specific goals people have when engaging in conflict. Conflict situations will rarely be characterized by pure goals of gain or preservation, but they may often be mixed and will often exist as a motivation for participants in varying degrees. We can envision an **absolute** motivation in which an actor desires all or nothing. If he cannot win completely and gain everything, he will not want to win at all; or if he cannot preserve everything, he will want to preserve nothing. More often, however, motivations will be relative and gradational, at least in the short run, even if the motives of the participants are absolute in nature over the long run. The actor who seeks gain will seek to gain as much as he can. Likewise, an actor who is motivated by the desire to preserve his resources or possessions will, if he sees that he cannot preserve everything, at least try to keep his losses to a minimum. But what does this mean in actual situations? Let us consider each of the two basic categories of motivation separately and then analyze how the two come together in conflicts.

GAIN

Gain is the motivation of the aggressive actor. It is the motive of acquisition, of expanding, or of getting or achieving something more than you have at the present. There are several types of goals pertaining to gain which people may desire to achieve. One, they may be concerned with increasing their **economic** position; that is, they may wish to make more money, to get a greater share of their society's wealth, or to gain control of a corporation. Two, they may wish to gain **status**; that is, they may be interested in increasing the kind of respect or deference they receive within their community. Hence, they may engage in the kinds of activity which are likely to result in an improved picture of themselves by their peers or by the community as a whole. For example, they may engage in time-consuming community activities, such as serving on the school board or leading a charity, not wholly with altruistic motives, but in part because there is a certain status to be gained from participating in these activities.

Yet economic goals and goals of status are but two of many types of goals which people may seek to attain. Human beings are complex and pursue multiple goals, or at times desire one goal and at other times forsake it for another goal. Goals are complex and multifaceted, and it is not always easy to say what goal or goals a person is pursuing at any given time. Similarly, it is not always easy to characterize an event in terms of the goals which motivate the participants. If we look at the Crusades of the Middle Ages, it is obvious that some participants were motivated by the economic gain to be derived from joining in this project, others were prompted by the status conferred on people joining a holy expedition, and still others were moved by a genuinely idealistic zeal for bringing salvation to others. One would have to be completely cynical to assume that all participants in the Crusades were motivated by the desire for economic gain. Similarly one would have to be totally idealistic to assume that all were moved by a burning spiritual conviction. Because the Crusades were large and complex events, the motives of the participants were mixed. Yet, in the case of the participants in the Crusades, all felt that there was something to be gained by joining in what was called a Holy War.

PRESERVATION

The second major category of goals which motivate people to engage in conflict is preservation. Preservation is by nature a defensive motivation and could alternatively be termed avoidance of deprivation. It may seem a strange motivation or goal at first, yet it is merely an extension of the most primitive and continuing aspect of life: the instinct for self-preservation. Each of us desires to preserve that which we already have. Obviously, we do not care equally about all our possessions or values and would not fight with equal fervor to maintain everything we possess. The desire to preserve our possessions and values need not always lead to conflict, but it cannot be denied that, when threatened, people will tend to react in whatever way seems most likely to assure their preservation—whether or not conflict ensues. They will seek to protect not only themselves but also their territory, possessions, and family.

Certainly this motivation (or instinct) is not peculiar to man. Animals will fight to protect not only themselves and their young, but also to protect the nest. They often engage in activity designed to demarcate certain areas as their own. This demarcation acts as a warning to all potential intruders. The calls or cries of birds or animals are often very specific in meaning. They establish territory as the province of a particular being or herd and indicate the willingness of the individual to fight for his domain. In many species there are rather elaborate mechanisms by which members define borderlines and show themselves willing to engage in conflict with anyone who crosses them. Such overstepping of boundary lines is regarded as a threat to the survival of the animal or group. Note that much of the conflict-avoiding behavior in the animal world is a response to **perceived** threats: The animal reacts to a perceived threat whether or not a threat actually exists.

Many animals have evolved a highly complex system of defense of self and territory. Bees, for example, cluster together in hives. The hive, or colony, cannot survive if the leader of the hive, the queen bee, is killed. Therefore, in response to threats, the bees will envelop the queen in a living blanket, making it very difficult for any intruder to find her. They will attack and sting any intruder who enters their domain. Ardrey notes that there is a similar willingness to fight to preserve territory on the part of the cicada-killer wasp. The wasp will take up the fight against any intruder either by threat, his buzzing sound, or by actually giving chase, and if that is not sufficient, by "butting him in mid-air . . . or in the last resort, grappling with him, tumbling to earth and trying if possible to bite out his eyes." The wasp will defend his territory against anything. "He will attack a pebble rolled across his border."[1]

It is evident that engaging in conflict in order to preserve oneself, one's possessions, or one's position or territory is a strong motivation common to many species. Similarly, we can note that animals, like man, engage in conflict over goals such as status, often with one animal seeking to preserve his preeminent position among the herd and other animals seeking to displace the leader and increase their status. Often animals cluster in such a way that there is one dominant male leader who is periodically challenged for his leadership. Seals, for example, form such clusters. It is interesting how often leaders are able to defeat intruders from outside the territory. Perhaps this is because there is a particular passion which animates man and animals when defending their homeland or their position on their home ground. There is of course the additional factor that the challenger is on unfamiliar ground and at a disadvantage.

Self-Preservation in Man

We have focused on some examples in the animal world particularly because they illustrate that some of the characteristics we think of as peculiarly human seem to be quite common among many species. The engaging in conflict by men to protect territory and possessions is, of course, a process evident throughout history. Not only do men respond to actual intrusions on their territory or attacks on their person or property, but like the animals they engage in an intricate system of warning signals to potential enemies in the hope of avoiding conflict. Sometimes nations find themselves faced with conflict because they have failed to give adequate notice to their potential enemies. For

---

[1] Robert Ardrey, **The Territorial Imperative**, New York: Atheneum, 1966, p. 65.

example, the question of the stockpiling of arms and munitions can be seen in some respects as a means of preserving and defending one's resources. Nations stockpile both offensive and defensive weapons in the hope that such preparedness will deter war. The assumption is that if you can convince any potential enemy of your strength you will deter him from attacking you. In the event that your strategy of deterence should fail, you then have at your disposal the weapons which allow you to enter into the conflict and successfully defend yourself.

Churchill made the point that the policy of many European countries, particularly Britain in the period between World Wars I and II, was self-defeating in that it pressed for the disarmament of the victorious powers such as France and England while at the same time allowing Germany to violate the provisions of the Treaty of Versailles, which ended World War I, and to rearm. Churchill claimed that this policy destroyed the ability of the Allies to threaten Germany and thus paved the way for German aggression. He felt that had the Allies been willing to engage in greater military preparedness they could either have prevented the war or stopped Hitler at much less cost of human life. Churchill's basic point was that Britain did not realize the steps she should have taken to defend herself. She should have realized that her vital interests were threatened and taken appropriate steps to meet that threat and increase her credibility as a foe to the German war machine.[2]

Certainly one could hardly accuse the victorious Allies of World War II of failing to build a military capability to meet real or potential threats. Whether or not this has reduced the possibility of global conflict is a far from proven premise. Whether the major powers, the United States and the Soviet Union, have perhaps overstockpiled and overcommunicated their capabilities is a question which many people have asked. Much of the foreign policy of the Western and Eastern blocs in the post-World War II era has been dictated by perceptions of self-preservation and protection. Both the Soviet Union and the United States have sought to gain strategic advantages during this period but, in general, both countries have sought to avoid direct confrontation and have respected the implicit and sometimes explicit

[2] Winston Churchill, **The Second World War**, vol. I, **The Gathering Storm**, London: Cassell, 1948.

threats of each side. The armaments race, the building of missile fleets, and the controversial development and deployment of antimissile systems have all been motivated by consideration as to whether or not such policies will protect the country and avoid direct conflict. In a sense nuclear deterrence is similar to the primitive screeches or cries of animals in marking their territory and warding off threats. We boast of weapon advances, numbers of weapons, first-strike capacity, and even second-strike capacity as means of asserting our capability for defending our possessions, status, and resources. As evidenced by the events in the Dominican Republic, in Hungary, Czechoslovakia, and the 1962 missile crisis in Cuba, both the Soviet Union and the United States have been willing to engage in minor conflicts to demonstrate their ability to act strongly in the preservation of their perceived interests, while both have at the same time sought to avoid an all-out conflict.

Taxation and the Avoidance of Deprivation

In many ways the desire to avoid deprivation and protect one's resources can be seen in the behavior of individuals who vote on tax referendums. Most local school systems support themselves on the basis of the property tax. Under such a system of taxation, all property in a community is assessed and the school tax is a percentage of the assessed value of one's property. Usually such percentages are set by the school boards within limits determined by the state. The locality is periodically asked to continue or to raise the present tax rate in order to support the school system. Recently, within the United States, we have seen a wave of what can only be called taxpayer revolts as more and more requests for additional taxes are defeated in local elections. Interestingly it seems that the greatest source of resistance to such increases comes from the middle class and the lower-middle class. Often such people find themselves with limited resources and in a situation where any additional money is a highly valued commodity. The proposals for increased taxation cut into that supply of additional money, and one finds that in community after community there is increasingly less tolerance toward continuing to support increased levels of taxation for schools and other local services. Election campaigns over such proposals have often been intense and have aroused great hostility. Those who oppose increased taxation rates often see such taxation as the means for subsidizing nonessential programs and feel that given the scarcity of their resources they will refuse to support such programs. As the choice narrows to providing increasingly higher levels of private funds to support collective enterprises such as schools or to use private funds for private goods and enjoyment, the choice seems to be for the latter.

Organizational Survival

The motivation of preservation can even be seen in organizations and bureaucracies. Organizations have a will to survive and maintain themselves and indeed to expand their level of operations. In the United States government's bureaucracy, we can see many cases of overlapping jurisdiction—of agencies and divisions pursuing similar tasks and even duplicating efforts. Yet these agencies have been able to maintain themselves and ward off threats of merger and restructuring. One interesting example of an agency's fight for organizational self-preservation is the Army Corps of Engineers. In the United States, the Army Corps of Engineers has long been charged with such projects as irrigation and flood control, harbor widening, and construction or improvement of harbor facilities. When the Department of the Interior was created, its Bureau of Reclamation undertook work which was similar to the Corps' and soon challenged the Corps' claim to sole jurisdiction over many projects. The Corps of Engineers responded to this threat with an obvious willingness to do battle with the Department of the Interior and even the President, in order to save its projects and, of course, itself. The Corps had developed close relationships with congressmen over the years. To the congressman such projects as river and harbor development represented tangible, visible evidence of the efforts he was making in behalf of his constituents. Thus his relationship to the Corps was very important to him. Indeed the ties between the Corps and Congress had become so effective that in at least one instance a President was unable to win jurisdiction for a particular project for the Department of the Interior.[3] The Corps used whatever means it could find to maintain its supremacy within its field. It felt its existence threatened and was fighting to assure its survival. In this fight it was even willing to engage in conflict with other executive agencies within the bureaucracy to which it belonged.

---

[3] Arthus Maass, "The King's River Project," in Harold Stein (ed.), **Public Administration and Policy Development,** New York: Harcourt Brace Jovanovich, 1952.

There is a thrust for survival in large organizations which often continues even after the organization has completed the task for which it was originally formed. For example, the March of Dimes was created to fight infantile paralysis. When, after years of research and testing, polio vaccine was developed and infantile paralysis was no longer a great problem, the organization did not die. Rather it has attempted to maintain itself by finding a new cause—birth defects and arthritis—and has become quite active in these fields. Its struggle was not a conflict in the usual sense, since the March of Dimes was fighting time and obsolescence of purpose—an intangible, elusive combatant. And perhaps its struggle for survival was justified since the organization had become highly skilled in medical fund-raising, and such experience is a useful commodity. Nevertheless, its behavior reflects a characteristic of many organizations. They do not simply complete a task and then disband. Rather they seek to persevere and develop even after the completion of a task, and may even try to redefine their goals in such a way that they have an eternal function to perform.

CONFLICT AND RISK TAKING

In Chapter 2 we discussed the fact that the intensity of conflict is a function of the stakes involved in the conflict. As the stakes increase in value to the participants, the likelihood of conflict becoming intense or violent increases. There is an additional factor which affects the intensity of conflict and that is the degree of risk associated with attaining various potential payoffs in conflict situations. In seeking to gain certain payoffs or in preserving existing payoffs there are various degrees of risk involved. While we each may, in any given situation, desire to gain as much as possible, we are constrained by the costs in achieving that gain and the risks associated with it. Let us look at the following example.

If we consider the case of a television quiz show we can note that the contestants are not risking any of their own money. The payoffs of the game are economic, but they are provided externally to the contestants, who are competing with each other to determine how the prize money from the show shall be apportioned among them. The loser of the game is assured of some consolation prize to compensate him for his time. We therefore have a situation in which it is possible for both loser and winner to gain something as the result of their participation in the game. Let us assume that this is a two-person game. Under the rules of the game, the contestants may pursue a cooperative strategy with each other and divide the money equally or they may pursue noncooperative strategies and try to win all the prize money available. The noncooperative strategies may include bluffing or trying to convince your opponent that you are cooperating with him while in actuality you are preparing to doublecross him at the strategic moment. In this situation there are two strategic options to choose from: (1) a cooperative strategy which assures you half the winnings; and (2) a conflict strategy which offers either complete victory or complete defeat. Because the payoffs are not provided by the players— that is, player A's winnings are provided by the program—there is less risk involved in choosing alternative 2. Alternative 2 offers the chance to make great gains while being relatively costless to the participants. The gains from noncooperation are greater than the gains from cooperation. This does not mean that strategy 2 will usually be preferred to strategy 1, it only indicates that the situation has been structured in such a way that the risks of noncooperation are not particularly high. Whether the individual participants choose strategy 1 or 2 depends upon their utility for money and their psychological predisposition toward adventurous strategies or toward conservative strategies.

Contrast this situation, however, to a game in which the payoffs are not externally provided to the players but rather in which the costs of pursuing a strategy are borne by the participants. We can look at the classic nonzero-sum game, the Prisoner's Dilemma. In this situation two men are arrested and placed in separate interrogation rooms. The police do not have enough evidence to convict the men of the crime. During the course of the questioning the police point out to each prisoner, separately, that he has two options, to confess or not to confess. If both prisoners do not confess, then the police will book them on some minor charge and both will receive minor punishment. If both confess, they will be prosecuted, but the district attorney will not press for the maximum sentence. If one confesses and the other does not, the one who confesses will get lenient treatment and the other will get the full penalty. The options are presented in Figure 3-1.[4]

---

[4] R. Duncan Luce and Howard Raiffa, **Games and Decisions,** New York: Wiley, 1957, pp. 94–95.

FIGURE 3-1
PAYOFFS IN THE PRISONER'S DILEMMA GAME

		PLAYER A	
		Confesses	Does not confess
PLAYER B	Confesses	Both *A* and *B* get less than maximum sentence on major charge	*A* gets maximum sentence *B* gets lenient treatment
	Does not confess	*A* gets lenient treatment *B* gets maximum sentence	Both *A* and *B* get off with light sentences on minor charge

In this case there is no communication allowed between the prisoners. Therefore, each has to calculate not only what his best strategy is but also what the probable strategy of the other prisoner will be. The high-risk strategy is to confess, hoping that the other prisoner will not. However, if in the absence of communication both confess, each winds up worse than if they had adopted the lower-risk strategy of not confessing. In this case the maximum gain, that is, the least possible sentence, also poses the risk of being the highest loss if the strategy is unsuccessful. In this case the risks of choosing the wrong strategy are borne by the participants and the nature of that decision is likely to require far greater concentration and intensity of feeling than is the case of the television quiz show.

These two situations are illustrative in several ways. In the example of the television quiz show each of the participants has nothing to lose for pursuing an unsuccessful strategy except his time. In the Prisoner's Dilemma, each of the participants must weigh his choice of strategy and pay careful attention both to the potential favorable payoffs as well as to the risks involved in each particular strategy.

The introduction of the element of risk indicates that in most conflict situations the stakes are not necessarily fixed. The stakes may vary according to the willingness of each participant to increase his risks for potentially higher rewards. Obviously there are certain goals we desire to attain or attain at higher levels of satisfaction and we are usually unwilling to face loss of our possessions or present resources Generally, people prefer gaining to losing. Our feelings about these matters, however, are not the same for all goals and all levels of gain or deprivation. Where the stakes are high and the conflict concerns a highly desired goal, we may be willing to tolerate much higher degrees of risk to satisfy our goals than in situations where the stakes may be high but we do not think the goals are worthy of risk taking. On the other hand, we are often not willing to go to much trouble for what seems to be a relatively minor threat or deprivation about something we care only slightly. For some people, status is so important that they are willing to risk both security and status in order to attain it.

CATEGORIES OF CONFLICT SITUATIONS

It is essential to remember that the distinction between the two basic motivational categories, gain and preservation, is strictly an analytic one. As the case of the Prisoner's Dilemma illustrates, participants who have to consider risks must often consider both these motives simultaneously. Indeed we may find very few examples of motivation only for gain or only for preservation. Mixtures and gradations of the two are much more common. For example, a person seeking gain, because of the risk involved, may engage in behavior which allows him to reach a level of satisfaction which falls short of his full goal. He is balancing, maximizing his gain against minimizing the risks involved.

Nevertheless, from the analytical viewpoint it is necessary to set up some sort of model and to establish the basic categories of conflict situations. Although the categories are abstractions and therefore somewhat oversimplified, they are highly instrumental in helping us to understand the process of conflict. If we set up a simple matrix for two actors in a given conflict, each of whom may be motivated primarily by gain or by the desire for preservation, we can see that three basic conflict situations emerge: (1) gain-gain, (2) gain-preservation, and (3) preservation-preservation (see Figure 3-2). For the sake of completing the matrix, there is the additional category of preservation-gain but since this is just a mirror image of situation 2, with

FIGURE 3-2
MOTIVATIONAL CATEGORIES OF CONFLICT SITUATIONS

		ACTOR 1	
		Gain	Preservation
ACTOR 2	Gain	Gain-Gain	Gain-Preservation
	Preservation	Preservation-Gain	Preservation-Preservation

the motives of the actors reversed it can be considered simultaneously with gain-preservation.

Gain-Gain

We have discussed this type of conflict earlier. It occurs in a situation where individuals, in seeking a particular gain, are brought into conflict with each other. Both participants are seeking to gain something, but because of limited resources only one can win. Our television quiz show is an example of this type of conflict situation. Similarly, sporting events could be classified in this manner. However, it is true that while both teams are desirous of winning, each is also concerned with maintaining its standing within its particular league. In all strictly competitive games, each team wishes to win and each is motivated by the desire for the gain which winning entails.

Gain-Preservation

In a gain-preservation situation the motivating factors behind each actor's behavior are different. One actor desires to attain a particular goal; however, the attainment of it poses a distinct threat to other individuals or groups. For the goal can only be attained by depriving others or by making others worse off than they are at present. For example, proposals for nationalization of industries or land reform fit into this category. If we assume an existent state of affairs in which land may be unequally distributed or where industry is in private hands, demands for breaking up large estates and distributing the land to the peasants, or nationalizing industry and distributing the profits among the workers fit into this category of conflict. One set of actors, those pushing for reform, is seeking gain either for itself or in the name of some segment of the population. This can only come at the expense of those who presently control the land or industry. The latter forces mobilize not to increase their land distributions or control of industry but to preserve the status quo.

Preservation-Preservation

The preservation-preservation conflict is probably the most difficult to understand since at first glance it would seem that if neither actor is concerned with gaining anything from the other actor, there would also be no threat of loss and therefore no motivation for conflict. Nevertheless, conflict situations of this type do exist. In some respects they represent competition or conflict between actors as a means of avoiding intense conflicts which would threaten the relative positions of the actors. The preservation-preservation conflict is born out of an atmosphere of fear and mistrust. In international relations nations often distrust each other and seek to protect themselves from possible or potential aggressive action by other nations. Even in the absence of immediate threats such behavior is not uncommon. In the post-World War II period it is possible to suggest that the Soviet Union and the United States do not have territorial designs on each other. Yet, because of differing social, economic, political, and legal systems, there is great distrust between the two nations. Such distrust could exist between any two countries because of the potential for aggressive actions or because of a history of bad relations between the countries. In this situation, while both countries do not desire territorial gains, each perceives the other as a threat, as a potential aggressor. The conflict exists because each of the participants feels that it exists and thinks it necessary to act in whatever way it perceives will best preserve its present strategic position. One may react to potentially aggressive behavior on the part of another country, while the latter country perceives that reaction to be a justification of fears of the aggressive intent of the former nation. Consequently, the two countries raise armies, strengthen their territorial defenses, and engage in rather elaborate strategic planning. While each of these acts may really be defensive in nature, in a climate of mutual suspicion it will probably be perceived by the other nation as potentially aggressive and of evil design. Thus, the activities of defense or preservation serve as a fulfillment of the perceptions of aggression to the participants. This is obviously a simplification of the tensions which lead to an armaments race between the two countries, such as the United States and the Soviet Union. While it is probably true that each has no territorial designs on the other, both do compete for influence in various parts of the world. However, one can suggest that part of this competition is a result of mutual distrust and the desire to achieve strategic advantages against a potential enemy.

Certainly much of America's present-day theory of deterrence is an example of strategic defense. The assumption of most deterrence theories is that if you raise the risks of potential gain high enough, you can deter aggressive activity. The attempt is made to establish a situation in which major powers cannot afford a nuclear war, and each nation maintains this situation through a balance of armaments. While each side feels that its strategy is rationally sound, each fears that mere parity in arms might bring with it the introduction of irrationality, the willingness to engage in risk taking. Thus, there is a constant striving by each side to develop an edge of security, of superiority, and it is this desire which so strongly fuels an armament race. While one may question the meaningfulness of deterrence theory, the basic assumptions have formed American military and foreign policy during the entire postwar period and are a dominant element of our present environment.

CONCLUSION

We have focused in this chapter on the motivations of conflict. Our categories are based on the motivations. It is possible that various motivations may be present in either zero-sum or nonzero-sum situations. The response of the participants to various conflict situations will in part depend upon the nature of their motivations and the risks associated in achieving favorable action of those goals which motivate action.

SUGGESTED READINGS

Ardrey, Robert, **The Territorial Imperative,** New York: Atheneum, 1966.
Hobbes, Thomas, **Leviathan,** ed. Michael Oakeshott, Oxford: Basil Blackwell, 1960.
Lorenz, Konrad, **On Aggression,** New York: Harcourt Brace Jovanovich, 1966.
McNeil, Elton (ed.), **The Nature of Human Conflict,** Englewood Cliffs, N. J.: Prentice-Hall, 1965.

Chapter 4

The Environment of Conflict

In the previous chapters we have discussed the structure of conflict situations and the motives for engaging in conflict. Before we use this conceptual framework to analyze political phenomena, however, we must ask ourselves a few more questions pertaining to the conflict model. What types of variables do actors consider before deciding whether to engage in conflict? Once conflict has begun, what types of calculations affect its nature, duration, and intensity? These factors are numerous, but can be grouped into broad categories: (1) **goals,** (2) **resources,** (3) **institutions and structures,** (4) **norms and mores of conduct,** and (5) **strategies.** Such factors concern all conflict situations although, of course, their importance and interrelationships are determined by the particular situation. Nevertheless, each of the five categories deserves individual attention.

GOALS

As we indicated earlier, human beings, like all species of life, are goal-seeking by nature. In many species a single goal may be pursued: **survival.** Survival will depend upon such simple needs as food, shelter, protection from predators, and procreation of the species. Even within the framework of these elementary goals, however, conflict will inevitably arise. For example, the creature may be forced to decide between his need for food and taking risks which expose him to danger. He often needs to leave the protection of his shelter in order to seek food. Good or more bountiful food sources may exist in a particular location but that location may also abound in predators. Each animal must cautiously balance the elements so that the pursuit of one goal does not jeopardize the other interrelated components of survival. What we are suggesting is that not only is there conflict among animals and men on the basis of their goals, but that the individual animal or man must also face up to internal conflicts concerning the satisfaction of various goals.

Certainly, if this state of conflict exists even among the most elementary goals, how great must be the cross-pressures for human beings involved in the pursuit of multiple goals. Man, like the animals, needs food, shelter, and offspring to ensure his own survival and the survival of his species. However, his goals and his level of satisfaction tend to be higher than animals. Man's acquisitiveness extends beyond the need for a survival level of satisfaction, and because of his intellectual capacities the range of goals which he may pursue is larger and more complex than that of the animals. Man is a comfort-seeking creature and this demands higher levels of satisfaction than mere subsistence.

If we consider again how the pursuit of a few goals such as shelter and food often creates conflict for the lower animals, we can see how the many and diverse goals of man cannot help but pull him in several directions. For example, the pursuit of wealth may not be congruent with the desire for status or power. In pursuing numerous goals, man continually must balance his desire for one thing against his desire for another. Similarly, he has to balance what he has already achieved against what may be lost in striving for new or different goals. Fortunate is the man who can structure his environment so that he can simultaneously pursue several goals while avoiding conflict among them.

As we indicated earlier, the stakes involved in a given conflict may not and often are not just economic; they can as easily be symbolic or ideological. Some people may be willing to forego economic gains, even to accept economic privations, yet they will be adamant about fighting for their spiritual, moral, or aesthetic values. Thus the political scientist must remember that all men pursue numerous goals, and their behavior, while perhaps not consistent in all cases, is guided by how important they consider a particular goal to be in any given context.

RESOURCES

The resources at the disposal of the individual combatant also influence his behavior and attitude toward engaging in conflict. The attainment of a particular goal may be important to an individual but his choice of arena for the satisfaction of that goal will vary according to his resources. For example, a man may crave status and admiration. He may choose to compete in the athletic arena to satisfy that craving. However, if his physical resources make such competition futile, it is likely that he will choose some other arena to achieve this satisfaction. This is an additional complexity involved in any analysis. Even knowing what goals an individual desires to attain will not necessarily indicate the manner in which he will go about achieving or satisfying those desires. The arena he chooses is a calculation based on his estimation of himself and his resources and the requirements for success in the various arenas from which he may choose. The resources available to each person necessarily affect his ability and desire to maintain his present level of accomplishment and to achieve advancement. He must consider not only his final goal but also the means he will employ to attain it. No action is costless. Costs, however, may be of several kinds, yet all costs involve expenditures of resources. These may be as simple as time. We often don't think of time as a cost, yet it is a consideration as to whether certain actions are or are not feasible for the individual. Costs may include the expenditure of such resources as physical energy. Costs may also be psychological ones, such as the amount of stress or pressure which the individual will have to endure to attain his goal. Often the costs for one goal will be viewed in terms of other goals. The attainment of one goal may involve the commitment of resources which cannot then be committed in the pursuit of other goals. Some resources are capable of being replenished while others, once expended, cannot be reclaimed. In making a decision as to whether to pursue a high-risk strategy, the individual must consider not only what resources he will have to commit but what this commitment of resources means to his ability to simultaneously or sequentially pursue alternative goals.

The Relation of Resources to Power

The particular goal of human behavior upon which political scientists have focused most attention is the desire for **power.** Their concern has been with who has power and what power is. A principal factor in answering these questions lies in a third query: In any particular society, what resources are necessary for anyone wishing to compete for power? If we know what the necessary resources are, and if we know how these resources are distributed throughout the society, we can begin to make assessments as to who is advantaged or disadvantaged and who is in a position to compete for political power.

Several definitions of power have been suggested by political scientists. Perhaps one of the clearest is that put forward by Robert Dahl. Dahl defines power in a two-person sense. He says that "A has power over B to the extent that he can get B to do something that B would not otherwise do."[1] Someone therefore has power over another if he has the ability to **change behavior.** This definition is an economical one but it often fails, in specific situations, to enable us to identify who has power over whom. Political power is not a single-faceted phenomena. Furthermore, not all instances of the application of power resolve themselves neatly into two-person situations. The appearance and manifestation of political power may be quite different in different arenas. The simple definition does not get to the problem that the resources necessary to exert behavior may vary enormously from setting to setting. The essence of political power in a party organization may require resources very dissimilar to those needed for political power in an administrative bureaucracy or in a legislature. We can still speak, however, of power as a situationally determined factor which

---

[1] Robert A. Dahl, "The Concept of Power," reprinted in Nelson Polsby, Robert Dentler, and Paul Smith (eds.), **Politics and Social Life,** Boston: Houghton Mifflin, 1963, p. 107.

through the application of specific resources allows one individual to affect the behavior of others.

In some situations the resource for exerting power over other individuals is a function of hierarchy. Those at the top of the hierarchy can issue commands to subordinates and exert power over their behavior. However, it is in the more subtle areas of power that the question of resources and the direction of power become difficult to assess. Bargaining situations, particularly where both participants are relatively equal, are examples of situations where both participants are seeking to use their resources to modify each other's behavior. Consider the following example.

If I want someone to perform a service for me, I may have to use certain resources to change his behavior so that the service will be performed. Without payment of resources he probably will not be willing to help me. To the extent that, by the expenditure of resources, I can get people to do things for me which they would not ordinarily do, I have power over them. A business executive's power over his subordinates is based upon his control over their salaries. Without the resources to pay these employees, he would be unable to persuade them to do the work he desires to have done. Thus it is his ability to commit the necessary resources which enables him to exert power.

Often, however, power is not so easily defined. For instance, suppose that the executive above is desirous of having a service performed and has to contract privately for that service. He is willing to pay one hundred dollars for it. Unfortunately, those workers who are able to perform that service state that they will not do so for less than two hundred dollars. An arrangement is finally reached, and the service is performed for one hundred and fifty dollars. Who has exercised power over whom? Our executive has induced his worker to do something which he would not otherwise have done; that is, the worker has performed the service for him for less than he originally wanted. The worker has forced our executive to do something he would not otherwise have done; he has spent more of his resources than he originally had wanted to spend. In this case both actors seem to be exerting power, and the question of who has power over whom is difficult to answer.

One can find similar analogies in the bargains that are struck in a legislature, the exchanging of support for bills among members. In this case, members of the legislature engage in negotiations whereby they get support for their bills from other members by expending their own resources—often by agreeing to support other legislation or by promises of present or future favors.

The separation of resources and goals into two distinct categories is purely for analytic purposes, as are our other categories. Any decision to engage in conflict and the extent of that conflict depend on perhaps the subconscious ways in which individuals calculate the importance of their goals and the relevant resources. If we assume that most people are not masochists, then we can note that most individuals set themselves goals which they perhaps see as attainable in the light of their calculations as to their own resources and the resources necessary for success.

INSTITUTIONS AND STRUCTURES

The attainment of goals and the kinds of resources necessary to achieve particular goals in a society depends largely upon the institutions and structures within that society. Whenever we are seeking a particular goal, we tend to ask ourselves what are the normal channels for achieving success. Any society specifies certain conduct as legal or illegal. Robbery is one way to achieve a goal of wealth, but in our society it is regarded as wrong. Therefore the institutional framework for achieving wealth is through routes other than robbery. Societies specify the acceptable channels for gaining rewards and use their resources and coercive powers to punish those who use extralegal means. In this way the societies specify what kinds of activity are approved of and will be rewarded and what kinds will be punished. This is one of the primary purposes of political order: to provide meaningful, regular, and predictable channels through which people may achieve specified goals.

Societies and governments develop institutions in order to implement and regularize the desired norms of conduct. The nature of the political order is usually characterized by the basic charter or constitution of the society. A constitution stipulates the institutions comprising the political structure, the procedures of government, and the appropriate channels for the exercise of political power. In the United States the Constitution stipulates the Presidency and the Congress as the seats of executive and legislative authority respectively. It not only establishes the organs which may legitimately exercise political power but also stipulates that those seeking to exercise such authority must contest for office through an electoral process. The Constitution also establishes a judicial branch to ensure that deviations from the established institutional pattern are punished.

Political parties in democratic societies provide the institutional framework for settling political disputes and handling the problem of succession of authority within the electoral process. Persons aspiring to political office almost always work through political parties. In the context of our discussion above, the society has designated the political party as the legitimate instrument through which one can seek to achieve the goal of political power. Parties disappear and are replaced by new ones when they no longer serve as effective institutions through which members can seek and win office. When a particular political party no longer functions as an effective channel for the satisfaction of political ambitions, it tends to be superseded by a more electorally viable organization. After the War of 1812, the Federalist party ceased to be an effective electoral organization. The existence of competitive political parties provides multiple outlets for the ambitions of those seeking political office. Where parties are competitive, that is, where each party has a reasonable chance of winning, rotation of party control of elective offices is usually frequent enough to provide effective channels for those who have political ambition.[2] In many respects one could say that the existence of contested elections provides not only a means for ambitious individuals to attain political office, but also serves the function of providing participation for the general population in the process of deciding who the national leaders shall be. The victory of one's preferred candidate is in some respects a vicarious victory for his supporters.

One of the sources of instability in one-party regimes is that the party is capable of absorbing only a limited number of persons who have political ambitions. There is no competition for office and consequently no promise of alternation in office holders. Therefore, the official structures of that society seem to block political advancement. Conflict may result between those who occupy office and those who see the legitimate path to office as being blocked. This is why such societies are often characterized by revolt and by coups d'état. The society offers a channel for the satisfaction of political ambition, but that

---

[2] Joseph A. Schlesinger, **Ambition and Politics**, Skokie, Ill.: Rand McNally, 1966. Schlesinger discusses the manner in which the opportunity structure conditions whether a society will be able to satisfy the political ambitions of its citizens.

channel is in many respects inadequate to handling the demands of those who seek success through such channels.

In the United States the institutions and procedures of party competition are well developed. The nominating and electoral process indicates the channels by which the contest for political power is institutionalized. The existence of a federal system with independent federal, state, and local governments provides numerous outlets for the energies of those desirous of political authority. The competition and the open structure of opportunity, which demands very few prerequisites as a condition for running for office, have tended, at least until now, to give the United States a fairly high degree of political stability. The channels have been perceived by most citizens to be legitimate and adequate. Not only is there the possibility of alternation in power between the parties, but the existence of the primary offers the opportunity for competition within the parties for nominations and the chance to contest elections. Therefore, those desirous of political office must calculate their chances of attaining that goal within the accepted structures. In other countries, resorting to violence or nonparty activity, while not perceived as legitimate, is done so frequently that it may not even arouse the indignation of the population.

Once an American citizen has decided to seek political office, he must subscribe not only to the procedures of his political party but also to the accepted methods of political campaigning. These procedures and methods stipulate the nature of the resources which are required for his winning political office. Recently many people have maintained that the monetary resources necessary for high political office inhibit all but the wealthiest men or persons who have access to large sums of money from running for office. As a political fact, the cost of campaigning requires that the candidates have large financial resources at their disposal in order to be able to compete for office. One of the objections which has been raised to the idea of direct national primaries for nominating Presidential candidates is that this structural change would increase the need for a candidate to have large personal resources. That is, a change in the structures would change the amount or kinds of resources necessary to try for the Presidential nomination. We can see the importance of financial resources for running for major office when we note that in 1952 the combined expenditures of the Democrats and Republicans for the Presidential election exceeded $11 million. If anything, this figure is an understatement of the actual amount of money spent.[3] The amount of money has, of course, increased over the years and completely dwarfs that $11 million figure. The addition of a nation-wide primary would add immeasurably to the costs of campaigning. It would require each contestant for the party nomination to mount a national campaign for the nomination whose probable cost would be similar to the costs of an actual Presidential campaign. This would place an enormous burden on the individual candidates' resources and make it almost a prerequisite of office that individuals have large amounts of personal wealth at their disposal. Much of the money available to the candidate in the general election is raised either by him or channeled to him through the regular contributors to the party. This second channel would probably not be available to contenders in the primary. The party leaders could not endorse a particular candidate and all party money would be withheld pending the outcome of the primary. This seemingly simple change would vastly alter the resources which are necessary to achieve success through the channel of contesting the Presidency.

The alternative of having government provide, out of tax revenues, funds for the candidates' campaign costs in order to remove reliance on personal wealth or big contributors, poses many other additional problems. Some means would have to be found to screen out the frivolous or nonserious candidate from the potential contender. Such a system of government financing would lower the resources necessary to contest for office and thereby probably increase the number of people willing to contest the office. If a sufficient number of contestants entered the field, the drain on resources would be quite large and would pose significant problems. What we are suggesting is that the nature of the institutions and the laws structure the resources necessary for success. Any change in the institutional structure changes those resource patterns sometimes with positive and sometimes with negative results.

Basically the institutions and structures in a society determine the structure of opportunity. They indicate what offices are available and what the prerequisites are for those offices and positions. It is important to note that having the motivation for political office and the resources for attaining political office would be meaningless unless there were opportunities in the political arena for achieving office.

---

[3] Alexander Heard, "The Costs of Politics," reprinted in William J. Crotty, Donald M. Freeman, and Douglas S. Gatlin (eds.), **Political Parties and Political Behavior,** Boston: Allyn & Bacon, 1966, p. 320.

NORMS AND MORES OF CONDUCT

Cultures and societies may have similar structures of opportunity but may differ in terms of what they consider to be permissible standards of conduct for attaining goals. For example, in a culture that places an emphasis on the avoidance of violence and stresses the need for compromise and conciliation, the use of violence to achieve a goal obviously will be regarded as illegitimate. Thus, other means have to be developed for the attainment of goals. Yet another society may place an emphasis on strength and greatly respect the use of physical force. In such a culture it would be regarded as legitimate to resort to force; indeed, persuasion or gentler techniques might be thought of as illegitimate since they could be interpreted as acts of cowardice.[4]

The norms of conduct exert an official and unofficial power in determining the type of conduct which will be pursued by persons or parties in conflict situations. Combatants are expected to adhere to these norms, and violating them often brings punishment.

In the United States, formal political power is obtained largely through the electoral framework set out by the Constitution and elaborated by various state and federal laws. Nevertheless, laws cannot completely dictate the style of a campaign nor can they wholly prevent fraud or the use of innuendo or smear tactics. Fair campaign laws and committees do exist, but those who desire to evade these laws can do so fairly easily. It is interesting to note, however, that increasingly few candidates do evade them. United States voters seem to place a premium on fairness, on a willingness to abide by rules, and on avoiding foul play. One can note a sharp decline from the previous century in illegal practices such as stuffed ballot boxes, forged registration lists, and malicious or unfounded accusations against candidates. Candidates for elective office may not all conduct their campaigns as paragons of virtue nor are the instances of vote fraud no longer with us, yet there can be little doubt that the frequency of fraud and misconduct has declined.[5]

---

[4] For an interesting discussion of alternative authority patterns, see Walter Miller, "Two Concepts of Authority," **American Anthropologist,** vol. LVII (April, 1955).

[5] An example of how much restraint is used by candidates in campaigns and how they try to avoid smear tactics can be seen in the 1968 Presidential campaign. In late October, 1968, Mrs. Chennault, the Chinese widow of the late General Claire

STRATEGIES

The fifth and final factor to be discussed is strategy, and it, of course, is interrelated with the other four factors we have examined. A strategy is the particular set of tactics, moves, or behavior which the actor adopts to achieve his goal. The type of strategy a person pursues may be varied. He may employ a single strategy or multiple strategies. Whatever his final choice, however, he must consider whether it is an **insider strategy,** that is, one that can be pursued within the acceptable framework which the society has set up, or an **outsider strategy**, one that the society may regard as illegitimate. Both types of strategies have distinct advantages and disadvantages.

For example, let us once again consider the costs, the drain on resources, of pursuing a goal. Often a person may reason as follows: "If I desire money, what are the costs of gaining it through the channels prescribed by the system? What are the costs and probable benefits if I can take some shortcuts: cheat or go outside the prescribed norms? If I work through the approved channels, I am bound by the rules of the game and the costs that those rules impose. If I go outside the system, then the rules of behavior no longer bind, and I have great freedom of maneuver. But what happens if I get caught?" Such a person will consider the costs as well as the advantages involved in an outsider strategy and will act accordingly. Indeed, the purpose of criminal law is to make the risks, the cost of engaging in antisocial, "outside" behavior high enough so that people will be deterred from going outside the approved channels.

The designation of what is an outsider and what is an insider strategy changes over time with changing laws, institutions, and norms of behavior. For example, initially organized labor was viewed as a sinister

---

Chennault, had been active in raising money for Richard Nixon's campaign. Mrs. Chennault was opposed to starting peace negotiations with North Vietnam and the Vietcong in Paris. She was in communication with several influential people in the Vietnamese government. Consequently, several Vietnamese legislators announced that they favored Richard Nixon's election, and President Thieu raised several obstacles to the Paris Peace conference. This information could have been a significant issue for Hubert Humphrey. However, while aware of the issue, he did not raise it. He felt that Nixon was unaware of Mrs. Chennault's activity and would have forbidden it. He therefore refused to use the issue in the campaign. For a more complete account of this episode, see Theodore White, **The Making of the President, 1968,** New York: Atheneum, 1969, pp. 443–445.

force which would disrupt the American social, political, and economic system. The strike was seen as an outsider strategy, and United States courts were quite ready to issue injunctions against this "unlawful activity." Since that time unions have become not only accepted but powerful organizations, and the strike has been recognized as a justifiable tactic which labor may resort to in bargaining with management.

Today, however, most state governments have passed legislation stating that strikes by public employees are illegal. In recent years public employees (school teachers, sanitation men, transit workers, and even police and firemen) have felt that the existing procedures were inadequate for the satisfaction of their grievances. They have resorted to what was essentially an outsider strategy. They defied the laws, engaged in strikes to secure their demands, and dared the state government to enforce its weapons against them. Most states faced with such situations have recognized the inadequacy of their legislation and are seeking to establish appropriate channels for negotiations with public employees so that fair contracts can be achieved and strikes prevented. Although the establishment of new channels takes time, it is noteworthy that, faced with an outsider strategy, the government authorities have recognized the inadequacy of the existing procedures. They have tried, without giving sanction to the tool of the strike by public employees, to develop alternative channels which will be satisfactory.

In the contest for political power, groups may decide that they do not have the resources to compete effectively within the prescribed channels, or they may feel that the established procedures work too slowly, or that the changes they wish to see enacted are too sweeping to win acceptance through legitimate channels. Consequently, they may resort to revolutionary and conspiratorial activity. They forsake the strategy of pursuing change within existing institutions and organize themselves as an outsider group to overthrow that institutional structure. This has been the pattern for most conspiratorial groups, and this is the pattern which most Communist parties have adopted at one time or another in non-Communist countries. Interestingly enough, however, in several Western countries such as Italy and France the Communist party has sought to present itself as a party of change but one which is legitimate in that it is willing to abide by the rules of the game and advance its cause through elections and participation in parliaments. The Communist party in France was probably as surprised as anyone else at the revolutionary rhetoric and tactics of the students in the 1968 uprisings.

The choice of working within or outside of existing channels is a primary decision, but it certainly is not the only decision of strategic importance. For example, having decided to work within the system still leaves an actor with an array of tactics from which to choose. A man desirous of having a particular piece of legislation passed may find several alternative strategies available. He may work through existing pressure groups to mobilize support for the proposed legislation, organize new groups to fight for it, support legislative candidates who will vote for it, or even run for office himself. He may pursue any or all of these strategies. Here again his choice of strategies will be influenced by the importance of the goal to him, the resources available, the receptivity of various institutions to these goals, and what is considered acceptable conduct for achieving results.

Often a person will be forced to use competing strategies to achieve a particular goal. This situation frequently faces the candidate of a minority party in a predominantly one-party area. Republicans who run for election in large cities may be confronted by this problem. They have to activate the party faithful, the staunch Republicans, and get them out to vote. This kind of partisan appeal, however, is apt to reduce the possibility of getting the votes of independents and Democrats. Therefore, the candidate must simultaneously pursue two different strategies. To Republican audiences he must emphasize his belief in Republican principles and establish his credentials as a good Republican. To Democrats and independents he must play down his partisan affiliation, stress his own personality and ability, and assert that the proper running of City Hall is not a partisan question but rather a question of who is the better man. This is a difficult strategy to follow, but the minority candidate cannot be elected if he fails in it. Without pursuing multiple, and perhaps even competing, strategies he cannot attain his goal.

A further question must be kept in mind no matter what strategy an individual or group decides to use. How binding is this particular strategy? Once he has adopted it, can he reverse or alter his course of action? Strategies require commitment of resources, and the actor's ability to abandon or modify that strategy is limited by his ability to absorb the loss he has sustained in using such resources as well as by his psychological commitment to a particular goal or strategy.

There are many examples one can cite to demonstrate the impact of irreversible strategy. The man who decided to become a medical doctor is required to go through four years of college, four years of medical school, one year of internship, and usually several years of residency. It is relatively easy for an undergraduate to modify or change his career goals. By the time a man is an intern, however, it is quite difficult to reverse these decisions because of the amount of time and money spent and the emotional commitment involved. By the end of internship, a doctor probably will be willing, at most, to change specialties. At the end of residency even a change here is unusual because so much time and effort have already been invested in a particular specialty. The longer a given goal is pursued with one strategy, the more resources that are invested, the less reversible that commitment becomes. Thus the man choosing strategies may lean toward one which does not foreclose, or forecloses the fewest number of, alternative strategies.

One comment often made about the war in Vietnam is that it illustrates how a strategy, when pursued over time, can lock you in and foreclose options. Many of our activities and the level of involvement in Vietnam were the result of several small decisions which cumulatively created a strategic situation that was difficult to reverse. The decision to introduce fighting troops of the United States into that war led to further demands that more troops be introduced to protect and sustain those that we had already sent. As the number of troops became larger and larger, it became increasingly hard to talk about withdrawal. This had the effect of Americanizing the war to the extent that the reputation of United States fighting forces as well as the prestige of the country were at stake. The decision to bomb the North followed a similar pattern. Strategic considerations led the government to decide it had to retaliate against North Vietnam. Once bombing began, it assumed, as in the case of troop deployment, a momentum of its own which was difficult to stop. Bombing was thought to be important and, since initially it was not doing the job it was supposed to do, the administration felt that we were not doing enough of it. As the bombing increased in scale, although not necessarily in effectiveness, the strategy became difficult to reverse. Continuing the bombing was a justification for beginning it. To unilaterally end the bombing would be to state openly that this strategy, costly in terms of material and men, was a failure. In other ways, too, our decisions committed us more and more deeply and made changing tactics nearly impossible. Ultimately it appeared that the only way to begin to turn around United States strategy was to replace the administration which was so heavily committed to justifying it. The decision that Lyndon Johnson announced in March, 1968, to renounce the bombing of North Vietnam was presented as a tactic which might increase the chance for peace. The rhetoric had to be changed in order to justify the reversal of a strategic decision. One can note that it was difficult to make this transition. Numerous efforts had been made to convince the administration to cease the bombing. These had all failed until, in March, Johnson announced that he would indeed cease the bombing and not be a candidate for reelection.

It is important to note that a series of small decisions can have the cumulative impact of locking one into a particular strategy. In conflict situations, particularly international conflict where the stakes are so frighteningly high, involved parties must consider the cumulative impact of decisions. Retaining the capacity to redefine goals, to reconsider commitments of resources, to maintain options, and to feel free to call off a strategy as a bad bet is an important factor in successfully achieving a goal.

CONCLUSION

The five factors we have discussed are obviously highly interrelated. It is almost impossible to consider one without simultaneously considering all others. The separation we have made is for analytic purposes. Every day, in most of our activities, we do make decisions concerning conflict behavior which involve these variables. These factors become particularly salient and complex when we are faced with decisions of vital importance. The more important the conflict, the more we tend to weigh each of these factors and, of course, try to determine their interrelationships and relative importance.

SUGGESTED READINGS

Coleman, James S., **Community Conflict**, New York: Free Press, 1957.
Dahl, Robert A., "The Concept of Power," **Behavioral Science**, vol. II, no. 3 (July, 1957).
Dahl, Robert A. (ed.), **Political Oppositions in Western Democracies**, New Haven, Conn.: Yale University Press, 1966.

Dahl, Robert A., and Charles E. Lindblom, **Politics, Economics and Welfare**, New York: Harper & Row, 1953.

March, James G., "The Power of Power," in David Easton (ed.), **Varieties of Political Theory**, Englewood Cliffs, N.J.: Prentice-Hall, 1966.

Riker, William, "Some Ambiguities in the Notion of Power," **American Political Science Review**, vol. LVIII, no. 2 (June, 1964).

Chapter 5

Conflict
&
the Political
Process

In the first four chapters we discussed the phenomenon of conflict as it pervades all human life and activity. We now turn to the specific case of political conflict. The political arena is the ultimate sphere for the resolution of competing claims, values, demands, and desires. Figure 5-1 provides a schematic diagram of the process of conflict resolution within the political arena. We shall first trace through the different states involved in the process and then study each phase in greater depth.

Figure 5-1 begins with the components of society: individuals and organizations, and institutions and structures. The first two are the potential actors; the second two represent the channels through which such actors can operate. Given any society, we know that conflicts naturally will arise as these individuals or groups, each with their own goals, interact. Many of these conflicts, however, do not become

FIGURE 5-1
CONFLICT RESOLUTION AND THE POLITICAL PROCESS

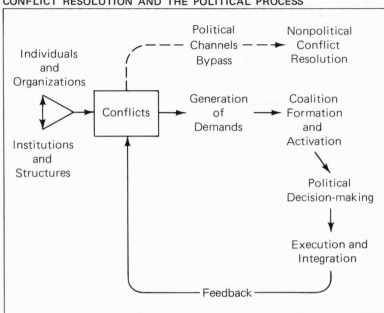

political in nature. They will either be unimportant and tend to fade away or they will be worked out by the parties to the dispute through the use of nonpolitical channels. This is indicated in Figure 5-1 by the "Political Channels Bypass."

Let us confine ourselves, however, to those disputes which do enter into the political process. Each actor has certain goals and demands which may clash with those of other interested parties. At first, his desires may be diffuse and unarticulated, but as he sees that the conflict is important and has political ramifications, he will tend to enumerate his demands as positively and distinctly as possible. It is here, with the **generation of demands,** that the first phase of conflict within the political process actually begins; it is here that the participants strive for **activation** or **politicization** of their conflict. They will attempt not only to state their demands in politically attractive terms but also to formulate strategies and enter into political coalitions in hopes of winning their case. They will try to put themselves in the most advantageous position possible as they enter into the second phase of the process, **political decision making.**

In the decision-making process, the coalitions and alliances (or individuals, where no alliances are formed) present their demands and direct them toward those institutions which are designed to handle such demands. If the coalitions are successful in reaching the "political elites," some form of decision will be made. This decision may be favorable or unfavorable, satisfactory or unsatisfactory, and it may be the result of compromise or coercion. Of the many demands reaching the political structure, only a few receive favorable and detailed' consideration.

Assuming, however, that a decision has somehow been made, we then enter the third phase of the political process: the **execution and integration** of decisions. As we see in Figure 5-1, this phase can be the end or, in a sense, the beginning. Sometimes the decision will be executed or implemented; the new status quo will be integrated into society, and the conflict will be effectively resolved. On the other hand, attempted execution of a decision may lead to new stumbling blocks and new conflicts will emerge. In this case the entire process will begin again.

Each solution and its resulting action affects the status quo, alters relationships among people, and may itself generate new conflict. Any political decision may become the basis for further activity. Even indecision or failure to take action can change the existing environment. It may encourage a mood or feeling about the responsiveness of political institutions and thereby influence the level and nature of future demands.

The model we have set out delineates three phases within the conflict process: (1) activation and politicization, (2) political decision making, and (3) execution and integration. In order to understand the relationships among these three phases, it is necessary to examine the dynamics which are operative in each. During each phase there are questions of strategy, tactics, and goals which must be decided. As we discuss these various considerations, we shall enlarge upon our initial diagram of conflict resolution and the political process.

PHASE 1: ACTIVATION AND POLITICIZATION

As we noted earlier, most conflicts do not involve political action. It is true that in any society the ultimate arbiter of all conflicts is the political arena; nevertheless, even within this arena societies seek to institutionalize procedures for the resolution of conflict so that no one political institution is overloaded. The purpose of a civil as well as a criminal code of law is to establish normal procedures and channels for the resolution of conflict. Indeed, much of societal conflict is resolved through the courts. Personal arguments, marital problems, and labor-management disputes are usually settled either outside the political arena or in the courts. In a sense, a legal code is the society's answer for conflicts which tend to be repetitive. It is the political system's attempt to resolve conflict and enforce decisions in an institutionalized, judicious manner. In this sense the courts are traditional channels of conflict resolution and are empowered to interpret decisions made by other political authorities. If we exclude legal cases, however, how do issues become political and require governmental action? We can discuss this process with relation to Figure 5-2.

When conflict emerges, participants may ask themselves whether this type of dispute is normally handled by political means. If the answer is no, then they probably will consider whether the usual channels of conflict resolution are appropriate. If the channels are appropriate, they simply will use them, and the conflict will not become political. If the regular means seem ineffective, however, they must consider whether the issues at stake are important enough to warrant recourse to further channels of conflict resolution, and particularly to political action. If the participants feel that the problem is important and that political channels are the only effective means for resolving it, they must redefine the conflict in such a way as to secure political attention and to show that the dispute should be handled through political action.

Coalition Formation

In this phase of activity the parties to the conflict are in the process of **generating** their **demands** in politically relevant terms. Once having made those demands, however, they must consider whether or not they have sufficient resources to secure action favorable to their cause. Most people have limited resources (limited time, money, and organizational skills) and therefore find it necessary to form coalitions— to seek out allies among like-minded men in order to strengthen the case for their demands. This **coalition formation** allows the participants to multiply their resources and thereby to compete for rewards in an arena where their single cries might have gone unheard. Once coali-

FIGURE 5-2
THE POLITICIZATION OF CONFLICT

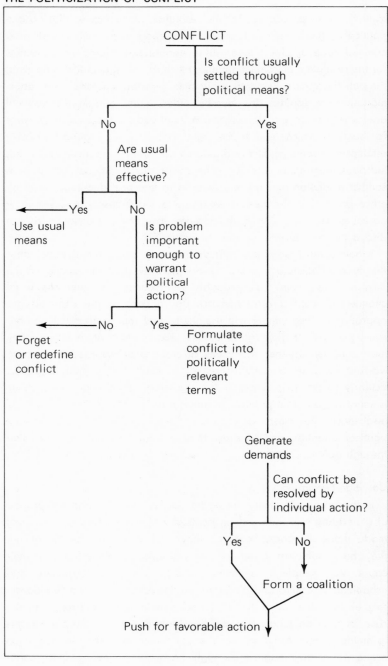

tions which seem reasonably strong are formed, the disputants are ready to present their case for political action.

The appearance of coalitions in all conflicts is not inevitable. Rather the structure of the coalition and the eventual size are a function of the nature of the conflict and of the resources necessary to resolve it. A disputant may have sufficient influence over decision makers to resolve his problem without the formation of any alliance. For example, in a small town a citizen may be interested in getting a zoning restriction lifted or waived. He may be able to do so simply by using his personal resources. If it appears that substantial opposition is developing to his proposed zoning variance, however, he may have to form a coalition. The size and strength of the opposition forces him to seek out help in order to emphasize that his position also has support within the community.

Since individuals often find that they must form coalitions to secure favorable action, why do they ever try to avoid forming them? In our example above, why did the citizen not form a coalition immediately to generate support for his zoning variance? The answers to that question involve several subtle aspects of political conflict. The formation of coalitions is not a costless enterprise; inducements must be offered to potential members, and time must be spent in gathering allies. An individual may be willing to use his own resources to gain favorable action on a zoning change, but may feel that the additional expenditure of resources to gather a coalition of support may not be worth the gain he would receive if the variance were granted. At the onset of a conflict, one is often unaware of the size of coalition that will be necessary to gain favorable action. If it looks as if the individual will be faced with a constantly increasing set of costs in order to achieve his goal, he may forego building a coalition and let the issue die. After all, the size of a coalition should correspond in part to that of the opposition, and the depth and full scope of the opposition may not be easily ascertainable at the beginning stages of conflict. The size of coalitions change as each side responds to the strength of its opponents. There are, therefore, costs of coalitions which may continue to grow as additional efforts are required to achieve favorable action.

Costs of Coalition Formation

Note some of the problems and even paradoxes involved in coalition building. We have mentioned the difficulty of predicting the full amount of resources which may be necessary to see the conflict through. As the coalition expands in size, the resources necessary to induce members to join the coalition and to hold it together may become burdensome for the leadership. If the leaders of the coalition have to continually pay out resources to gain members by buying support, or by agreeing to trade off support on other issues, the process of coalition formation may become prohibitively expensive. One way to solve this problem is to form a coalition on the basis of a collective good: that is, to define the conflict in such a way that the broadest number of people have a common stake in achieving the same outcome. If such a definition of conflict is successful, members should join not because they are induced to join but because it is in their self-interest to join. For example, membership in a labor union offers a share in a collective good to the workers. All share in the final contract which is negotiated between management and labor. The stronger and more inclusive the union is in membership, the greater will be the pressure on management to respond to union demands. However, coalitions formed on the basis of providing collective goods face an essential paradox. Since all coalition members will share in the rewards if their side wins, why should any one member work harder than the others? He will get an equal share of the prize even if others do the work. While the collective good may provide the stimulus for people to join an organization, it often is the motivating force in dissuading them from active participation.[1]

When labor unions were being formed, the leaders had to face the problem that any benefits they achieved for their members would be shared by the entire work force whether or not all of the labor force was unionized. Why, then, should any one worker pay dues or devote extra energy to the union if he will share in its success even though he does nothing? The labor leaders fought not only for unionization but also for the **closed shop.** The closed shop system meant that a worker could not get a job in an industry or factory until he joined the union. This was a coercive tactic which the unions developed as a means of resolving the paradox of a collective good organization. If all workers have to join the union as a condition of employment, then all have to pay dues in order to get a share of the benefits provided by unioniza-

[1] Mancur Olson, Jr., **The Logic of Collective Action,** Cambridge, Mass.: Harvard University Press, 1965, chap. 2, "Group Size and Group Behavior."

tion. Even so, "required membership" cannot force workers to participate more actively or to put forth any extra effort for their union.

The provision for the closed shop is an example of organizational leaders applying negative sanctions to those who do not join the coalition. This is the reverse side of the coin from the provision of collective benefits by the organization. In the instance of the closed shop, the union is able to say that if you do not join you will not be able to work in this industry or in this factory. Similarly, professional associations provide collective benefits to their members but also impose sanctions or make life difficult for nonmembers. It is not necessary to be a member of the American Medical Association in order to practice medicine within the United States. However, in many areas nonmembers may find it difficult to get hospital privileges; that is, they are not allowed to use hospital facilities. This, of course, is a factor which is likely to depress a doctor's practice and is a strong stimulus for him to join the county medical association.

Strategies of Coalition Formation

Given the problem of expenditure of resources, the question of the size of the coalition becomes highly significant. While size may fluctuate throughout the political process, at least two basic strategies of coalition formation merit consideration. The first is the strategy of the **minimum winning coalition**; the second, that of **coalition maximization.** We shall consider the effects of each separately.

A strategy which seeks to build the minimum winning coalition attempts to reduce the costs of victory. A minimum winning coalition is one in which the loss of one member makes that coalition no longer sufficient for victory.[2] Such a coalition is based on the assumption that the addition of each member imposes costs on the coalition—that is, the individual share of the rewards to members will be smaller as the result of additions—or that the additional members impose costs on the leaders, that is, costs involved in securing their support. The theory behind the minimum winning coalition is that once you have secured exactly that amount of support which assures victory, the utility of additional votes is negative. It is rational to refrain from ex-

---

[2] The theory of the minimum winning coalition is best developed in political terms by William Riker. See his **Theory of Political Coalitions,** New Haven, Conn.: Yale University Press, 1962.

pending resources for votes whose costs to the leaders is greater than the benefits derived from having those votes.

Coalition maximization, on the other hand, is the attempt to secure the largest basis of support possible.[3] A maximizing approach obviously is more costly but it allows for defections. The maximizing approach has a built-in insurance policy—it can suffer the defection of some members and still be of sufficient size to achieve victory.

What considerations enter into the decision as to which of the two strategies to pursue? One key factor is the completeness of information available to the participants and the consequent degree of certainty under which they are operating. This factor is particularly important when pursuing a minimum winning strategy. Individuals, leaders of interest groups, such as unions or voluntary associations, political decision makers trying to get a piece of legislation passed, all have to make calculations as to what is the necessary degree of support which will bring them victory. To win with a minimum-size coalition requires leaders to know how each of the participants stands. Although one never operates under conditions of total information and therefore total certainty, forming a minimum coalition is easier in some cases than in others. The smaller the political arena, the fewer the number of participants, the easier and more rational it is to adopt a minimum strategy. Thus it may be possible to pursue a minimum winning strategy to get a bill passed in a state legislature, but the degree of uncertainty in a statewide referendum campaign would give us pause about pursuing a similar strategy there.

In the activation phase, however, it usually is difficult for groups or individuals to pursue a minimum winning strategy. The range of participants is large, information is sketchy, and the issue has not yet become a part of the formal political agenda. We can note that in many ways general elections, in terms of the issues which are raised, set the political agenda. However, in most political elections, the electorate is so large that the degree of certainty concerning the behavior of the actors, the voters, must be relatively low. This is particularly the case in competitive regions where often a shift of 1 or 2 percent of the vote would be sufficient to change party control of the office. Lacking

---

[3] Anthony Downs, **An Economic Theory of Democracy,** New York: Harper & Row, 1957. Downs devotes an extensive amount of discussion to the impact of maximizing strategies.

precise information, the parties seek to appeal to as broad a segment of the electorate as possible. They seek a maximum coalition under the assumption that they must allow for imprecisions in their calculations about probable voter behavior.[4]

There are other reasons for participants in conflict situations trying to achieve a maximum-size coalition. Causes which activate large segments of the population seem to gain greater legitimacy or acceptance when decisions are made by large majorities. In seeking to bring about action, in trying to place an issue on a political agenda, it helps to demonstrate strong support: Political decision makers can overlook the question of legitimacy at their own risk. Note that in this case, leaders seek to maximize their support because the utility of additional votes beyond the point of winning is greater than the costs of those votes. What we are saying is that winning and acceptance may be two separate things. In many cases it may be necessary to build large coalitions to ensure that the decision will not create an even more conflictual situation than the one it was intended to resolve.

A man or group wishing to form a coalition must weigh the considerations of both costs and strategy. For example, he may determine the size of the coalition necessary to win his case only to discover that he needs additional resources or inducements to gain him enough supporters. What methods can he use in getting additional support? First, he can recast the terms of the conflict in such a way as to alter perceptions of individuals as to the stakes involved. Through broadening the base of the conflict, he can win more people to his side by convincing them that their self-interest is at stake. In the process, however, his own immediate goal may become only one portion of a larger conflict.

Alternatively our organizer might form a coalition by promising support for issues not necessarily relevant to the present dispute. We discussed this approach before. It involves enlisting the aid of people who are indifferent to the outcome of this conflict by promising them future support on issues which are important to them. This is the common procedure of logrolling, the trading of support on one issue for the promise of support on another.[5] Such maneuvering is typical among most legislative bodies. In Congress, for example, members from urban

---

[4] Ibid. Downs differentiates between strategies based on complete information and strategies where complete information is impossible.

[5] Grant McConnell, **Private Power and American Democracy,** New York: Knopf, 1967, pp. 111 ff.

areas often offer support on farm issues to which they are relatively indifferent in return for the support of farm state representatives on issues of direct concern to urban constituents. Or representatives from agricultural states with one predominant crop, such as cotton, may support senators from corn-growing states on the assumption that such support will be reciprocated. The basis for the coalition is a trade-off of support.[6]

PHASE 2: POLITICAL DECISION MAKING

When the demands have been articulated, the strategies drawn up, the coalitions formed, and all the necessary resources mustered, a conflict is at last ready for the political battlefield. It is here that the second phase of political activity, **decision making,** begins. Demands and their resultant decisions tend to range along two dimensions: the **ideological-pragmatic** dimension on one hand; and the **comprehensive-incremental** on the other.

The ideological-pragmatic dimension encompasses the following questions. Does the conflict challenge existing ideologies or strongly held beliefs? Does it require an affirmation or change in the ideological predisposition of large segments of the population? Or is it one which is relatively devoid of ideological overtones, which can be approached unemotionally and pragmatically?

The comprehensive-incremental dimension, on the other hand, is concerned with whether the resolution of the conflict would require large-scale change in the political, social, or economic institutions of the society. Does the solution require a restructuring of institutions or bold entry into new areas of governmental activity? Or is the conflict one which is incremental in nature? Does it involve only marginal changes in the direction and focus of existing programs: altering existing governmental commitments, appropriating larger sums of money to various programs, or amending a given legislative statute? Such changes do not result in large-scale innovation; they are likely to involve only a revaluation of priorities.

Political demands arising from conflicts can range the full length of

---

[6] Donald Matthews, **U.S. Senators and Their World,** New York: Random House, 1960, paperback ed., p. 99.

both dimensions. Seldom does either a demand or the solution to a conflict fall at either pole. Instead demands exhibit a tendency toward one side or the other and may fall anywhere in the continua. How conflicts will be presented along these dimensions depends upon what both proponents and opponents believe to be the best strategy, whether it be for getting positive action or for blocking action on others' demands.

The options available in this stage of the political process can be divided into four major categories. These are **avoidance, tabling, acceptance,** and **rejection.** The first two, avoidance and tabling, are responses of political elites to sets of demands. These two responses are similar, but can be separated for analytic purposes.

Avoidance

Avoidance as a response is based on the assumption by political authorities that they can ignore a conflict. They may feel that the issue is unimportant and will fade away on its own; there is no need to expend energy and time in coming to grips with the particular question. Avoidance may be practiced by both opponents and proponents of a particular issue. In one case, proponents of a favorable course of action may find that sentiment is building against their position. It is then to their advantage to avoid any premature action and wait until sentiment changes. Conversely, proponents of an issue may be pushing for an issue and decision makers may decide that the issue is unimportant or not worth the effort involved in resolving the dispute. Indeed, avoidance is a more common response than we may wish to admit. Many people in their personal lives seek to avoid unpleasant stimuli because they do not wish to respond to them. It is more than just a cliché for someone to say, "If it's bad news I don't want to know about it."

Tabling

Tabling is similar to avoidance, but the motives for action are somewhat different. Issues may be tabled not because of any unwillingness of decision makers to respond to a particular conflict but rather because a particular conflict is seen as a lower-priority issue than other existing conflicts: Issue A is not as important as issues B, C, and D. For example, there is greater concern for aesthetic questions, conservation, and similar issues in affluent societies than in poorer societies. A country which is having problems providing a subsistence level of living for its population and is struggling to build an industrial base and simultaneously increase the food supply in order to feed and shelter its population will usually place aesthetic questions as low-priority issues. Tabling an issue does not necessarily mean that the issue has been ignored. The very act of tabling or postponing action indicates that the issue warrants enough consideration to require a formal decision to defer action. It represents a recognition that this is a valid political issue.

Indeed a conflict may be tabled even if it is of high priority if there are, in the opinion of political decision makers, insufficient resources to deal with it now. This is often the case when the conflict is of such magnitude that decision makers either do not have enough information to deal with it effectively or feel that they cannot commit the resources necessary to solve the problem. For example, many countries are severely burdened with overpopulation. Yet in most of these societies the topic has been avoided or, at best, tabled until very recently. Why? The forces opposed to any form of birth control are strong, and many decision makers are reluctant to lead a battle against them on an issue which is not likely to elicit widespread support. Enormous resources are required to educate a semiliterate population in techniques of birth control and the concept of family planning, and any commitments have been doubly difficult to make because the most pressing needs to all the inhabitants are food and shelter. Birth control and family planning have always been a particular concern of the upper classes. It is very difficult to convince those in the lower economic strata that the future of unborn generations depends upon expending vast sums of money for birth control; they see only the need to use present resources to provide decent levels of shelter and food for the generations now alive. The counterpressures to birth control have not only been a result of present generations unwilling to make sacrifices for future generations. There are counterpressures in affluent as well as poor societies. In many religions the use of birth control techniques, particularly artificial forms of contraception, are disallowed. The question of birth control has been intimately connected with religious questions and this connection is one reason again for the frequent tabling or avoidance of this issue in many countries.

Within the United States the demands for environmental controls to limit pollution, contamination, and the waste of our limited natural resources have only become of great political importance in recent years. Conservationists and ecologists have been concerned for years about such problems as pollution and its effects on the balance of life. Such questions were not given priority in the early years of this country, however, because land and resources seemed to be inexhaustible. And they did not seem urgent problems compared to the more basic issues of taming and controlling the excesses of a very rapid period of industrialization. Problems of ecology and conservation and the consequent conflicts they raised did not disappear, of course; indeed, as wastefulness and pollution became increasingly apparent, these problems multiplied rapidly. Only recently, however, have they caused sufficient concern to spur political action. Today we see the passage of water and air pollution legislation and the expansion of the national forest programs. Such issues are no longer being tabled; nevertheless, many people feel that these issues are still not receiving the priority they deserve.

Both avoidance and tabling are responses which assume that particular conflicts can be treated in a summary way. In either case the decision is that, for whatever reasons, resources should not be committed to resolve this conflict now. In some cases even, demands and conflicts are raised without any expectation of achieving immediate political action. Proponents fully expect the issue to be avoided or tabled, and raise it now in the hope that this will lead to future consideration and action. This strategy of introducing conflicts prematurely is an educational device designed to acquaint people with the existence of a problem and to build the basis for future support. In a sense it is staking a claim, so that when resources are available or immediate high-priority conflicts are resolved, this issue will be deemed appropriate for political activity.

Acceptance

Acceptance can have several dimensions. We may be talking about action in the form of resolutions, legislation, programs, bureaucratic decisions, and so forth; and whatever the action, we may mean either temporary or more permanent resolution of conflict. For example, governments must often respond to situations of conflict in ad hoc and piecemeal ways. This type of response is easily understandable when we consider the range of governmental activity in a modern society. The number and complexity of problems often force decision makers to cope with situations by giving only temporary solutions. Indeed there are several types of temporary acceptance of demands or temporary resolution of conflict.

TEMPORARY ACCEPTANCE.   Temporary action may be **marginal** in nature. Decision makers often take recourse to this makeshift response when they do not have the luxury of avoiding or tabling the particular conflict—when the problem is so important and of such widespread significance that it demands an immediate response. Marginal action, therefore, is designed to handle the surface manifestations because, for whatever reasons, political decision makers are unwilling or unable to tackle the problem in a comprehensive or lasting way.

One example of marginal action is the recent change in the draft system in the United States. Proposals and demands for abolishing the draft or selective service system became increasingly strong in recent years. There have been periodic rumblings of dissatisfaction with the quality of and inequities within the selective service administration. Yet reform has been slow in coming. The problem had been avoided or tabled for years. In the late 1960s the demands became more persistent. President Nixon responded to such demands with the inauguration of a draft lottery system. This system—the establishment of a lottery system for induction of men into the armed services—is at most a temporary and marginal solution. It is a temporary measure in that it does not address itself to the basic issues raised in the draft controversy; namely, the right of the government to conscript labor in periods of peace or at least in periods of undeclared war. The continuance of selective service, the movement to an all-volunteer army, the low pay for enlistees and officers (this has been recently raised, but only marginally), and the need for restructuring military service are still hotly debated issues which have not abated with the imposition of a lottery system. Institution of the lottery answers some of the most pressing problems of men of draft age: questions of inequity and uncertainty. Deferments are gradually being abolished so that all men of certain ages are equally subject to the draft. The uncertainty which exists under a lottery system is less than under the previous system, being limited to one year instead of extending from ages 19 to 26. But action such as the institution of a draft lottery is often designed to appease groups who are upset. It is an attempt by decision makers to reduce the level of hostility associated with a particular conflict. Possibly, although this seems doubtful, many of the proponents of the draft reform felt that such action would mute the conflict and prevent the necessity of reevaluating the entire structure of the armed forces and the system for procuring military manpower.

Recourse to marginal action does not necessarily mean an attempt to deceive or placate various parties. Often it indicates that decision makers feel unable to cope with the total dimensions of a problem or to devise permanent solutions to it. They feel that their only alternative is to try to ameliorate the worst excesses of the problem until such time as a more permanent and comprehensive alternative becomes practical. People are often forced to act when they are neither ready nor willing to make long-term commitments. Marginal action is a common response to such circumstances.

Another reason for temporary action which decision makers may take is to use such action as a **wedge for later action.** The "wedge" is obviously a future-oriented strategy. It may treat demands marginally or more comprehensively. What distinguishes it from other forms of temporary actions is that it is perceived as an immediate rather than a long-range response to a problem. The aim of the decision maker is to give legitimacy to the problem and create a base from which to build further and more permanent actions. This is sometimes a conscious strategy employed to gain acceptance for a program on a temporary basis when acceptance in long-range or more permanent terms is impossible.

For example, in the 1950s the Congress passed the first civil rights bill since Reconstruction. The 1957 civil rights bill did not provide a solid framework for handling the problems of either segregation or discrimination; it was merely legislation which offered initial relief. The legislation was used, however, as a wedge for further more sweeping legislation. Civil rights proponents argued that the bill represented the awakening of a commitment by Congress to eradicate discrimination. As support for this position grew, succeeding bills became more comprehensive and long-range in scope. Thus the original legislation was fed back into the political system as fuel for more legislation. Once the first civil rights bill had become part of the political and social environment, it provided the basis for activity of greater and more lasting significance.

Similarly, since the conclusion of World War II, American foreign policy has striven to foster cooperation among the nations of western Europe. Integration of western Europe has proceeded with varying degrees of success. Political integration and unification posed the greatest problems; therefore areas in which agreement was more easily attainable were developed first. Belgium, the Netherlands, and Luxemburg formed the Benelux system to promote trade and coordinate policies among themselves. There were various other agencies established to promote economic integration and defense strategies among the western European countries. The European Coal and Steel Community (ECSC), the European Atomic Energy Commission (Euratom), the European Economic Community (EEC, the Common Market), the North Atlantic Treaty Organization (NATO), are all examples of attempts at integrative and cooperative behavior. Although these organizations are permanent in nature, they can also be seen individually as a series of temporary actions each of which contributed toward the establishment of formal cooperative and more extensive institutions. Once the organizations were established, they became the means for achieving greater coordination and integration among their member nations.

The last category of temporary acceptance is action designed to handle crisis or immediate situations. Such action is temporary in that the conflict which it is designed to settle is itself considered a short-term phenomenon. Decision makers often respond to crisis situations with temporary solutions which are meant to continue only for the duration of the crisis. Analogously, often some relationships may be temporarily out of balance and therefore need a corrective. The draft instituted during the Civil War was perceived as a temporary program to respond to the manpower shortage raised by that particular crisis. It is only in recent years that the conception of a permanent draft has arisen and, ultimately, been challenged.

Many of the programs of Roosevelt's New Deal were also conceived of as actions for an explicit purpose. They were introduced to alleviate specific aspects of the Depression. Similarly, controls on prices and wages and on the supplying, procurement, and distribution of goods traditionally have been imposed to ease the strains and demands of a severe wartime economy. The tax cut which President Kennedy proposed in the early sixties, and which was finally enacted after his assassination, was another example of a temporary action. The goal was to stimulate the economy and prevent a recession. The surcharge which President Johnson asked for likewise had a temporary goal: to provide funds necessary for fighting the war in Vietnam, to maintain the level of domestic expenditures, and, at the same time, to act as a brake against inflation.

There obviously are drawbacks to taking temporary action, and the examples above point out a few of these. Through sheer inertia temporary programs often tend to become permanent ones, and a response to a crisis situation may be continued long after the immediate crisis has passed. Much of the debate in the United States Senate between supporters and opponents of Lyndon Johnson's policy in South Vietnam centered on the Gulf of Tonkin Resolution. This resolution originally was a response to the shelling of United States naval vessels by the North Vietnamese in the Gulf of Tonkin. After the shelling, the President asked for and was granted (through the resolution) the go-ahead by Congress to take appropriate action to protect American vessels and servicemen in the area. President Johnson interpreted the resolution as authorizing him to take any necessary steps with respect to the total Vietnamese problem. Senator J. William Fulbright and others, however, claimed that the resolution was a temporary action designed to cover the single set of contingencies arising from the shellings in the Tonkin Gulf. What Fulbright considered a temporary action became instead a seeming authorization of a more permanent and expanded United States presence in Vietnam. In this case, the action not only became permanent but also served as the vehicle for further and stronger action later.

PERMANENT ACCEPTANCE. Many responses, however, are intended to be permanent. The nature of permanent acceptance may vary greatly. Often, of course, the decision makers will not be able to choose the type of response a conflict requires. Much depends upon the way in which the conflict is phrased and the nature of the demands of the parties to that conflict. Resolution of conflicts may be phrased in ideological or pragmatic terms. By **ideological acceptance** we are implying that the resolution of the conflict involves a value commitment which transcends particular programs. Obviously any action taken will have pragmatic implications, but here we are concerned with the degree to which a conflict is resolved in terms of the affirmations or changes in dominant values. For example, in 1964 when Lyndon Johnson asked Congress for the passage of the civil rights bill, his use of the civil rights movement's slogan "We shall overcome" was particularly striking. As a symbolic gesture, this transcended the provisions of the bill itself. It indicated an ideological commitment to achieving equality of opportunity throughout the country.

Such ideological acceptance is difficult to achieve when it involves changing or reorienting existing values. People often avoid rethinking their basic values. Such a process of reevaluation can be difficult and even painful—increasingly so as one grows older. For example, during the period of the Great Depression, the Roosevelt administration enacted many programs radically different from those of the past. The federal government took a much more active role in the economy and in social welfare than it ever had before. In doing so, it repeatedly met with resistance—to social security, to the National Recovery Administration (NRA), to the Wagner Act, and to governmental regulation of minimum wages and hours. Such programs were resented because they represented a departure from the traditional role of the federal government. Indeed, the Supreme Court held that some of these programs were unconstitutional. Roosevelt had to gain acceptance not only for his particular policies but also for the idea that such programs fell within the power of the federal government. He probably succeeded in doing so only because the country was in a deep crisis where departures from normal were thought to be not only desirable but necessary.

This period marked the stormy beginning of the social security system. During the 1930s many Americans thought that providing social security was not a proper governmental function; it was surely tinged with socialism! Yet between then and today social security, other welfare programs, and above all the belief that government should provide help for its needy citizens have become so well entrenched that an attack on social security is believed to be an assault on basic American values. During the Presidential campaign of 1964, Barry Goldwater was charged with wanting to cut back or even abolish social security. It was reported that Goldwater wanted to make the system voluntary, which was felt by many to be tantamount to destroying the program. Whether such statements were campaign rhetoric or indications of planned policy is unimportant for our purposes; the mere possibility of this tampering with the social security system frightened many voters away from him.

Governmental activity in the welfare arena undeniably has gained at least limited acceptance among American voters. This does not mean that all succeeding social welfare programs have had smooth sailing. They have not. The possibility of medical care for the aged under social security was introduced in 1948, but not until 1965 was any such care provided. Theoretical acceptance of providing social welfare services does not mean acceptance of or agreement on the types of programs which should be undertaken.

Some social welfare programs have gained only a limited, particular acceptance. Some programs continue for long periods of time and build up permanent bureaucratic organizations, but never receive broad-based ideological acceptance. Welfare payments have been in existence for long periods of time, yet it is doubtful whether the majority of Americans feel strongly committed to the idea of welfare payments. For example, poverty programs have never received total or even overwhelming acceptance in the United States. The old Puritan ethic persists. This ethic maintains that hard work leads to success and that failure can only mean laziness or ineptitude. We think of welfare as charity which we dispense to those who are somehow perceived as being inferior. One of the reasons why our welfare policies have not been succeeding can be traced to this type of mentality. Furthermore, even those ideologically committed to a poverty program disagree as to what the program should mean. Consequently, it is probably easiest to graft new programs onto existing agencies, to change the level of funding for programs without rethinking the philosophy behind such programs.

In some cases, however, new agencies are established. Such agencies and programs come into being either because they represent the only feasible alternative in terms of money, personnel, or the scope of the problem or because the problem seems to be a long-range one and a more permanent separate agency is required to cope with it.

Thus **permanent acceptance** is at best a relative term. The acceptance of demands generated out of conflicts can have several different meanings and even acceptance itself may involve varying degrees of permanence and commitment.

Rejection

Rejection is our last category of action. Like acceptance, rejection may be on ideological grounds or may be pragmatic, or rejection may be comprehensive or incremental. Rejection along ideological grounds may stem from several roots. Perhaps an affirmative response to the demands would be a departure from the dominant value structure of the society. The program might be perceived as "un-American" or undemocratic, or the change in symbols and values that would result from acting on certain demands might be considered undesirable.

Let us return to our example of poverty programs. As we indicated earlier, the Puritan ethic has been a dominant ideological expression within the United States for many years. However, it has always co-existed in an uneasy way with a strong egalitarian belief. The Puritan ethic places great stress on individual achievement. Egalitarianism places stress on treating people equally regardless of their position or achievements. Values conflict, and the two positions often become irreconcilable. Many aspects of the poverty program have been rejected as a result of the supremacy of the individual achievement ethic over the egalitarian position.

Often, however, demands may be acceptable ideologically and yet be rejected on pragmatic grounds. In recent years it has become painfully obvious throughout the United States that local property taxes are incapable of paying for good public education. Most people now agree that the states and the federal government should provide larger shares of the revenues for education. Yet despite the broad-based acceptance of this position, programs of aid to education and financial reform of educational systems almost always face a hard struggle. The question is not whether raising the quality of education is desirable, but rather how it can best be done. If there is to be federal aid to education, should it be given to the states or directly to the localities? Should such aid be unrestricted, or should the government indicate the ways in which the money can be spent? Should the funds be apportioned on a per pupil basis, or should they be determined by the magnitude of the educational problems within the various school districts? Should aid be available to private and religious schools? What we are indicating is that even given widespread agreement concerning the need for states and the federal government to increasingly support public education, there are many dimensions around which conflicts may arise and demands may be rejected, on pragmatic grounds.

Thus a particular program may be rejected because it is inappropriate, unlikely to work, or too costly or because it specifically conflicts with other values. One's belief in aid to education, for example, may come crashing against a particular program which seems unfeasible or which while promising aid to public schools also involves aid to private schools, a program to which one may be quite opposed. Often an idea or value may gain wide acceptance and yet not be acted upon because in the process of implementation it comes into conflict with other programs or agreement breaks down on the specific means of achieving a desired goal.

As with acceptance, demands can be rejected comprehensively or marginally. The idea of federal aid to education may be vetoed as being too costly or too unwieldy. In this case the whole program has been rejected; the rejection is comprehensive. More commonly, however, rejection is incremental in nature. Legislators or large groups of the population may be in favor of a particular program and still vote to decrease the budget for such programs. Or they may vote to maintain the budget at the present level and thereby block expansion of a program. In such cases there may be both an ideological commitment to the program and acceptance of the way in which the program is administered, yet decision makers may feel that, because of higher-priority issues, they must reject demands to increase the scope of the program. Often the question of monetary appropriations is fundamental to both acceptance and rejection. The funds appropriated to each agency determine its ability to perform the tasks it was designed to handle.

Often institutional structures exist which are designed to cope with certain types of conflicts. However, they often may lack the funds to adequately perform that role. With this in mind, it is easy to see how an agency can be crippled through a series of relatively minor budgetary decisions. Often a budget cut is the government's method for phasing out programs and institutions without undergoing the necessity of publicly announcing this intent. It is a quiet although often painful means of killing a program: death through starvation. In any given administration or political system, the degree to which budgets for various programs grow or decline and the number of new programs initiated within agencies usually tells us something about the commitment of decision makers to certain problems and the priorities they attach to them. A budget is a political document and represents the results of several incremental decisions and much bargaining. It reflects the degree of commitment to and priority of existing programs and gives an indication of the areas which are likely to expand or contract in the near future.

With the above factors in mind, let us consider why sometimes it is strategically better to present demands and decisions as incremental in nature while at other times the best strategy, for both decision makers and concerned publics, is to characterize them as dramatic departures from past experience. For example, in the Vietnamese War, both the Johnson and Nixon administrations have consistently portrayed their decisions and actions in Vietnam as the logical continuation of policies started many years ago. When the bombing raids on North Vietnam began in 1965, they were presented not as a departure from but as the logical consequence of a series of decisions reached earlier—indeed, as the inevitable outgrowth of the international peace-keeping responsibilities which the United States assumed at the close of World War II. The bombing represented a response to North Vietnamese actions and was presented as a logical continuation of our commitment to aid the South Vietnamese. As we introduced increased numbers of American troops, the bombing was defended on the basis that such tactics were essential to protect our fighting men and represented no real widening of the war. Similarly, in 1970 the Nixon administration portrayed the United States efforts in Cambodia not as an extension of the war but rather as a necessary step in protecting troops already there and as a step which would hasten the departure of our troops.

The Vietnamese conflict, according to both the Johnson and Nixon administrations, could not be considered as a separate phenomenon. It was part of the overall problem of dealing with the threat of Communist expansion throughout the world. The rhetoric maintained that the activity of the United States in Vietnam was similar to the same overall strategy and goals which motivated our intervention in Greece and Turkey in the late 1940s as well as our role in the Korean War. Our commitment in Vietnam, it was maintained, flowed from this larger commitment to prevent the forceful and aggressive expansion of Communism. This rhetoric represented an attempt to tie the Vietnamese conflict to earlier, well-established policies. It was further maintained that the present policy was a logical continuation of that begun under President Eisenhower in 1954 and reaffirmed by President Kennedy. Far from being a departure from American policy, our war efforts were consistent with the highest American ideals of defending freedom throughout the world!

Opponents of the policy, of course, wove a different tale. They maintained that United States activity in Vietnam had changed drastically under President Johnson. The United States had begun to engage in active combat and become involved in the Asian land war which the general staff had warned about for years. In asserting that Johnson's policies represented a large-scale change from previous policy, opponents sought to differentiate Vietnam from Korea: South Vietnam was a country in the midst of a civil war, whereas Korea had been a country which was invaded from without. Similarly, opponents sought to contrast our Vietnamese policy with all previous policy. It was only relatively late in the debate over the war that doves began to raise the larger questions of all United States commitments abroad.

Johnson, and Nixon after him, realized that in the game of political conflict it is good defensive strategy to portray your actions as part of a larger, more accepted mode of behavior. This could be characterized as the "We've always done it this way before" ploy. Opponents, in seeking to change or block policy, made the most of a useful offensive strategy: to attack the disputed actions as being a departure from established procedures, as somehow being unpatriotic and ill-conceived. This can perhaps best be called the "revisionist" or "deviationist" ploy. Such a strategy involves portraying oneself as the true defender of the orthodoxy and one's opponents as the sinister revisionists or deviationists. This is essentially the ploy that China has taken with respect to the Soviet Union.

In times of stress governments may decide to take exactly the opposite tack. Decision makers often feel pressed to present programs as radical departures from the past, as innovations which are important and necessary for the time. During the course of the New Deal, Roosevelt recognized that the Depression had badly shaken confidence in government. New programs were required—programs which were presented as bold departures from the past, programs which could create a feeling of government actively and successfully seeking to surmount the crisis which the country faced. It was the only strategy which, from an electoral standpoint, seemed to make sense in the face of the events. Yet, as we indicated earlier, the fact that many programs were departures from the past still aroused a great deal of opposition. It was, however, the magnitude of the crisis which allowed for departures and even made it necessary for such programs to be presented as departures from the ordinary.

PHASE 3: EXECUTION AND INTEGRATION

A piece of legislation, an executive pronouncement, or a settlement to a dispute does not in itself bring about the end of a conflict. Every day in every society countless decisions are made and countless conflicts "resolved." Yet what occurs after these decisions are made—the effort, care, and relative priority which is given to their implementation—will determine the effectiveness and significance of their ultimate resolution.

We have been interested in the first two phases of the political process because we have assumed that the ways in which conflicts are raised and politically resolved mean something—that the decisions which are made will be implemented. Indeed people nearly always make this assumption when they place their faith in a political system. They believe that the decisions made by their system have meaning: that they will be followed through. If citizens could not count on the implementation of decisions made by political authorities, they would see little reason to pursue conflicts through political channels.

The Political Structure

The significance of this final phase of the political process becomes increasingly clear when we consider the numerous ways in which a political system can be organized. No one political structure is ideal. Each implies certain costs and certain benefits. Whether one structure will be preferred to another depends in part upon the values and ideals which are prevalent in any particular society. Furthermore, a political structure which is most responsive and best equipped to handle one type of conflict may be relatively inefficient at handling others. In the United States, for example, debates continually rage as to whether the federal government is too big or too limited in its powers. Advocates of more federal authority argue that federal control is more efficient and assures that legislation will be equally implemented in all states and localities. Their opponents contend that these benefits are outweighed by the importance of local control and local individuality. Administering everything from a national center, according to critics, tends to make programs unresponsive to variations in local conditions, cumbersome, and overly bureaucratized. In such a debate there can be no absolutely correct position. Both centralization of control in the federal government and decentralization to the local communities have advantages and disadvantages. Which type of administrative structure is chosen depends upon the population's perceptions of what is an advantage and what is a disadvantage. In any case, however, the structures affect the ways in which conflicts are resolved and legislation is implemented.

Within the United States a federal system has had mixed results. In the case of race relations, the dual system of political authority obviously has allowed segregation and discrimination to last longer than they might have under a more centralized political system. The federal government for years gave great latitude to the states in this area. When the Supreme Court handed down its ruling against segregated education in 1954, the administration of that order was in effect left to the state and local authorities.[7] As a result, some fifteen years later the pace of integration in education was still slow and in some areas practically nonexistent. This prompted a Supreme Court decision in 1969 demanding an immediate end to segregated educational facilities.[8] Obviously, though, within a federal system in which education remains under state and local control, desegregation continues to be a slow and difficult process.

On the other hand, the existence of a federal system often has led to innovations and experimentation with programs on the state level which only later were adopted by the federal government. Women's suffrage existed in several states before the adoption of the constitutional amendment extended that suffrage throughout the country.[9] Similarly, many states at an early point in time have experimented with a voting age which is lower than the traditional 21 years. Many social welfare programs were introduced in specific states and became models for adoption by the federal government. In this sense a federal system provides flexibility and sometimes an innovative quality to government. It is not easy to draw up a balance sheet and decide whether the costs of federalism have outweighed the benefits.

Opponents of increased federal control also base their argument, in this country, on the fact that in such a diverse and heterogeneous society as ours, account must be taken of local variations in population characteristics, climate, topography, and similar factors. This can only

---

[7] **Brown v. Board of Education,** 347 U.S. 483 (1954).

[8] **Alexander v. Holmes County Board of Education,** 396 U.S. 19 (1969).

[9] Alan Grimes, **The Puritan Ethic and Woman Suffrage,** New York: Oxford University Press, 1967.

be achieved where state and local governments exert a reasonable degree of autonomy.

In any case, looking at the existing structure in the United States, we cannot deny that the federal system has meant that laws and decisions made at the federal level may be enforced differentially in different states. A victory in Congress or in the courts does not necessarily assure one of the desired results, and often conflicts must be resolved in several arenas. Also, as we noted earlier, once a commitment has been made to a specific program or form of action, that commitment has to be related to other governmental programs and expenditures. This often results in weaker programs than originally planned. The 1969 appropriations bill for the Department of Health, Education, and Welfare was some $1 billion higher than President Nixon had requested. Education groups fought to gain greater funding for their programs and Congress voted that they should be given it. This, however, distorted what the President had set as his priorities and provoked a veto from him. What we are suggesting is that not only does a federal system create the problem of winning in several arenas, but that the separation of powers which exists in this country means that a victory in one branch of the government may not mean that the ultimate goal of a group has been met. What looks like a political victory may be short-lived when it enters another political arena.

The Arenas of Conflict Resolution

The above example illustrates how conflicts, even after they have been resolved in one political arena, may have to be fought not only in other levels of government but also in other branches within a given level. The "checks and balances" set up by the United States Constitution give rise to certain costs as well as benefits in the resolution of conflict. The result is a strange set of paradoxes. Because of the existence of multiple levels of and branches within government, the raising of demands and the politicization of conflicts are relatively easy. By virtue of these same levels and branches, however, conflict resolution is often very difficult.[10] A lasting resolution tends to require coordinated action among the various levels, and this is often difficult to attain. Furthermore, as more agencies or persons become involved,

---

[10] James D. Barber, "Some Consequences of Pluralizaton in Government," unpublished paper, mimeo.

it becomes increasingly difficult to innovate. As in any decision-making process, the greater the number of people who have to participate in a decision, the greater the likelihood for stalemate. The difference between the ease of two persons versus twenty persons making a decision is far larger than a factor of ten. Consider again the dimensions along which conflict may range and the various responses which political decision makers may make and you can get an idea of the magnitude of disagreement that can ensue. Arguments may arise over whether a specific course of action should be adopted, whether that action is adequate to meet the problem, whether the level of funding is appropriate, whether this action should have higher priority over other programs, how the program should be administered, how responsibilities for the program should be apportioned, and even how long-range a commitment should be made to a particular program. The list could go on indefinitely. The result is that as the dimensions of actions required and the number of decision makers involved increase, the probability of achieving any positive coordinated and comprehensive action decreases. In a highly or even reasonably decentralized decision making structure, any one of several groups may veto an action.

On the other hand, decentralized decision making is not without its virtues. When action finally is taken on a program, there tends to be general agreement that such action is desirable and necessary. Actions thus gain greater legitimacy and are reasonably sure of being executed. The result is a stable society—stable in that changes in leadership from one party to another usually do not mean that all programs face repeal and the enactment of opposite programs. When programs may be changed completely every few years, long-range planning becomes nearly impossible; and such planning is necessary if we are to solve the problems of a highly complex and sophisticated society. Even the rhetoric of Barry Goldwater in 1964 would not have enabled him, had he won the Presidency, to repeal many of the programs he was said to oppose. Support for most of these programs was too engrained. The curse of stability, however, is that, because of the amount of coordination necessary to achieve innovation, whenever conflicts require large-scale change, governments tend to avoid action until the conflict reaches the near-crisis stage. This lethargy can be seen with respect to urban problems, environmental pollution, race relations, and other such enduring questions. The machinery is complex and often only an acute problem can compel political decision makers to act. And when they do act, most programs will be constructed in such a way as to cause minimum havoc with the existing administrative structures. This situation is not unique to the United States. Most societies seek to channel change in the least upsetting way.

There are many societies which do not exhibit great stability in political authority and policies. Throughout much of France's modern history, political authority has been highly unstable. Regimes and governments have often represented abrupt changes; and when a new regime came to power, it occasionally sought to radically change the political and social environment. More frequently political coalitions were so fragile that meaningful change and the development of a consensus regarding that change were impossible to achieve. This presented in many respects a political vacuum, one which was filled by the French bureaucracy. That alone was a permanent and continuing force. It was senseless for civil servants to adjust to political authority, since this was regularly displaced. Unfortunately the bureaucracy, the only force of stability, became increasingly unresponsive to elected officials and, through them, to the electorate.

This reveals a second paradox of administration. At the same time that a regularized bureaucracy provides continuous and regularized channels for the resolution of conflict, their very routinization and in some sense insulation makes them perhaps unresponsive to changes in the political environment. In a decentralized administrative system there are numerous points of access. Nondemocratic groups or ideas may find it difficult to win support in all the significant decision-making arenas. Very seldom can they gain control of the entire political machinery. Thus James Madison argued in the Federalist Papers that even should one form of tyranny take root at one level of government, it would have great difficulty in capturing control of the whole political structure.[11] Madison's argument still seems valid. On the other hand, the multiple levels and branches open any conflict to vetoes at various levels and branches. Consequently, the system may become unresponsive to the demands of citizens—and in this sense undemocratic. Often only after a conflict has assumed great importance and mag-

---

[11] **The Federalist,** Jacob Cooke (ed.), New York: World Publishing, 1961, no. 10, pp. 64–65.

nitude will the many levels of government coordinate their efforts to solve the problem.

Highly centralized administrative structures are able to respond to conflicts at earlier stages and are able to implement their decisions and introduce changes more swiftly. Yet centralized government also has its costs. A central government's solution may not consider local variation and therefore may not be applicable all across the country. Also, participation in the political process, beyond merely voting, is limited to those who possess the resources necessary for such participation. In a centralized society, only those interests which can develop a broad base of support or persons endowed with great personal resources can make their presence felt. A decentralized system allows for more participation since the costs of participation are likely to be less at the lower levels of decision making.

The institutional arrangements which exist in any society inevitably impose costs in terms of the society's ability to respond to the legitimate demands and aspirations of its citizens. Over the years patterns emerge which indicate to political actors what strategies are likely to be most successful in particular contexts. It is important to stress, however, that few problems are ever **finally** resolved. There is a dynamic quality to politics which precludes final solutions (except in the most barbaric sense) and easy answers. The problems which beset most modern societies—the environment, technology, ethnic and racial tensions—are not new problems. They are complex and repetitive problems.

Any model of the political process must account for the fact that problems persist. This is why we have indicated that each new decision becomes a part of the environment and conditions the next level of conflict. Conflict arises from our living in societies and interacting with each other. Political systems define the ways in which conflict may be raised, indicate the resources necessary to engage in conflict, and provide channels for the resolution of conflict.

CONCLUSION

In discussing the formation of coalitions, the patterns of decision making, and the nature of administration, we have, of necessity, engaged in a certain amount of oversimplification. We have presented a somewhat static model with sharply demarcated phases of activity and a clear progression from one phase to another. This model is useful for analytic purposes but the actual politicization of conflict is by no means so clearly defined. In contrast, it is an ongoing process where the formation of coalitions and the presentation of conflict are constant. Also, for ease of presentation, we have stressed the two-sided character of conflict. In an actual dispute there may be numerous coalitions, each espousing different viewpoints and demands on any given issue or set of issues. Despite these oversimplifications, however, our model should help us to picture and to understand the various elements and sequences of the political process.

SUGGESTED READINGS

Groenings, Sven, E. W. Kelly, and Michael Leiserson (eds.), **The Study of Coalition Behavior,** New York: Holt, Rinehart & Winston, 1970.

Olson, Mancur, Jr., **The Logic of Collective Action,** Cambridge, Mass.: Harvard University Press, 1965.

Riker, William, **The Theory of Political Coalitions,** New Haven, Conn.: Yale University Press, 1962.

Schelling, Thomas, **The Strategy of Conflict,** Cambridge, Mass.: Harvard University Press, 1960.

Chapter 6

The Conflict of Distribution

In Chapter 5 we diagrammed and discussed the nature of conflict within the political system. We introduced a model for the way in which demands are presented and rejected or accepted; and, using this model, we analyzed the level of acceptance or rejection which characterizes political decisions. Nevertheless, our discussion remained primarily theoretical; we never delved into the actual causes of political conflict. In this chapter we shall attempt to examine some of these.

We have been studying the political system as the ultimate arbiter for conflict. Political decision makers, administrators, and judges, however, are more than arbiters; they are active participants in the **distribution of values and of wealth** within a society. This distribution and redistribution is the meat of political conflict—the reason that political battles often rage with a fervor surpassing that of other types of conflict, and the reason that political conflict can mobilize an entire population.

As we discussed previously, the character of a political system inevitably affects the distribution of resources, and the values within a society. Political authority determines which types of conduct are rewarded and which are punished. It also plays a role in the nature of wealth and its distribution throughout the society. Not only does the political system designate which channels are appropriate and which channels are inappropriate for the accumulation of wealth, but it also specifies how the wealth of the country will be distributed. Through **taxation,** the government can promote programs designed to distribute wealth equally among the population, it can pursue programs designed to maintain the present or pretax distribution of wealth, or it can pursue programs which divide wealth unequally but on the basis of criteria which are different from those affecting the pretax distribution of income and wealth. Taxation is an excellent example of the political system's power of distribution and the conflicts which can arise from that power. It is to this question of taxation that we now turn our attention.

TAXATION: DISTRIBUTION AND REDISTRIBUTION OF WEALTH

Taxation is a process which either redistributes or fails to redistribute the wealth of a society. There are several forms that taxation may take and any of these various forms may be used in a particular society either singly or in combination.

Progressive Taxation

One form of taxation is based on the proposition that all citizens are entitled to the same basic governmental services and should have these services equally available to them. However, payment for these services should be based on the earning capacity of the individual. Such taxes have been called progressive taxes. An example of such a tax is the graduated income tax. The man who earns $100,000 might have to pay 65 percent of his income in taxes, while a man who earns $10,000 and enjoys the same governmental benefits and services might be taxed only 15 percent of his income. The tax money collected comes disproportionately from the wealthier segment of the society, while the services of government are provided on a more or less equal basis for the entire population. Such a system of taxation has not necessarily redistributed income in the sense that it takes from the wealthy and gives to the poor; what it minimally does is deflect the burden for the provision of collective services on the more affluent members of the society.

Graduated taxation, such as that described above, violates one principle of equity in favor of another. It denies the principle that all who share equally in a service should contribute equally towards its provision. It is, however, based on the proposition that governments should provide equal levels of services to all of its citizens regardless of their ability to pay for such services. For example, fire protection is a collective service provided by governments out of tax revenue. Assuming that such fire protection is financed by a graduated income tax system, what would happen if it were offered to citizens on the basis of the amount of taxes each paid? On this basis, those who paid higher taxes would be entitled to better fire protection than those who contributed less, and the man who paid no taxes would receive no protection. Obviously, adherence to such a principle would be ill-advised. It would doom the poor to death and misery. Few people would maintain that a person's poverty should be the basis for deciding whether he and his family will live or die in case of fire. Instead taxation is differentially collected from the population, while services are provided, or ostensibly provided, on an equal basis to all members of the community. Should a taxpayer refuse to pay his taxes under this system, the government can apply sanctions such as attaching his assets, levying fines, or imposing a jail sentence until the taxpayer complies with the law.

There is an additional proposition associated with progressive taxation which insists that government should go beyond merely providing equal services in its effort to achieve economic equality. Advocates of this theory believe that taxation should be used as a means of raising the standard of living of those less fortunate through taxing heavily those who are economically most fortunate. We can see how such a system might work if we look at Figure 6-1, which depicts the distribution of wealth among the population before taxes. Even from a brief glance it is easy to see that the wealth of the society is not at all evenly distributed. The first 50 percent of the population has only 20 percent of the nation's wealth, while the upper 10 percent of the population also holds 20 percent of the wealth. The shaded area between the hypothetical line of total equality and the actual-wealth curve shows

FIGURE 6-1
DISTRIBUTION OF WEALTH BEFORE TAXES

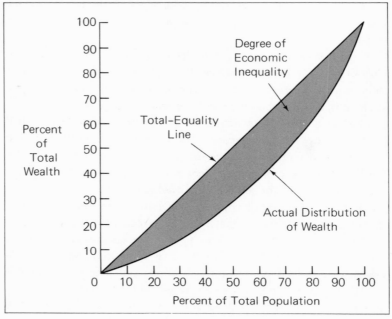

the degree to which the actual distribution of wealth differs from that of total equality. A redistributive scheme of taxation would be one which uses taxation as a means of lessening that shaded area: of moving the actual-wealth curve closer to the total-equality line.

Note that the total-equality line is drawn at a 45-degree angle from the point of origin on the graph. Thus any point on this line is equidistant from both axes. On the total-equality line, 10 percent of the people have 10 percent of the wealth, 25 percent of the people have 25 percent of the wealth, and so on. No society has ever achieved such a perfect distribution of wealth. Nevertheless, political decisions and the ultimate form of taxation can and do affect the degree of economic inequality. Indeed, before-and-after tax graphs will clearly indicate whether or not a country's tax program strives toward economic equalization. In studying such curves, however, we must not forget that the primary activities provided by taxation, namely goods and services, cannot be seen in this type of chart. What this chart explains is the distribution of wealth. It is possible not to redistribute wealth as such but to use differentially collected tax revenues as a means of providing differential or equal levels of service to the population.

Regressive Taxation

It is possible, of course, not to use a taxation system which is progressive. Direct levies, such as uniform sales taxes, are a common alternative. Such taxes have been called regressive by their critics. A government may set forth a general sales tax in which certain consumer items will be subject to a flat-rate tax. For example, let us suppose that a state government has enacted a basic 4 percent sales tax payable upon purchase of all goods and services, including food and clothing. At first this may seem a fair, nondiscriminatory tax. All taxpayers are paying the same tax for the same types of goods and all are sharing equally in the collective goods and services produced and provided as a result of this taxation. The direct levy, however, does challenge another principle of equity. If all goods are taxed at a fixed rate, poorer people are likely to pay a greater proportion of their total income in taxes because a greater part of their income must go toward the purchase of basic goods. Saving, for example, is not being taxed, but food is; and after paying the tax on food, they may have no income left for saving. A general sales tax is particularly hard on those who must devote a great percentage of their total income to buying basic necessities. The adoption of regressive or direct sales levies often is not a conscious decision to avoid taxing the wealthy. Rather, from the standpoint of legislators, who see any tax package as a source of voter irritation, the sales tax and similar levies have the virtue of appearing as hidden taxes. The individual does not see such taxes withheld in a lump sum from his paycheck. For most purchases the tax is relatively small and the individual usually does not bother to calculate what it has cost him over the year in sales tax, while he can clearly see what it has cost him for an income tax.

DISTRIBUTION AND CONFLICT

One of the most significant and recurrent sources of political conflict involves the distribution of political power within a society. Who has access to political power, and what are the rules and procedures which determine that access? How widely is political power dispersed or

concentrated? If we agree that the political system can and does allocate resources and values, then political power is the ability to have
at least partial control over that distribution and to determine the
basis of that particular distributional system.[1]

Criteria for Distributive Justice

The importance of distribution and the conflicts which can arise over
the distributive process have been noted for long periods of time.
Aristotle devotes enormous detail to the problems of distribution and
says that the basis for the distribution of goods and services in a
society comprises the justice of that society. Aristotle does not argue for
an equalitarian distribution system. Rather he notes that the basis for
distribution and distributive justice should be of proportionate equality.
"As A and B have given to the state, in the way of personal merit and
personal contribution to its well-being, so A and B should receive from
the state in the way of office and honour."[2] If A's contribution is greater
than B's, he should get that much more proportionately than B. Aristotle
lays down as the basis for his system of distributive justice the criterion
of achievement. Societies differ in terms of the criteria they use or
enunciate as the basis for their system of distribution. Some societies
have been characterized as achievement oriented; others have distributed rewards on the basis of birth. Noble birth entitled one to a
greater share of rewards than those who did not come from the
nobility. Still other societies have proclaimed that the only just form
of distribution is that based on need. Such is at least the Marxist
position. There are probably several other alternative systems of
distribution which one might want to use as the guiding principle of a
political system.[3]

One major source of conflict throughout history has been between
those who have differing conceptions of what the appropriate basis
for the allocation of values should be. The additional major source of
conflict has been in the actual allocation of values; that is, in determining the best means for achieving adherence to an agreed idea of

[1] The definition of politics as the "authoritative allocation of values" is developed
by David Easton. See his **The Political System,** New York: Knopf, 1953.
[2] Ernest Barker, **The Politics of Aristotle,** New York: Oxford University Press, 1946
(1962 paperback ed.), pp. 120–121.
[3] I am indebted to my colleague Professor David Bell of Michigan State University
for some interesting insights into the implications of various criteria for distributive
justice.

distributive justice. We can note that societies whose idea of distributive justice is based on immutable criteria often encounter great conflicts. For example, the category of race is immutable. Race is genetically determined and it is impossible for an individual to change his race. A society which ideologically and practically enforces an unequal distribution of values and resources based on race structures its society in such a way that perhaps large portions of the population know that it is impossible for them to better themselves. Such a situation can build frustrations to a dangerous level. Similarly, societies which claim to distribute rewards on the basis of mutable categories, but which in practice seem to do so on the basis of immutable categories, invite conflict for those who subscribe to the dominant ideology and feel that they are being unfairly deprived. In the United States, for example, we have proclaimed as a basic tenet of our ideology that the basis for the distribution of values and resources is achievement. This is a mutable category in the sense that, given equality of opportunity, all people would be capable of achieving within the limits of their ability and would be proportionately rewarded. Our treatment of black Americans has in many areas tended to belie this proposition. Often equality of opportunity has not been present and often the achievements of blacks have not received rewards commensurate with similar activity by white Americans. In this case, the contradiction between the ideology and the actual allocation of values and resources has been a persistent and growing source of conflict in this country.

The Allocation of Values and Resources

We have spoken of wealth as an example of the resources which a society may distribute to its population. However, other values and rewards also are distributed by government. Status is one obvious example. Governments do bestow honors and awards upon their citizens. The basis for these awards often gives an indication of what traits or actions are likely to be approved. Some societies may offer rewards to those who are innovative, or intellectually stimulating. Other societies may base their rewards upon such characteristics as obedience and loyalty. In the United States we see several instances of the awarding of medals and citations by the President to individual citizens. The symbolic content of such awards cannot be overestimated. In Great Britain the receipt of an award from the sovereign, the place-

ment of one's name on Her Majesty's Honor List, are marks of achievement and the means by which a society rewards those characteristics
it wishes to foster among the population.

Similarly, governments distribute health care within a population.
Governments today build hospitals and clinics, license physicians, provide support for medical education, engage in medical research,
provide a network of public health officers, and help supply a wide
range of medical care. People want good health and therefore want
good and readily accessible medical care and facilities. The way
in which a government distributes health services, which are a scarce
resource, is a potential source of conflict. Where should hospitals be
built, how general or specialized should they be, how are they to
be linked to transportation routes, and how extensive should their out-
patient facilities be? These are factors which can vitally affect the
quality of health care in a community and the fact that these are
questions which are often decided by political authorities makes the
question of health care a source of political conflict.

Educational facilities are another service provided by government.
Where should they be placed and what degree and type of training
should they provide? The answers to these questions determine not
only the educational structure of the society, but also, to the extent
that jobs are dependent on education, the allocation of jobs within a
society. Schools vary significantly from town to town and region to
region. Not all schools are geared to preparing children for higher
education, and this variance in the quality of education affects the distribution of other values as well. A school system which consistently
fails to meet the needs of certain groups of students, gives vocational
training to some, and prepares others for professional careers has
consequences for the way in which rewards will be distributed among
the population. A government's decision to move to comprehensive
secondary education for all or to maintain or set up selective secondary
education will affect many aspects of its society. Much of the recent turmoil in education in the United States is a reflection of the crucial
role which education plays in determining the distributional system
within the country and the role of schools in socializing individuals to
the norms and approved behavior of a society.

Just the few examples described thus far give us a clear idea of
how important the values and services provided by government are to
its people. It is from government's involvement in dispersing or con-

centrating these benefits that the basis for political conflict grows. Conflict is inevitable since politics is largely a process of governmental distribution in which no citizen wants to get left out or shortchanged.

Distribution and Control of Education

When political conflict emerges and becomes salient in a community, existing predispositions and biases are activated. Since conflict involves distribution, as the conflict is raised the predispositions or biases toward each possible system of distributions begin to surface and make themselves felt. In any community or society there exist differing but often unarticulated opinions. When a conflict arises, these opinions and predispositions emerge and must be expressed. Suddenly the opinions one has are relevant to the existing conflict. Political conflict, therefore, initially serves a mobilizing function. It awakens people to their predispositions and opinions and begins the process whereby those opinions are publicly and consciously articulated.

An example of this process of mobilization can be seen in the recent disputes over the relationship of community control to the American educational system. This is a conflict concerning the distribution of power —a conflict over who is to control the distribution and nature of education in any given community. Wherever this conflict has arisen, particularly in large cities, it has mobilized many existing predispositions. There are at least two basic conflicting conceptions of education. One maintains that the educational process is a professional one which must be controlled by professional educators. The growing militancy of teacher organizations is in part a reflection of this position. The second conception of education insists that since education is vital to the future of children, parents have an important stake in determining how the educational system is to be designed. Here the feeling is that in some settings the professional ethic is not responsive to the needs of the children. Particularly in ghetto areas, parents and community leaders have felt that a large centralized school system has ignored the specific needs of their children. Whenever the question of decentralization and community control has been raised, parents, teachers, and all interested parties have become mobilized into articulating and fighting for their views.

Such conflicts are not new. Indeed, they are not restricted to inner-city ghetto areas. Perhaps one of the most difficult situations regarding professionalism and community control exists in upper-income suburban communities. Such communities are composed of well-educated, university-trained citizens who feel themselves to be equal to professional educators at running the school system. Consequently they are usually unwilling to grant any status to teachers or to defer to school professionals in the running of the school.

The entire educational establishment has certain built-in conflicts. There is a professional hierarchy which extends from the individual teacher through principals, district leaders, administrators, and superintendents. This professional hierarchy, however, is usually overseen by a lay board. Herein lies one source of conflict. In the cities, local communities are demanding that there be several lay boards, each composed of members from the local community rather than from the city at large. It is hard to claim that the principle of lay control at the community level (**decentralization**) is unprofessional while upholding lay control at the citywide level. On the other hand, what size should the community be, and what areas will be subject to lay control? Once again we see a conflict arising over the way in which certain services or goods, in this case education, shall be distributed and controlled.

A good example of a conflict over the distribution and control of education could be seen in New York City in September, 1968. With the opening of the school year, a struggle broke out among the teachers union, the city Board of Education, and the administrators and board of the experimental Ocean Hill-Brownsville school district. The original conflict concerned who was to control the schools within the experimental district.

Ocean Hill-Brownsville is a predominantly black section of Brooklyn. Under a special grant an experimental local school district was set up within this area. The initial explicit dispute arose when the local administrator of the experimental district dismissed ten teachers. The teachers union demanded that the teachers be reinstated, and the city Board of Education denied the right of the local district to fire teachers. Nevertheless, the local board refused to reinstate the teachers. From this grew a bitter dispute between the district and the union which resulted in a lengthy and tense teachers' strike throughout the entire New York City school system.

The teachers maintained that vesting control over hiring and firing in the hands of the experimental board would be a violation of their professional rights and the master contract negotiated with the citywide board. The representatives of the community retorted that the central school board was too distant and was insensitive to the needs of their children. They maintained that a local board was important and that it had both the right and the responsibility to function like any educational board: to assure that the teaching staff met the standards and needs of the community. The parents in Ocean Hill-Brownsville felt that they were demanding only the same kind of control over education which had been exercised by white middle-class parents in other areas within and in most suburbs of New York City.

The conflict soon included the entire city educational system. When all the city school teachers went on strike, they brought the significance of the dispute to all parents who had children in the city school system. The conflict which initially was local and specific soon became broad and general in scope. The question of the ten suspended teachers became broadened to include questions of general control, of how children should be educated, and of what kinds of education they should receive. All these factors began to change the nature of the conflict, to broaden its contours, and to mobilize existing predispositions and biases throughout the total community. Both groups, the union and the local district, tended to expand the nature of the conflict. The union talked about whether professionals were to be told how to do their job by nonprofessionals. The local district emphasized the rights parents have in deciding how their children are to be educated. Both sides sought to manipulate symbols, to form the largest possible coalition of support to bring about a resolution of the conflict favorable to it. The teachers union raised the specter of the complete collapse of the educational integrity of the school system if the experimental board were allowed to control the hiring and firing of teachers and if such a concept was extended throughout the city. This argument was designed to arouse the sympathy of all residents who supported the city school system as well as to convey a sense of immediacy and urgency to those who had school-age children.

Supporters of the local school board sought to manipulate other symbols to increase their basis of support. They emphasized the position of blacks as historically being out-groups in the educational process and maintained that the destruction of the experimental board would perpetuate such a situation and show that the city was unwilling to respond to the educational needs of blacks. Many maintained that the experimental school district in Ocean Hill-Brownsville was a start toward allowing black citizens some say in the educational process and that therefore it would be disastrous to dissolve it. This generalization of the dispute and the invocation of symbols and rhetoric were designed to activate predispositions among the population in order to elicit support for one group or another. Unfortunately, as such conflicts become more general, more important, and significant to larger sectors of the population, they also carry with them a growing divisiveness which is often difficult to bridge even after the conflict has been resolved. As additional issues are introduced, disagreement moves toward antagonism.

Using the example of the Ocean Hill-Brownsville school conflict, let us arbitrarily designate four points in time and discuss the distribution of attitudes and biases at each time (see Figures 6-2 through 6-5). The first point, time **T,** is depicted in Figure 6-2. The curve represents a distribution of opinion in the city. The left-hand side indicates those people who strongly support community control while the right-hand side depicts those strongly subscribing to greater teacher and professional control. In Figure 6-2 we can see that at time **T** most people's views fall somewhere midway between the two poles; the issue obviously is not overly important to many city residents.

Now we move to a situation later in time, designated as time **T+1.** At this point questions of school decentralization and community control are being raised. Looking at a curve (Figure 6-3) similar to the previous one, we can note that the distribution has changed, but that the bulk of the population still remains untouched by the particular issue. Disagreement exists, but there has yet to be an overt conflict

FIGURE 6-2
THE DISTRIBUTION OF BIASES AT TIME *T*

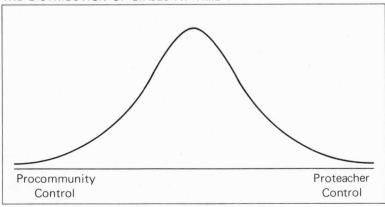

Procommunity
Control

Proteacher
Control

FIGURE 6-3
THE DISTRIBUTION OF BIASES AT TIME *T* + 1

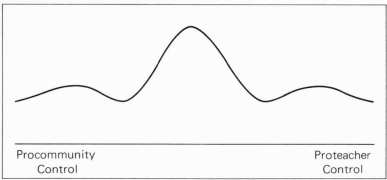

| Procommunity Control | Proteacher Control |

sufficient to activate the predisposition of most people within the community.

The third stage has been labeled time.T + 2 and is graphed in Figure 6-4. This is the point of the dismissal of the ten teachers and of the union's objection to this action. As can be seen in Figure 6-4, the conflict is being polarized by the specific issue. The middle ground is gradually being flattened. As the issue becomes more salient, it activates predispositions, involves greater numbers of people, and begins to force people to choose sides in the dispute—to shift their view toward one pole or the other. The final point in the conflict is time **T** + 3 and is depicted by Figure 6-5. At this point the teachers have struck, and the local school board is defying the central-city school board by refusing to reinstate the teachers. Symbols and rhetoric are being invoked on both sides. The conflict, because of the actions taken, now has direct impact on greater numbers of people. The initial mild disagreement has been

FIGURE 6-4
THE DISTRIBUTION OF BIASES AT TIME *T* + 2

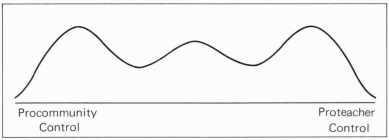

| Procommunity Control | Proteacher Control |

FIGURE 6-5
THE DISTRIBUTION OF BIASES AT TIME *T* + 3

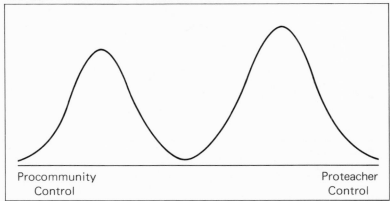

Procommunity
Control

Proteacher
Control

exacerbated and the community, as shown in Figure 6-5, is divided
into two hostile groups.

Thus we can see how the conflict has progressed from a limited dispute into a more general and widespread struggle. As the series of
distributional curves have illustratively shown us, as the conflict spreads,
the middle ground begins to dissolve and more and more people find
themselves moving toward one pole or the other. With the generalization of the conflict, the introduction of new issues, and the invocation
of symbols, few people remain in the middle. There is a dynamic aspect
in conflict which tends to foster an increasing polarization and which, if
unchecked, can lead to disastrous consequences.

New York's battle over educational control has been repeated, perhaps with less stridency, in many other communities. The demand for
school decentralization has become a significant national issue. It has
melded into the larger issue of citizens in ghetto areas demanding
greater community control over local services and governmental programs. These are also conflicts over distribution, and they have arisen
with ever-increasing frequency because of altered conditions in our
cities. The growing concentration of nonwhite groups in urban areas
has precipitated disputes over the distribution and nature of services
there. Since, as was indicated, conflicts arise from the nature of the
distribution of rewards and values by the political system, it should be
helpful to look at the kinds of factors which tend to lead to such distributional battles.

CHANGE AND CONFLICTS OF DISTRIBUTION

We know that conflict mobilizes certain predispositions and biases among a population. Conflict itself is a response to changing conditions and demands for new patterns of distribution of goods and services. Change may be sharp and abrupt, resulting from a catastrophic set of events, or slow and gradual. In either case it can sharply alter the circumstances or environments in which people live. Such change can occur along several dimensions. We shall study the way that a few of these alter the environment and generate demands for redistribution of goods and services.

Population Growth and Movement

Perhaps one of the most simple and yet significant factors to look at is the impact of population growth and movement on political structures and the distributive process. As a nation's population grows faster than its capacity to feed and shelter it, as population growth outpaces the distributive capabilities of society, the pressure for amelioration of conditions heightens. The rapid and unchecked growth of population places increasing strain on resources. An exponential growth of population tends to bring about severely stressful situations where the capacity of resources to meet such stresses is inadequate. Unfortunately, over-population is most acutely felt among the least economically advantaged segments of a society. Symptomatic of such a situation is the scarcity of food and the consequent food riots and the undermining of political and social authority. Most simply put, increased population strains a system's capacity to provide the goods and services essential even for a subsistence level of existence. The fact that the poorer classes tend to reproduce themselves at faster rates than the wealthier segments of society is what made Thomas Malthus (1766–1834) formulate his rather dismal prediction that the poor were perpetually doomed to live at the margins of subsistence. He noted that population tends to increase geometrically while the food supply tends to increase only at an arithmetic rate. The only thing which temporarily affects the situation is the occurrence of some natural disaster such as plague or earthquake or some man-made disaster such as war, which thins out the population and temporarily reduces the demands of overpopulation. However, Malthus felt that this was a temporary correction and that the threat of overpopulation would return and the process of misery and subsistence living would begin again.

This propensity of the poor to have large families was not necessarily irrational. Contrary to the view that most Americans have today, in past years children were perceived as economic assets. They were sent out to work at an early age and very young children soon became an additional source of income for the family. Children were nurtured and then put on the labor market to provide for the family. This is in marked contrast to the United States today, where the whole extension and the prolongation of education keeps children off the labor market until later in life. The more demanding the occupation, the longer the delay until the individual is on the job market. The high infant mortality rates (always higher for the poor) also accounted for the larger number of births recorded among that segment of the society. These differential mortality rates are still reflected in present-day American society. Infant mortality rates are related to the economic level of the parents. It is interesting that one political observer, Samuel Lubell, felt that these differential birth rates were a significant factor in building the triumphant Democratic coalition of the 1930s. Lubell noted that the immigrant classes in eastern cities were reproducing at higher rates than the native population. The children of these immigrants reached voting age just when the Democratic party was forging its national urban, ethnic coalition and they contributed in no small measure to the strength of that coalition.[4]

Population Conflicts and the Heterogeneous Society

Differential birth rates and rapid changes in the composition of a society induce certain strains which go beyond the problem of population growth. Consider Switzerland, which is a country geographically divided into three distinct cultural and linguistic regions. There are French-, German-, and Italian-speaking sections of the country. The French and German groups are larger than the Italian minority. This potentially explosive mixture of populations (these nationalities have spent inordinate amounts of time waging war upon each other) exists

[4] Samuel Lubell, **The Future of American Politics**, 2nd ed., New York: Doubleday, Anchor paperback, 1956, pp. 29 ff.

in a delicate balance of compromise. It is a compromise facilitated by the federal nature of the country which grants great autonomy to the various local **cantons** (states); the cantons, in turn, are essentially French, German, or Italian in composition. This is an uneasy balance which is subject to stress as the population ratio among the three groups becomes disturbed. In recent years there has been a marked emigration of Italian workers into Switzerland in search of higher-paid jobs. This large influx of Italians threatened to upset the delicate balance and to necessitate a reevaluation of the distribution of resources and services among Switzerland's ethnic groups. Consequently, the government has placed limits on the number of Italian workers who could enter the country.

Differential growth rates in any multinational or multiracial society will put strains on that society and eventually raise demands for the redistribution of basic rewards and services. The mere presence of a population heterogeneous with respect to language, race, ethnicity, and nationality poses problems for the political system. Such conflicts are continuous and lasting so long as the divisions among these groups remain salient.

There are countries which have consciously tried to forestall problems which arise from a multinational population. Australia and Canada through most of their history have enacted restrictive immigration policies. Such policies have been intended to restrict the number of non-whites entering these countries. Australia and Canada, which are relatively underpopulated, have feared that unrestricted immigration would place the white citizens in those countries in the minority within a relatively short period of time. Canada and Australia have also had immigration policies which not only favor whites but which favor professional and skilled labor. Such policies are designed to avoid the conflicts of the multinational society. Obviously Canada has not been spared such problems since it has always had a tension between French and English Canadians. Until recently, Canada had encouraged the immigration of American professionals and academics. With a rising spirit of nationalism, Canadians have begun to complain about the dominance of American educators at Canadian universities. A conflict has developed between the desire to bring in as many professionals as possible and a growing resentment of foreign, and especially American, influence and dominance. Britain has recently experienced problems resulting from the increased immigration of Asiatics and blacks into the country.

Immigration has been more tightly controlled as the demands for keeping Britain homogeneous have become more strident. Within the United States the passage of immigration quotas in the 1920s and in succeeding years were designed to maintain somewhat of a balance among the major groups within the population. The quotas of the 1920s were particularly inspired by the massive exodus of eastern Europeans into the United States.

Underpopulation

Even underpopulation can bring problems. Countries which find themselves relatively sparsely populated often need to import labor and encourage immigration in order to develop the resources of the country and to raise the standard of living. Such a policy, of course, may bring future difficulties, as it has to Canada. Underpopulation may also have an impact on important services, such as the protection of the country. France during the years of the Third Republic and especially in the period between World Wars I and II found itself with a declining birth rate and a population which was stagnant or decreasing. During the same time, the German population was growing and the Germans were rearming. By the time the two countries went to war, it is estimated that for every man of age for military service in France, there were two in Germany. Such manpower inequities might not be so important if one were talking about a relatively advanced society and an underdeveloped one. When such a situation exists between two hostile and developed societies, however, it poses grave problems for the smaller nation.[5]

Internal Population Migration

Even beyond population growth, the balance among nationalities, and underpopulation, there are other aspects of population which affect the distributive process and can become sources of conflict. Internal population movements have enormous impact on the development of the country and the consequent strains on the distributive process. Perhaps because of its size, the United States provides us with many examples of the impact of such movements. This is especially true since Americans tend to be unusually mobile people.

---

[5] William Shirer, **The Collapse of the Third Republic,** New York: Simon & Schuster, 1969, pp. 142–143.

EAST TO WEST. The initial and continuing thrust of population movement in the United States has been from east to west. There were many reasons for this movement. As population increased along the eastern seaboard, land became less available and its value began to rise. The presence of relatively cheap and available land did much to spur the initial westward migration. From the beginning this migration had an impact on governmental services. A larger army was needed to protect those moving westward, and in many cases to drive the Indians off the desired lands. One horrible cost of the westward expansion was the displacement of the Indians, who were either pushed further and further westward or killed. Indians were often placed in reservations and then evicted from them when that land also was desired. Amid the excitement and grandeur of the westward sweep the treatment of the Indians was and still remains a sorry chapter in American history. On the other hand, westward expansion had positive side effects beyond the questionable strengthening of the army. It led to the development of transportation networks which included the transcontinental railroad. This system was subsidized by the government and represented a shift in resources to aid the westward movement.

Indeed, westward migration continues today. The most rapidly growing area of the country is the Far West and the Pacific Coast. While movement may no longer be for cheap land, it continues relatively unabated. Obviously this movement and the concomitant spread of population through a large area places strains on governmental distribution. The sheer amount of populated territory in this country creates problems. There are different demands for governmental activity. Where governmental resources are limited, regions compete with each other for existing funds and services, and bitter conflicts may ensue. Locations of government installations and projects become a keen source of competition. Positioning of aerospace facilities and the awarding of contracts are one example. Californian corporations have been awarded many defense contracts. This has created resentment in other states like New York, which feels it is not getting its fair share. The location of the Manned Space Center in Houston instead of Florida or Massachusetts was a highly contested question as various states lobbied to secure the benefits of the giant governmental complex. Similarly the decision as to whether to award the contract for the controversial TFX swept-wing plane to Texas-based General Dynamics or the Boeing Company (based in the Seattle, Washington, area) evoked conflict and competition.[6] Senators and representatives of the various states as well as company representatives became involved in these conflicts. The awarding of contracts and the placement of government installations have enormous economic consequences for a community. Success in gaining a contract can mean sustained high levels of employment, and loss of a contract can mean a substantial cutback in a particular locality. The loss of the TFX contract and the general slowdown in the aircraft industry has particularly been felt in the Seattle area, where unemployment figures are very high. The dispersal of population over a large geographic area strains the capacity of a political system to meet the various and diverse needs of the regions.

SOUTH TO NORTH.   Along with the east-to-west population movement, other significant population patterns have emerged. One such pattern is the south-to-north migration which developed after the Civil War and accelerated in the Depression period. This was basically an emigration of black citizens from the South into northern urban areas. The migration was an attempt, all too often unsuccessful, to move to better conditions, better-paid jobs, and better housing. The choice of northern cities was often a function of the proximity of rail lines. For example, those living along the southern coast tended to move up the seaboard to Washington, Baltimore, Philadelphia, and New York. Others further inland tended to migrate to Detroit or Chicago or Saint Louis. We can see this movement of population reflected in Table 6-1.

---

[6] Robert J. Art, **The TFX Decision: McNamara and the Military,** Boston: Atlantic-Little, Brown, 1968.

TABLE 6-1

POPULATION CHANGES BY RACE FROM 1870 TO 1960 BY REGION

YEAR	TOTAL POPULATION	WHITE POPULATION (%)	BLACK POPULATION (%)
Northeast			
1870	12,298,730	98.5	1.5[a]
1880	14,507,407	98.4	1.6
1890	17,406,969	98.4	1.6
1900	21,046,695	98.1	1.8
1910	25,868,573	98.0	1.9
1920	29,662,053	97.6	2.3
1930	34,427,091	96.6	3.3
1940	35,976,777	96.1	3.8
1950	39,477,986	94.7	5.1
1960	44,677,819	92.9	6.8

Table 6-1 (continued)

YEAR	TOTAL POPULATION	WHITE POPULATION (%)	BLACK POPULATION (%)
North Central			
1870	12,981,111	97.8	2.1
1880	17,364,111	97.7	2.2
1890	22,410,417	97.8	1.9
1900	26,333,004	97.9	1.9
1910	29,888,542	98.0	1.8
1920	34,019,792	97.5	2.3
1930	38,594,100	96.5	3.3
1940	40,143,332	96.3	3.5
1950	44,460,763	94.7	5.0
1960	51,619,139	92.8	6.7
West[b]			
1870	990,510	91.9	0.6
1880	1,767,697	91.2	0.7
1890	3,102,269	92.6	0.9
1900	4,091,349	94.7	0.7
1910	6,825,821	95.9	0.7
1920	8,902,972	96.2	0.8
1930	11,896,222	96.0	1.0
1940	13,883,265	96.2	1.2
1950	19,561,525	95.0	2.9
1960	28,053,104	94.3	3.9
South			
1870	12,288,020	64.0	36.0
1880	16,516,568	63.9	36.0
1890	20,028,059	65.9	33.8
1900	24,523,527	67.4	32.3
1910	29,389,330	69.9	29.8
1920	33,125,803	72.9	26.9
1930	37,857,633	74.9	24.7
1940	41,665,901	76.0	23.8
1950	47,197,088	78.1	21.7
1960	54,973,113	79.2	20.6

[a] Figures may not equal 100 percent due to rounding. [b] The missing percentages come basically from Orientals who were not included in the figures for the West.

Sources: **Historical Statistics of the United States, Colonial Times to 1957,** Washington: D.C.: U.S. Bureau of the Census, 1960; **County City Data Book,** Washington, D.C.: U.S. Bureau of the Census, 1967.

This migration of blacks has had enormous consequences. The shift in population meant it was no longer possible to regard race relations as purely a southern problem or complacently criticize the South for its doctrine of white supremacy. When the test came for northern cities, the patterns of discrimination became established there as firmly as in the South. At times these patterns were more subtle, but the impact was the same. Essentially this population movement nationalized the black population. As a result, their demands for redistribution of goods and services among whites and blacks could no longer be dealt with as a peculiarly regional problem. All regions of the country had to face up to these demands. The demands for redistribution and the strains caused by this migration would have been great without considering the question of race. It is tragic that an additional and in many respects irrelevant factor, namely that of race, was allowed to become a problem and a source of conflict. The migration of blacks into northern cities left those cities to handle the diverse demands of a population which was racially and ethnically heterogeneous.

With the migration of blacks to the cities came additional problems, some of which earlier waves of immigrants did not have to face. There was, of course, the problem of racial discrimination. Additionally, however, the greatest waves of black northern migration occurred just when unskilled jobs were disappearing—both because of the Depression and because of the increasing mechanization of work previously performed by men. Unskilled labor had been the traditional first-opportunity level for those who migrated to the cities. Many of the European immigrants, like black Americans, came from rural backgrounds. However, when the European immigrants came to this country, unskilled jobs were readily available. By the time of the Depression such jobs were disappearing. We can note that today large cities are increasingly becoming service and communications centers instead of manufacturing centers. As a result of this change they no longer need large pools of unskilled labor. Unskilled jobs are relatively scarce, particularly low paid, and the heavy population movement of unskilled labor into cities often means that the unskilled will have to be provided for by social welfare services. Discrimination has brought about resentment which, when coupled with the demands for scarce resources and economic deprivation, have made conflicts greater and more intense in most American cities.

More recently, this south-to-north pattern of migration has been reinforced by the migration of poor whites from depressed rural areas such as Appalachia into northern cities. The decreased need for coal as a primary source of fuel has depressed many of the mining regions in the mountain country of Pennsylvania and West Virginia. This movement of unskilled workers again adds to the demands for increased governmental services. Furthermore, as unskilled workers have moved into the cities, the middle class has in turn been moving out to the suburban areas. This suburban migration received great impetus after World War II and has continued unabated since then. The loss of middle-income families has tended to diminish the tax base of the cities at the same time that the increased number of poor and unemployed has added to the demands for city services. As cities find it more difficult to raise sufficient funds and as demands for services become stronger, frustration mounts rapidly. In situations such as this, political conflict can and has turned to violence.

NORTH TO SOUTH. In the last few decades there has been a reverse movement of population from north to south. A recent migration pattern, this trend has also accelerated since the close of World War II. It is the result of the movement of industry from northern to southern cities. The high costs of labor, land, and fuel for power in the North were factors which made many manufacturers decide to relocate their plants. In many cases the choice was relocation or eventual bankruptcy. Many southern states have made attractive offers to companies to get them to relocate. These offers have included special tax incentives and write-offs, readily available and inexpensive land, the existence of cheap hydroelectric power, and a pool of nonunionized labor in a low-wage area. That these inducements have been successful is obvious from the mass movement of textile manufacturers to the south. New England, which once was the base for the textile industry, is dotted with old mill towns in various stages of decay. Similarly, we can note that most of the furniture production in this country has shifted to the South, particularly in the Carolinas and Virginia. Likewise the location of aerospace facilities such as those at Cape Kennedy, Florida, and Huntsville, Alabama, and the Manned Space Center in Houston, Texas, have been a continuing spur for the movement of related industries to these areas.

This population movement has differed from the others in that it tends to be dominated by well-educated professionals and semi-professional workers. While the basic labor force comes from the new area, industries often have moved their top management and professional staff south. This has brought an influx into the South of northern-educated professional people. Furthermore, this industrialization promises to break down the regional distinctness of the South. As it does, new conflicts and problems similar to those of other regions will emerge.

Not only industrialization but also urbanization seem to be moving south. At a time when national statistics show almost every major city in the country losing in population, southern cities such as Atlanta have been growing rapidly and have been vigorously annexing adjacent territory. This growth of urbanization in the South has brought about substantial political conflicts. For years the basic political strength in the South was based on the dominance of rural interests. The enormous population growth of cities has threatened the rural-state domination and created significant conflicts over the pattern of distribution within these states.

RURAL TO URBAN AREAS.   Underlying all of these population movements has been the general trend in this country of population migration from rural to urban areas. The United States began its history as a primarily agrarian society. However, it has had a continuous and at times dramatic rate of urban growth and an equally constant decrease in rural population. The twentieth century has seen a continuation and reinforcement of this trend. The number of people living in urban areas continues to grow. Small towns are being deserted as younger inhabitants move away to larger cities.

The migration from rural to urban areas has resulted in part from better-paid jobs in urban areas and in part from the increased efficiency of American agriculture. Each year fewer and fewer farmers and agricultural workers are needed to produce sufficient food and agricultural commodities for the country. Consequently subsistence or marginal farmers are increasingly abandoning agriculture. Agricultural units have grown in size while the number of individual farmers and workers has diminished.

This increase in urban population has strained the traditional dominance of rural interests in state legislatures and in the United States Congress. By the turn of the century the balance in this country was shifting to a dominant urban society. Many state legislatures, dominated by rural interests at the time, often wrote specific laws and provisions into state constitutions which guaranteed the maintenance of rural dominance in the legislatures. This was done, first, by maintaining the basis for apportionment in at least one house of the legislature on the basis of territorial units such as towns or counties. Such a stipulation required that any county, regardless of size, was entitled to at least one representative. This provision, coupled with a limitation on the maximum number of representatives any county could have, was usually sufficient to dilute urban strength. In most states urban population is centered in a few counties. By limiting any single county to no more than three representatives, for example, and requiring that each county have at least one representative, it is relatively easy to block urban power and to assure rural control of at least one house of the legislature. Because both houses have to agree on any legislation in order to make that legislation law, the rural interests by controlling one house assured themselves of a strong veto over bills which were not in their interests.

In addition, even in the house of the legislature which is apportioned on the basis of the population, it is possible to draw district lines (**gerrymander**) in such a way as to dilute urban influence. Many states simply refused to reapportion their legislatures to correspond to population changes. Such situations were a continuing source of conflict between urban and rural areas, particularly since the rapidly growing urban areas found that their ability to get needed state revenues was blocked by rural domination of the legislature. Rapid population growth brought far more demands for additional services than it did additional revenues to the cities.

Until the 1960s citizens who keenly felt the imbalance caused by rural overrepresentation in legislatures had little meaningful action that they could take. In a series of landmark decisions the Supreme Court of the United States overturned the arrangements which had allowed rural domination. In 1962 in **Baker** v. **Carr**[7] the Court held that a citizen could file suit in federal court against a state which denied equal representation in legislative districts. In 1964 in **Wesbury** v. **Sanders**[8] the Court held that all Congressional districts had to be relatively equal in population. Again in 1964 in **Reynolds** v. **Sims**[9] the Court held that the only acceptable basis for representation in both houses of a state legislature was that of population. This in effect could work to break the stranglehold which rural forces were able to secure in one house of a state legislature. The Supreme Court decisions were opposed by many. The late Senator Everett Dirksen proposed legislation to remove the question of apportionment from the jurisdiction of the Court or to hold a constitutional convention which would allow for

[7] Baker v. Carr, 369 U.S. 186 (1962).
[8] Wesbury v. Sanders, 376 U.S. 1 (1964).
[9] Reynolds v. Sims, 377 U.S. 533 (1964).

bases of representation other than population. The decisions, however, brought about in many states the first reapportionment in almost fifty years. Reapportionment, however, is just a device to have representatives more accurately reflect the population distribution within the state; it does not solve the conflicts which emerge from the differing needs of urban and rural areas.

SUBURBIA.   Interestingly enough, the Supreme Court decisions were less useful to the cities than they would have been had they been issued several years earlier. While it is true that for long periods of time cities have been underrepresented, the suburban migration has been of sufficient magnitude that prior to reapportionment most cities had about the same number of seats as their population would justify. The most underrepresented areas in most states were the suburban areas. In many respects the cities had won their victory too late. While suburban communities share many of the same problems as urban centers, their representatives do not always identify with cities. While suburbanites are concerned with transportation facilities into the larger city, they tend to be unconcerned about the problems of mass transportation within the city itself. The original underrepresentation of the cities cost them much in terms of funds, and the present reapportionment does not seem to offer hard-pressed mayors of large cities much hope for additional funds from legislatures dominated by rural and suburban interests.

It becomes increasingly clear that as population characteristics change, demands made on specific governmental units also change. The nature of coalitions formed to elicit action on demands must likewise be altered. Since the political process involves a delicate balance among various demands, factors such as population growth, decline, and movement can radically alter the relationships among groups, the pattern of demands, and the nature of conflicts in the society.

TECHNOLOGICAL CHANGE

While population changes can and do lead to political conflict, there are other societal changes which are equally significant. **Technology** by its very nature produces change. Industrial technology has provided the basis for large industry and consequently fostered the concentration of workers in urban areas. In England the industrial revolution changed society from an agrarian to a basically middle- and working-class urban one. The advent of new forms of power, of steam and electrical generating capacities, spurred industrialization and, in turn, led to urbanization.

There have been many interpretations of the impact of industrialization. Karl Marx noted that industrialization rang the death knell for the old feudal system. He maintained, however, that industrial capitalism, even while a force of innovation, carried within it the seeds of its own destruction. Marx noted that industrial society changed the nature of work. Men no longer dealt with products as artisans, carefully fashioning a product from raw material to its finished state. Instead they worked piecemeal, turning out larger numbers of goods but deriving little satisfaction in the process. With the advent of the factory system, work ceased to be an enjoyable activity and became merely a means for pursuing other activities. This created a sense of alienation from work which, Marx maintained, could not be alleviated except by substituting a communistic society for a capitalist one. Marx assumed that just as it was inevitable for feudalism to be succeeded by capitalism, capitalism because it contained unresolvable inner contradictions was destined to be succeeded by a communist society. Whether the Marxian dialectic is inevitable is, of course, highly questionable. Nevertheless, the industrial revolution did sharply alter the nature of society. It created new classes, that of the capitalist and the large urban working class; it fostered a movement of population into urban centers and, in the process, introduced new conflicts into society. By focusing on two aspects of technological change, transportation and communication, we can get an indication of the type of factors which are set in motion by large-scale technological innovation and the consequent problems and conflicts which are generated.

Transportation and the Mobile Society

The refinement of the internal combustion engine at the turn of the century offered endless possibilities for the changing of society. The development of mass production techniques by automotive pioneers such as Henry Ford made possible a mobility of population which years before would have been inconceivable. From its first putter, Henry Ford's "horseless carriage" was considered an interesting device. Yet few people were aware of the enormous significance which the automobile and the internal combustion engine were to have. Within the

United States the automobile opened up the continent in a new and much more meaningful way. Today's urban sprawl would be inconceivable without the automobile. The increasing size of metropolitan areas becomes possible only where distance and travel are relatively modest barriers. The automobile made it possible to live at a distance from one's work. Compare the sprawling nature of a relatively new city such as Los Angeles to that of an older "pre-automobile" town such as Boston. Before the automobile, cities tended to be more compact and citizens were dependent upon mass transportation routes. One could live only as far as the bus or subway system extended. European cities similarly exhibit this compactness of size, although there the reasons extend back into the middle ages when the city was enclosed in walls and was the fortress to protect inhabitants from the onslaught of invaders. The compactness of the city became a significant factor in a defensive strategy. In Europe the growth of suburbs has, as in the United States, depended upon the development and ready accessibility of the automobile. We need not argue whether or not the automobile has caused the suburbs; the point is that suburbs would be nearly inconceivable without the automobile. The automobile has also changed leisure patterns of living. It has opened up vast new areas of leisure-time activity for many. The increased demand and use of national and local park systems and lakes can be traced to the mobility which has been generated by the automobile. The widespread availability of cars has caused the government to spend large and ever-increasing sums of money to build better and safer highway systems to link areas together.

The growth of air transportation has similarly changed in a profound way the nature of man's environment. Rivers, seas, mountains, and all such geographic barriers no longer isolate communities and nations from each other. This has resulted in greater communication among peoples of varying backgrounds and a greater awareness of the interdependence of individuals. The developments in transportation have also had an awesome impact on the technology of war. War, by virtue of the airplane and the mechanization of arms, no longer takes place on secluded battlefields such as Waterloo or Austerlitz. Rather it takes place in the cities and the densely populated production centers which are within easy reach of the bombers or tanks of an invader. London, Rotterdam, Dresden, Hanoi, Tokyo, and other cities unfortunately too numerous to catalogue have all felt the impact of technological change in the nature of warfare. It is, I suppose, one of the typically double-edged blessings of technological progress that things which can be so liberating for people can also be the instruments of mass destruction as well. Even in the absence of war, the horrifying weekly and yearly carnage caused in automobile accidents is appalling. The automobile, which was a factor in liberating man and giving him greater choice in where to live, at times seems to threaten his existence as the problems of pollution become increasingly severe in heavily settled areas and as the onslaught of new highways ties a slow noose of strangulation around many of our cities. Technological change itself is neutral; it is the use or abuse to which people put such changes which brings about conflicts.

Communications

Technological advances in communication likewise have changed the nature of relationships on both a group and personal level. The advent of mass communications, of the telegraph, telephone, radio, and television, has had an enormous impact on life. Again natural boundaries are no longer barriers to other ways of life or to new and different ideas; most systems of mass communication have little respect for natural or national boundaries. The speed of communications creates a sense of immediacy about events both far and near which in the past was inconceivable. We have become more aware of the world around us and lost our sense of isolation. That awareness tends to create empathy, fear, passion, and a variety of other emotional and intellectual responses. News in distant places is no longer something which we only hear about occasionally; instead wars, famines, personal tragedies, and large-scale disasters are carried into our living rooms daily—often in frightening detail.

This communications revolution has had a particularly enormous impact in nonindustrial and semiliterate societies. Radio broadcasting to all areas of a country has become a significant aspect of government control in such countries. Through radio or television a government can easily reach its citizens, even the illiterate. Where previously the government had to rely on printed forms of communication which could only be read by a very limited segment of the population, it now can forcefully present its message to all regardless of the degree of literacy in the country. Indeed, given a governmental monopoly on broadcasting and the existence of illiteracy, it is easy to see how citizens in many countries will only be exposed to that information which their government decided that they should receive. In this sense control of communications becomes an important means of social and political control.[10]

Within the United States, television and radio have changed the news habits of the population. Surveys have demonstrated that in recent years a growing majority of Americans received their news primarily from television. The printed word has been displaced as the primary means of news transmission. This inevitably implies a large-scale change, since the nature of television and of television news coverage differs quite sharply from that of the newspaper. Television has a way of eliciting involvement from an audience which is much more difficult to achieve in a newspaper. We still do not know the exact effects of this change in news sources, but we can suggest that it is likely to be a potent force in changing attitudes and conditioning reactions. The mass media have changed the relationships among people and affected perceptions of events. Such factors are bound to have an effect on the nature of demands generated and on the level and tone of conflict within societies.

CONCLUSION

In this brief sketch we have indicated only a few of the ways in which technological change has affected the quality of life, the distribution of goods and services, the biases and predispositions which take root in communities, and therefore ultimately the sources of conflict. Conflict is the inevitable by-product of change. Change alters relationships, restructures thinking, and requires adjustments. In the process some form of conflict is inevitable. The greatest revolutionary forces may not be the ideologies propounded by philosophers but rather the technological innovations developed in the laboratory or through makeshift arrangements. If, for example, we asked who had more impact on twentieth-century society, Karl Marx or Henry Ford, it is quite possible that of the two, Henry Ford with his refinement of the internal combustion engine and the automobile and his development of the assembly line

---

[10] Daniel Lerner, "Toward a Communications Theory of Modernization," in Lucien Pye (ed.), **Communication and Political Development,** Princeton, N.J.: Princeton University Press, 1963, p. 344.

production formula has been the more significant source of change and of conflict.

Politics is a distributive process, and conflicts arise out of the nature of that distribution. We have briefly indicated some of the sources of change which may affect society in terms of mobilizing biases or predispositions. This change brings about demands for new services and for redistribution of old programs, creates tension between what was and what is emerging, and therefore is a continuing and ever-present source of conflict. In this sense conflict can be avoided only if a society freezes itself and refuses to change. Even this option is essentially foreclosed because changes in technology have rendered physical isolation almost an impossibility. The challenge for political structures is to approach such conflict constructively and to harness it to socially beneficial activities.

SUGGESTED READINGS

Barker, Ernest (ed.), **The Politics of Aristotle,** New York: Oxford University Press, 1946.

Easton, David, **The Political System,** New York: Knopf, 1953.

Fry, Brian R., and Richard F. Winters, "The Politics of Redistribution," **American Political Science Review,** vol. LXIV, no. 2 (June, 1970).

Lasswell, Harold, **Politics: Who Gets What, When, How,** New York: McGraw-Hill, 1936.

Lasswell, Harold, and Abraham Kaplan, **Power and Society,** New Haven, Conn.: Yale University Press, 1950.

Schumpeter, Joseph A., **Capitalism, Socialism and Democracy,** 3rd ed., New York: Harper & Row, 1950.

Chapter 7

Activation

THE PREDECISION MAKING PHASE

The distributive basis of politics involves both the raising and the resolving of conflicts. Since all societies suffer from some form of distributive inequality, we want to understand how problems about distribution of goods or values become politically significant conflicts. Citizen groups, government leaders, and even the institutional structures themselves all may be sources of conflict. Yet, as we indicated in our diagrammatic presentation of the political process, the mere raising or articulation of conflict will not bring about political action. Somehow each problem must move into the political arena and this depends, for success, on the manipulative skills of both proponents and opponents.

GENERALIZING THE CONFLICT

We have noted the trend in political conflict from the specific to the general. Most conflicts initially are highly specific. A person or group feels that it is being discriminated against in employment. Another is involved in a dispute over property rights. A third is fighting government officials about the terms and implementation of a legislative act. Each of these struggles is of limited scope. Yet often before the original dispute has been settled, all the participants may have lost sight of their original goal in their involvement in a broader and enlarged cause.

In Chapter 6 we traced the dispute over school decentralization in New York City from a specific disagreement concerning the firing of ten teachers to a general conflict concerning the nature of the educational process. A similar example of the trend from specific to general is America's debate over the antiballistic missile system (ABM). The ABM hassle began over expenditures for the construction of a new defensive weapon system. The point in conflict was clear: Can the projected ABM system provide effective protection against a missile attack? Scientists gave contradictory opinions concerning the workability of the system. As advocates on both sides sought to expand their support, additional issues were drawn in. For the opponents of the ABM, the proposed system represented one more case of misdirected priorities. The system would be ineffective, would be obsolete by the time it was built, and would waste resources urgently needed for such internal problems as fighting pollution, improving the quality of urban life, and easing racial tensions. The issue was presented as one of pitting military spending aganist important civilian needs.

Proponents of the ABM system also expanded their argument. They stressed that national security was the most important responsibility of any government. To them the deployment of new and more sophisticated Soviet weapons demanded an immediate response from the United States. Not to act would be a dereliction of duty and would open the country to rather unenviable consequences. Thus the proponents invoked the symbols of national security, common defense, and fear of the enemy in order to broaden the base of their support.

ELICITING COMMITMENT

We have observed this process of generalizing conflict in many examples. Indeed it is often a necessary strategy for anyone wishing to form a coalition large enough to achieve the desired aims. Yet the generalizing phenomenon has the effect of snowballing the conflict, in the process of drawing in supporters previously unconcerned. New issues are added to elicit commitment to a side of a dispute, to pull people away from their apathy and noninvolvement.

The significance of gathering such commitments deserves special attention. Even the first step, that of inducing a potential supporter to express a preference on an issue, may require the expenditure of considerable resources. This should not be surprising. Given any situation of stress, most people are hesitant to state a preference, particularly in public. Once they have done so it becomes very difficult, especially if one is a public figure, to retract a statement or reverse positions. As soon as they have made a commitment, people have a vested interest in justifying it. Indeed, they are more likely to deepen it. Perhaps this is the human instinct to rationalize decisions once they are made.[1]

For example, in purchasing an automobile, we may be restricted to a particular price range. Within that range there might be anywhere from five to twenty available models plus an ever-higher permutation of equipment and "extras." What automobile shall we buy? The decision is confusing and often frustrating. We may be forced to make a decision on the basis of very little information. In fact, we may simply rely on our "gut reactions." Nevertheless, as soon as we have made our choice, there is a strong tendency to justify it. We will convince ourselves that this particular car was the best one; we may even brag to our friends about the fantastic deal we just made. It is truly amazing how many "unbelievable" automobile deals are made daily. The subsequent performance of our car may force us to reevaluate this euphoric judgment, but our immediate reaction is to rationalize our decision and congratulate ourselves on it. Automobile dealers and salesmen are shrewd enough to display the appropriate grimaces and looks of pain over the deal we have forced out of them. The psychology is to make the buyer feel that he has gotten something at a bargain. Instead of merely buying a car, we participate in an elaborate ritual designed to make us feel satisfied with our purchase.

The same problems of commitment occur in other decision-making settings. For example, in diplomatic negotiations there is a real reason for quiet and even secrecy. Open negotiations tend to lock people in

---

[1] Jack Brehm, "Postdecision Changes in the Desirability of Alternatives," **The Journal of Abnormal and Social Psychology,** vol. LII (May, 1956).

rigid positions. When one negotiates in public, there is often a need or desire to make statements for one's constituency. Having made those statements, it then becomes difficult or nearly impossible to back away from them. Indeed, merely repeating a position often enough tends to intensify it. Suppose we make a statement which we only mildly support. Repeating that statement often enough may elevate it to a principle of firm belief. This is a tenet of modern propaganda. The Nazis were masters of it. Their theory was that if you repeat something long enough and incessantly enough, people will believe it. In much the same way, people propagandize themselves. In an election campaign, for example, voters are told of the dire consequences which will occur if the opposition wins. Why then is national opinion concerning the President-elect extraordinarily favorable immediately after an election? A decision has been made, and after-the-fact rationalization sets in. Perhaps this is not really a catastrophe at all; could the majority of the voters be so very wrong? Supporters of the losing candidate are willing to accept the decision of the voters and even justify it.

One decision often leads to further supporting decisions, statements, or commitments. Suppose an initial commitment involves an investment of time and money. This investment may lead us to further commitments in order to justify that which we have already spent. People who own stocks whose prices have declined, often buy additional shares at lower prices in the hopes of evening out or lessening their losses. Because commitments lead to other commitments, the addition of new issues in a conflict is designed both to add new support and to justify the increased expenditure of resources among those already committed. New issues are designed to elicit commitment, through the manipulation of symbols, from a larger segment of the community.

In this movement from the specific to the general, parties to conflicts try to gain the interest and support of people previously uncommitted and unconcerned. There are at least three critical aspects of the activiation phase that must be considered: (1) the use of symbols and beliefs, (2) the process of communication, and (3) the character of leadership. Each of these factors will be considered below.

SYMBOLISM

Perhaps philosophical or symbolic disputes are the most familiar form of conflict. Communism versus capitalism, Catholicism versus Protestantism, Judaism versus Moslemism—these are among the classical and most severe examples of conflict. In part, the severity and durability of these conflicts result from the fact that the dominance of one belief system may threaten the existence of alternative beliefs. From the standpoint of the capitalist, communism precludes individual dignity, suppresses creativity, and denies man the just rewards of his labor. Yet to the Communist, individualism is an outdated concept inapplicable to the needs of a highly industrialized society. To him capitalism does not allow the worker dignity in his work, denies the workers their share of the society's productivity, and suppresses the forces of innovation and change. Each system has its own symbols and these describe the two systems as being totally hostile and incompatible. The symbols of each affirm that it alone provides the only hope for salvation, that all alternative systems are evil and destructive. Religious conflicts take on the same tones. Christians pitted against Jews, Catholics against Protestants, Christians against Moslems, Moslems against Jews, all have developed their own symbolic language. All religions share basically similar goals, yet each historically has claimed that its methods are the only truly divinely inspired procedures. Symbols in these cases have been evolved by religious groups and other organizations as a means of identification for the group. These symbols serve two basic purposes. First, they unite those who share the same beliefs by emphasizing those beliefs and demonstrating their uniqueness. A feeling of uniqueness and distinctiveness strengthens group solidarity.[2] Second, symbols unite the group by portraying a common enemy. It is easier to fight for something when there is something or someone who is standing ready to oppose your beliefs or way of life.

How important is this notion of uniqueness to ideology? Before the Roman Catholic Church and Eastern Orthodox churches split, there were many points of difference between them. Most of these differences arose from peculiar customs and were not crucial doctrinal conflicts. Priestly celibacy, for example, was viewed as a Roman custom and nothing more. Celibacy later became a source of division and a symbol of the differences between the two churches. Similarly the doctrine of papal supremacy became a source of tension. The Pope maintained that he should have primacy over all other bishops. The Orthodox Church was not willing to grant such claims to Rome and this occasioned many arguments. However, during the early Christian

---

[2] Lewis Coser, **The Functions of Social Conflict,** New York: Free Press, 1956 (1964 paperback ed.), chap. 2, "Conflict and Group Boundaries."

period many of these differences in customs and interpretation were
played down in order to maintain the unity of the Church, particularly
in the early period where opposition to Christianity was strong. But
later, when the churches split, both sides emphasized their differences
and pointed to their own unique beliefs and customs as a means of
rallying their supporters. It is interesting that as a spirit of ecumenicism
has become prominent in the Catholic Church there have been attempts
to play down the differences between Catholicism and other forms of
Christian worship, and particular attention has been paid to reconciling
some of the differences between Rome and the Eastern churches.

Symbolism also plays a key role in the ideological battle between
the Chinese and the Russians. The Sino-Soviet dispute goes beyond
ideology; it is also a conflict over territory, a conflict which has endured
for centuries, regardless of dynasties or regimes in both countries. In
today's dispute, however, both sides have deemphasized the territorial
aspect of the conflict and invoked symbols to further their cause. Both
sides have branded each other as heretics to true Communist gospel.
Each maintains that it alone is applying the Marxist Dialectic and that
the actions and philosophy of the other nation are a threat to all real
Communists. The charges of deviation and revisionism are attempts to
unite supporters and widen the ideological chasm between the two sets
of leaders. In part the use of these particular symbols instead of the
arguments over territory is dictated by the fact that both countries are
Communist systems. According to Marxist doctrine it is impossible for
two Communist countries to be engaged in a border dispute, because
communism is supposed to be an international force which supersedes
nationalistic feelings. It is a force which theoretically brings about the
demise of national boundaries as a significant aspect of political life.
Given this constraint, the Sino-Soviet dispute cannot be presented as a
nationalistic dispute. Instead, the conflict, as we have indicated, has
been developed as one over which of the two countries is adhering to
orthodox Communist doctrine. By painting each other as deviationists
from true Marxist doctrine, each nation is able to ignore the constraints
which would exist in a dispute between two Communist countries.

In moments of conciliation, differences are downplayed and even
ignored, while in times of conflict, divergences become significant symbols used by each side to a dispute as a means of gathering strength
and support. The propaganda war between the two Communist states
is directed not only at each other but also toward a larger international

audience. The claims as to which country is truly revolutionary are aimed at forging alliances and gathering supporters throughout the world.

Thus, there seem to be two sides to the symbolism of conflict: (1) Symbols are invoked as a source of unification, and (2) symbolic unity is easier to maintain in the face of an external threat or common enemy.

All war and violence in and of itself is repugnant. Why is it, then, that some wars have enjoyed great popular support while others have only caused dissension? In World War II the ideology of the Fascists was totally and diametrically opposed to that of democratic nations such as the United States. Furthermore, their aggressiveness and military power represented a direct threat to all the Allies. The development of the airplane and German work on rocketry made it obvious that if the war continued without American aid, even the Atlantic and Pacific oceans no longer would provide any country with adequate protection. Both our democratic philosophy and the nation itself were threatened. Yet there was strong resistance to an early entry by the United States into the war. Many felt that the involvement of the United States in World War I had been wasted because it had settled very few of the age-old European problems. There was considerable reluctance to get involved in a European or Pacific war again. When the United States finally did enter the war, however, almost the entire population was mobilized and firmly united. Obviously the Japanese attack on Pearl Harbor solidified this unity.

This remarkable unity has been almost totally lacking in the war in Vietnam. Why? What has caused the resentment and real lack of support which have accompanied American efforts there? During the period from the end of the Korean War to the buildup of American forces in Vietnam, American foreign policy was aimed at increasing communications with the Soviet Bloc. The United States was seeking agreement with the Soviet Union wherever the two nations had mutual interests. Despite the rhetoric of the Dulles era, the continued arms race, and the post-World War II disillusionment over the possibilities for any real cooperation between the two countries, both nations did try to tone down the rhetoric of the cold war. This dual and often ambivalent position has been difficult to maintain. Yet at the Geneva summit meeting in 1954 and at several meetings since, both nations have tried to find common grounds for agreement and for a lessening of their conflicts.

This process continued in the 1960s despite the existence of the war in Vietnam. Agreement between the United States and the Soviet Union increased, and mutual interests were emphasized. Consequently, Americans who once thought of Russia as the "enemy" began to entertain much more complex opinions about that country. The strong sense of fear and distrust has declined somewhat and as a result the exhortations to fight the monolithic Communist enemy have become less successful a factor in mobilizing attitudes and uniting the country.

An additional factor in the Vietnam War has been that the ultimate enemy was the Chinese and not the Russians. Most Americans consider China to be far less an immediate and significant military threat than the Soviet Union. The military superiority of the United States over China is so overwhelming that few Americans feel that the Vietnamese war is essential to the security of the United States. Despite the advances in Chinese armaments, that country is still militarily far behind the United States or the Soviet Union. If it is difficult to picture the Chinese as an immediate military threat to the United States, how much more difficult it is to make the claim that the North Vietnamese or the Viet Cong represent a threat. We are suggesting that symbols were successful in mobilizing attitudes and creating unity in past wars, but that several events have made similar symbols unsuccessful in arousing support for the Vietnamese war.

The use of symbols as a means of generalizing conflict and extending support is obviously a common phenomenon. Certainly the invocation of symbolism will be more or less successful depending on the circumstances and on how appropriate the symbols are for the particular conflict. The population must be willing to accept the symbols put forth. In a sense they are a system of shorthand for reacting to the environment. In one setting the word "radical" may indicate support, in another setting the term may have a pejorative connotation, and still elsewhere it may elicit a neutral reaction. For example, administration officials may describe a new government program in the field of pollution control as a "radical" undertaking. Here the intent of leaders in using the word is to create a feeling of urgency, a sense that the government recognizes the gravity of the problem and is willing to take any and all steps to solve it. In this situation the word connotes a willingness to go beyond what has been done before, beyond the stale old programs to a new workable solution. Here the desire is to elicit support and create a feeling that the government is concerned and is taking action.

Alternatively, the word may be used pejoratively. For example, a government official may claim that an opposition group is planning a radical takeover of the government, or that the program of a group would radically alter the nature of our society. Here the symbolic connotation of the word is completely different. It is meant to convey suspicion and danger, to elicit a response of hostility toward this organization. The word is designed to create the impression that the government even has to defend the citizen against this dangerous group of people.

Yet it is even possible for the word "radical" to have no emotional connotations connected with it. The French Radical party, for example, was not radical in the sense that we commonly use the term. It was a center party which was fairly conservative in its program. Furthermore, a news commentator could state that a new program was "a radical departure from previous policy" and still not commit himself as to whether the program was good or bad.

If we look at the foregoing examples, it becomes clear that the same symbols will not always elicit the same response. Words may have several definitions and many shades of meaning, and often the context or the tone of voice is even more important than the word itself. Indeed, using symbols can be a difficult and involved art. The choice of words and symbols will be affected largely by the strata of the population which such symbols are supposed to arouse.

IDEOLOGY

Symbols are in part a condensed form of an ideology. By **ideology** we do not necessarily mean something highly structured and rigid (many Americans use the term only in a pejorative sense for systems like communism or fascism). An ideology is any system of beliefs or interrelated ideas.[3] Democracy can be as easily considered an ideology as fascism. Most people do subscribe to some sort of belief system which links in some manner their preferences, language, and ultimately their actions. Obviously people differ in the extent to which they can integrate their various beliefs. Some, and perhaps most, people subscribe to many beliefs but do not necessarily link them together into a con-

---

[3] Joseph LaPalombara makes a strong case for a broad definition of ideology. See his "Decline of Ideology: A Dissent and an Interpretation," **American Political Science Review,** vol. LX, no. 1 (March, 1966).

sistent or total pattern.[4] Nevertheless, it makes more sense to talk about reactions to the use of symbols in terms of the ideologies which people hold rather than in terms of whether or not they hold any. For our purposes, an ideology need be no more than a relatively consistent set of beliefs and symbols.

American Ideology

Within the United States, most surveys have shown that there is a loosely held set of beliefs or symbols to which most Americans do subscribe. This can be called the American ideology, the American Creed, or any other such name. It tends to center around the major tenets of democracy—that elections are the keystone of a democratic system and the appropriate means through which citizens should express their political preferences. Corollary to this, people must be free to gather information about the political system; they must be secure from unjust and arbitrary governmental action. The rights of free speech and assembly, protection from unwarranted or improper searches, the protection of due process, and the prevention of unlawful detention all are necessary if a society is to remain democratic and if the electoral process is to continue as a meaningful forum for political participation.

Because such freedoms are basic to democratic society, there is widespread agreement within the United States that such protections are important and worthy of being defended.[5] Perhaps, however, as a result of the relatively low degree of ideological thinking, these principles are not always related to specific problems. When freedoms are imbedded in specific situations such as the limits of dissent or the right of a Communist to free speech in public buildings, the level of support for these actions declines among the population.[6] People often fail to consider the abstract principle in discussing the particular event. Furthermore, actual situations are never as clear and unidimensional as are principles or beliefs. Often a problem will pose a conflict, for the individual, among several beliefs.

The degree to which people and therefore their societies are attuned to thinking in ideological terms and have consistent beliefs and

[4] Cf. on this subject Milton Rokeach, **The Open and Closed Mind,** New York: Basic Books, 1960, particularly chap. 2, "The Organzation of Belief-Disbelief Systems."
[5] James W. Prothro and Charles M. Grigg, "Fundamental Principles of Democracy," **Journal of Politics,** vol. XXII (1960).
[6] **Ibid.**

values conditions the ways in which symbols can be invoked in the conflict process. The movement from specific to more general and perhaps ultimately abstract conflict depends upon the dominant beliefs and the unity with which they are held.

Soviet Ideology

Let us look beyond the United States for a different example of the use of ideology and symbols as a means of defending action or of building support. The example we shall use is one which was not particularly successful. It concerns the use of symbols by the Soviet Union to justify their invasion of Czechoslovakia in 1968. The invasion was the ultimate outgrowth of events which were set in motion when party liberals such as Alexander Dubček were successful in ousting the old-line Communist leaders in Czechoslovakia. The new leaders found themselves faced with an economically stagnant society and a highly repressive structure. They decided that in order to build support for the needed economic reforms it would be useful to ease some of the restrictions of the previous regime of Antonin Novotny. They hoped that this liberalization would build a greater loyalty to the regime. Press censorship was lifted and statements were issued concerning the possibility of a relaxation of tensions with the West and increased trade with the United States and other western European countries. The lifting of press censorship, however, resulted in the publication of many anti-Soviet articles. The Soviets, already faced with a bitter ideological dispute with the Chinese, a relatively independent Rumanian Communist regime, a "revisionist" Yugoslavian government, and a pro-Chinese Albanian regime, began to fear that Czechoslovakia too would move away from complete Soviet hegemony.

What triggered the final confrontation? The anti-Soviet articles mushroomed and there was even speculation that the Dubček regime might reopen the case of Jan Masaryk, the Czechoslovakian foreign minister who died under mysterious circumstances, believed by most to be a phony suicide, just when the Communists took over complete control of that country in 1948. These were the specific issues, yet when the Soviets decided to take action, they altered the argument by invoking outside symbols in the hope of gaining support for their actions. The effort was not particularly successful but was, in a grim way, interesting.

The Russians maintained that their dispute with the Czechs was not one of whether Czechoslovakia would differ from Russia in its form of communism. Rather, they argued that the existence of communism itself was at stake in Czechoslovakia; some sort of concerted Soviet action was needed to prevent reactionary, anti-Soviet forces from destroying communism. This is why the Russians enlisted the aid of the Poles and East Germans, so as to provide a more international flavor to this campaign to save communism. The defense of communism was proclaimed as the justification for the Soviet invasion. Symbols and ideology beyond those of the original dispute were employed to justify Russian actions. The Russians sought to use a symbol of a common enemy, a revanchist Germany, as the basis for unifying support. Since most of the eastern European nations still feared German militarism, the symbol of the common German enemy was designed to win over all of eastern Europe. The effort was crude and it failed to convince many people, since few felt that Germany was about to invade Czechoslovakia. The action strained the relations of Moscow with many of the western European Communist parties. The French and Italian Communist parties felt it necessary to dissociate themselves from the Soviet actions and condemned the Russian action. What is significant in this example is the attempted use of symbols as a means of building support and justification for action. The failure in this case indicates that the manipulation of symbols is not easy.

As the conflict between the Soviet Union and Czechoslovakia grew, arguments and justifications also multiplied. When the Soviet Union felt that the differences between the two nations were no longer capable of being negotiated, it resolved to use force. But before doing so, it increased the level and tone of its ideological assault in the hope of generating support for its planned invasion.

The Constitution and the Court

Yet symbolism and beliefs are not always sources to broaden and intensify a conflict. They are also sources of unity, and as such may act to constrain conflict or maintain it within certain bounds. Within the United States, the federal Constitution is a strongly supported symbol and one in which many Americans take great pride. Indeed, such support among an entire population is a rather rare phenomenon. In any dispute, when one side challenges the constitutionality of the other side's position, it is presenting a powerful argument. Certainly many a school child has been heard to cry, "But that's unconstitutional!"

The Constitution is a source of both symbolic attachment and great constraint.

The same general halo surrounds the institutions which the Constitution enumerates. The Supreme Court, the Congress, and the Presidency all enjoy strong support as institutions, even though particular officials within these institutions may be attacked vigorously.

To glean some idea of the symbolic strength of and powers of constraint within the Constitution, let us review the famous court-packing case of President Roosevelt in 1936. In a series of decisions throughout 1935 and 1936, the Supreme Court of the United States had struck down as unconstitutional several of the key legislative programs of the New Deal, particularly the provisions of the National Recovery Act and the Agricultural Adjustment Act. Most of the justices, at the time, were of quite advanced age and formed a strongly conservative majority. After the election of 1936, which was a smashing landslide victory for Roosevelt and his New Deal, the President proposed to add additional justices to the Court up to a total of fifteen, for every justice who was above the age of 70. There was nothing radical or unconstitutional about this suggestion. The Constitution only specifies that there shall be a Supreme Court; it says nothing about the number of justices to serve on it. In fact, the number has not always been nine. Roosevelt's intent (though not announced as such) was, of course, to give a majority to the Court so that it would not continue to overturn his programs.

The President's timing seemed propitious. He was at a peak of his popularity and there was much resentment against the Court's decisions. Yet an astonishing degree of outrage greeted his proposal. Roosevelt's enemies, and even some of his supporters, felt that the Court plan was an inexcusable attempt by one branch of the government to force its will on another independent branch. His enemies decried the plan as unconstitutional; it would make a mockery of the separation of powers provided for in the Constitution. Thus, a President, at the height of his powers and after a landslide electoral victory, was constrained from taking action by the deeply held belief and symbolism which surrounded the Court. With the country in the midst of a depression and a Court issuing opinions which seemed to correspond to another and earlier historical era, people still refused to support a plan which seemed to challenge the constitutional separation of powers. The importance of ideology and symbols in conflict situations obviously is highly significant, even in a country which is ostensibly nonideological.

Whatever the particular situation, it is here in the activation phase of conflict that the symbolic contours of the dispute take shape. Symbols and ideology are invoked to achieve the broadest and strongest possible base of support. The success or failure of symbolism is, of course, dependent upon other conditions: the pattern of communications, the nature of the leaders, and their skills. Let us now turn to the next of these considerations.

PATTERNS OF COMMUNICATION

We have seen how symbolism and ideology are used to expand the nature of conflict and to encourage people to commit themselves to a particular coalition. The assumption underlying this process is that, having made an initial commitment in a conflict, people will feel that they have invested resources and that they have a personal stake in seeing that their coalition wins. The greater the investment of resources, the greater the desire to achieve a victory.

Group Mobilization

As a conflict becomes political, existing organizations and ad hoc groups tend to form around the issue. For example, in the schools we might see a mobilization of groups such as the PTA, teachers unions, student councils, and so forth. In addition, as the conflict becomes more intense, new and more specialized groups may form. Suppose the conflict concerns an increase in local school taxes. Supporters of the tax might form a parents' organization for better schools, while opponents might start a taxpayers' league to combat the proposed tax on the grounds that additional funds are unnecessary or that the school system is not making the most efficient use of their present funds.

An analogous national example would be the strong movement for gun control legislation after the assassinations of Martin Luther King and Robert Kennedy in 1968. Such legislation has been opposed in the past by very well-organized groups such as the National Rifle Association. After the assassinations many ad hoc groups, such as the Committee for a Sane Firearms Policy, were created to press for stricter legislation. Additional groups proliferated on both sides. Many conservation organizations were pulled into the struggle. Because of the support which they had received in the past from the National Rifle Association, they were called upon to help defend the NRA and block new gun control legislation.

Associational Activity

The conflict brought about a flurry of organizational activity. The struggle to extract commitment from the population extended beyond merely winning the sympathy of the population to encouraging citizens to join associations and to act. Some interesting and significant patterns emerged from this heightened associational activity, and insofar as they were typical of conflict situations, they deserve our attention.

POLARIZATION.   In the fight for gun control, the main antagonists were the National Rifle Association and the Committee for a Sane Firearms Policy. Other organizations and groups aligned themselves on both sides of the issue. Large and small organizations as well as loose associations of persons were formed. During the process, two striking factors about communications in conflict emerged. As the conflict became more heated, the amount of communication between the sides declined. Even if we include propaganda statements, there was less and less interaction among opposing parties. At the same time the amount and frequency of communications among like-minded groups and individuals increased. The two sides gradually became isolated from each other and turned inward more and more for both information and communication.

This pattern of separation is typical. Indeed, if the conflict is severe enough, a near-total encapsulation of the two camps may take place. During a conflict (see Figure 7-1), the natural reaction is to join organizations and associate with persons who agree with you. As the conflict becomes more important, the tendency to associate and discuss the topic only with those who share your views is heightened.[7] Association with people whose views differ from yours is a challenge and often an unpleasant one. Furthermore, since organizational membership and activity represent a commitment to a position, there is a need to justify that commitment. Association with like-minded persons reinforces that initial commitment and tends to convince you that you are indeed fighting a worthwhile cause. Where the conflict is strong enough, this process of polarization can break even family bonds. In the American Civil War, members of families severed all contact with each other when they found themselves on opposite sides. One of the horrible prices of any civil war is that it may often involve cousin killing cousin and brother fighting brother.

---

[7] James S. Coleman, **Community Conflict,** New York: Free Press, 1957, p. 11.

FIGURE 7-1
COMMUNICATIONS AMONG GROUPS THROUGHOUT THE COURSE
OF A CONFLICT

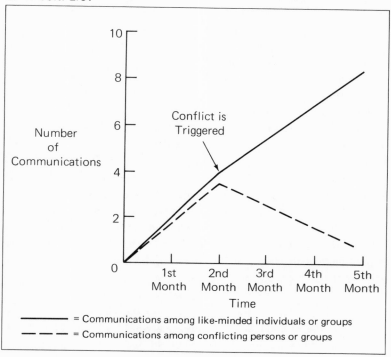

BREAKDOWN OF COMMUNICATION. Obviously, the complete ·breakdown of communication between antagonists represents an extremely polarized situation. In such a case, persons rely completely for their information on sources whose position is similar to their own. There is a sharp upsurge of internal publications specifically designed to reinforce the commitment and morale of participants to the conflict. Information from outside sources tends to be discarded, or at best, suspect.

Even a brief glance through history will show us that prior to the outbreak of war, communication between hostile nations becomes increasingly rare. This is why the breaking of diplomatic relations is a sign of fairly strong hostility. Except for the most formal announcements, all communications between the future belligerents may cease. Karl Deutsch, in his analysis of communications, notes that the breakdown of correspondence across national boundaries in times of tension can even be measured by the decrease in mail flow.[8] While this is a crude indicator, it does support the hypothesis that in times of stress opponents and potential adversaries decrease their level of communication with each other. At the same time, allies tend to increase their communications. Meanwhile messages between belligerents tend to be carried by intermediaries.

In 1938 when Hitler presented his demands for the Sudetenland to the Czechoslovakian government, communications between the two countries were practically nonexistent. It was the French and English who interceded between Germany and Czechoslovakia. The French were bound by treaty to aid Czechoslovakia in case of attack, and the English were committed to the French. The Germans agreed to negotiate with the French and English but refused to see the Czechoslovakian representatives. Indeed, at the Munich Conference of 1938, where Czechoslovakia's fate was sealed, there was no Czech representative. The Czechoslovakian emissary was allowed to sit in a waiting room outside the conference. Only after Hitler's demands had been met was he informed of the terms of his country's virtual surrender, and then only by the English and the French. France and England demanded that Czechoslovakia accept the decisions reached at the conference; otherwise they would consider their duty to the Czech regime to be at an end. The episode was a painful one which reflected little credit on the Chamberlain government in England and the Daladier government in France. Yet it must be noted that, at the time, the decision was warmly greeted by the inhabitants of both countries, who were fearful of war. Throughout the entire drama all major communication was carried on through these two intermediaries.

Lest we conclude that breakdowns of communication take place only on a grand scale, let us consider the following everyday example. An argument takes place between two friends. Each of the parties seeks solace in other friends, unburdening himself and asking, only rhetorically, "Was I wrong?" Of course the answer which he expects is "No." Should sympathy be expressed for the other side, the conversation often abruptly ends and the third party is also drawn into the dispute. In any conflict we tend to seek reinforcement. We want to be told that we are reasonable and correct and the other side is unreasonable, wrong,

---

[8] Karl Deutsch, "Shifts in the Balance of Communications Flows," **Public Opinion Quarterly**, vol. XX, no. 1 (Spring, 1956).

or in some cases, evil. It should not be surprising that the mechanisms which are operative among individual antagonists also exist on the community, societal, and even intersocietal level.

Organizational Encapsulation and the Potential for Conflict

Where a society is characterized by little interaction among major groups, the potential for hostility among groups, and therefore for conflict, is quite high. If both groups are subject to a common authority and may have to reach common decisions at some point in time, there is a likelihood that their insulation from each other will heighten the conflict when it occurs. The more that major groups in the society become organizationally encapsulated, the less those of different beliefs or opinions interact, the greater is the probability of severe conflict.

In Italy various explanations have been put forth for the success and durability of the Communist party. Most classical descriptions of Communist party support do not make much sense in the Italian setting. One such standard description is that the party has grown strong because of increased industrialization. This thesis depends upon Communist strength being drawn primarily from the most urbanized, industrialized areas of the country. In Italy this simply is not the case. There is no uniform pattern. In some industrialized areas the Communists are very strong while in others they are relatively weak.

An alternative explanation of Communist strength is that communism draws its support predominantly from poor rural areas. Here, too, there is information which both supports and refutes this contention in Italy; some rural areas have a strong Communist party while others have almost no Communist organization.

An Italian political scientist, Giovanni Sartori, suggests a third and more convincing explanation for the success of the Communist party in rather disparate regions of the country. To Sartori, the party's success cannot be explained simply by asserting some constant relationship between socioeconomic variables and Communist strength. Instead it lies in the organizational encapsulation which the party provides for its members. Sartori makes no comment on why people join the party; he is interested only in what holds this party together. When he speaks of organizational encapsulation, he means that the party provides a total life for its members. It supplies a full range of publications, including news, features, sports, and so forth. Likewise it furnishes a wide array of information for its members. All the material, of course, is designed to reinforce commitment to the party. News is interpreted and presented in a manner consistent with the position and ideology of the party. There is no need to consult "untrustworthy" non-Communist sources.[9]

Similarly, the Italian Communist party provides a whole range of recreational activities, cultural events, and discussion groups for its members. The party has some kind of organizational apparatus available for almost all types of human activity. It allows its supporters to live as much as possible in an ideologically homogeneous environment. The Communist party member can belong to many associations, take part in varied activity, and yet never have his ideological beliefs challenged. This perhaps explains the remarkable fact that the Communist vote in Italy for years has consistently ranged between 20 and 30 percent of the total vote cast.

This situation of organizational encapsulation is somewhat more prevalent in Europe than it is in the United States. In many European democracies, practicing Catholics find it possible to belong to a Catholic political party, a Catholic labor union or manufacturer's association, and several other Church-sponsored or -endorsed associations. Similarly, organizational networks exist for Socialists as well. As a result, vast segments of the population can lead lives almost entirely separate from those of other groups.

The perennial ethnic conflict in Belgium is in part a reflection of the geographical separation of Flemish and Walloon communities. There are few organizations which cross ethnic lines. Physical isolation breeds suspicion and hostility, associations develop almost entirely along linguistic and cultural lines, and sources of conflict are reinforced.

Holland is divided much like Belgium, except along religious lines. The Netherlands is populated mainly by Protestants in the north and by Catholics in the south (there is also a substantial nonchurch-affiliated group). Likewise Canada has a sharp division between French- and English-speaking citizens. French-speaking Canadians comprise a minority of the population and are concentrated in one province, Quebec. The assertion of French nationalism, of French culture and traditions, has been a continuing source of friction between the two

---

[9] Giovanni Sartori, "European Political Parties: The Case of Polarized Pluralism," in Joseph LaPalombara and Myron Weiner (eds.), **Political Parties and Political Development**, Princeton, N.J.: Princeton University Press, 1966, pp. 144 ff.

communities. Recently a French separatist movement has emerged, and it is strengthened both by the power of the French-speaking majority within Quebec and by their feeling of being discriminated against throughout the rest of the country.

In such cases, the potential for hostility and conflict is high because (1) there is little interaction among opposing groups, and (2) at the same time groups are subject to a common authority. Geographic isolation is not the only form of isolation which can lead to conflict. Psychological isolation can also be significant. Within the United States, for example, blacks and whites have lived in reasonable proximity for years and yet have remained psychologically isolated from each other.

Whatever the particular circumstances, however, isolation is a common phenomenon in conflict situations. Sometimes lack of communication helps lead to hostilities. In other instances people choose sides in an existing struggle; communications among hostile groups break down at the same time that interaction among allies increases. In any dispute, combatants associate increasingly with like-minded persons and in so doing continually reinforce and strengthen their beliefs.

LEADERSHIP

Both the use of symbols and the patterns of communication are obviously important in conflict situations. Leadership, however, is needed to unite these factors and to provide impetus to the conflict. Leadership is a highly difficult concept to adequately define. Most simply, it is the ability to induce others to accept one's directions and one's authority. This definition obviously covers a great deal of territory. It includes leadership where the followers voluntarily agree to someone or some group's preeminence, as well as situations where preordained relationships dictate who shall lead and who shall follow. There are certain positions in any society which, by virtue of the authority involved, simply are positions of leadership. A president may not be universally liked, admired, or even respected; yet he leads because of the nature of his office. In a tightly structured organization such as the army, every officer exerts a given degree of leadership by virtue of his rank within the hierarchy. Certainly officers may expand their leadership because they are admired and respected, but they always exercise some sort of power by virtue of their positions. In voluntary organizations where nothing intrinsic to a relationship provides for leadership, the would-be leader may have to gain the respect and admiration of his followers before his orders will be obeyed.

Prerequisites for Leadership

Who shall be a leader? This question becomes involved when we realize that the qualities which evoke admiration, respect, and a willingness to follow vary from society to society and even from one particular time to another. Some societies place a high premium on boldness, daring, and direct action. He who wishes to lead in such a setting must either posses these qualities or at least seem to do so. To appear devious, hesitant, willing to compromise would be to risk one's following. We need only look at most lower-order biological species to see how this principle works. Leadership among herds of animals involves physical prowess. As soon as the chief of the pack is defeated in battle, he falls from power and a new leader takes over. Leadership is based solely on brute force. For those who would argue the superiority of human life over that of lower forms of life, it is noteworthy that in many relationships we, as humans, demand these same qualities of force from our leaders and often take recourse to some form of battle in order to choose them.

In other contexts leadership consists of being cunning and wily. In such a setting, negotiation, patience, the ability to play factions off against each other, to always come out on top without risking anything, are characteristics which are admired.

In monarchial or aristocratic societies leadership is based on birth and "breeding." Even in the United States in the early 1800s, the Federalist party leaders maintained that they were better equipped to lead than the Jeffersonians by virtue of their better background and upbringing. Leadership as a result of birth or ascription, however, is largely fading throughout the world. Monarchs, and there are few of them, may continue in office but usually have very little real power.

At other times other qualities have been deemed essential for leadership. In theocratic societies such as Calvinist Geneva, piety and good works were the qualities which inspired leadership. This is not to imply that cunning and boldness were not also useful. Rather, the dominant theology dictated the characteristics which were essential in the leader. As late as the early twentieth century, it was assumed that no man could be the president of Yale University without being a Congregationalist minister—even if presidential designates had to be ordained the day before their inauguration, an event which occasionally occurred. Intelligence or intellect may also be necessary for leadership in some contexts, although one must admit that it has not always been particularly stressed as a requirement for political leadership.

The prerequisites for leadership, then, are highly varied and often situationally determined. Winston Churchill provided what was considered to be outstanding leadership for Britain during the war. After the close of the war, the British population turned Churchill out of office and voted for the Labour party. Most societies impose some limitations on leadership and disallow certain methods for gaining power. Murder, for example, is usually, but by no means universally outlawed. Each society sets its own limit, not only on leadership characteristics, but also on the style of leadership which it expects.

Evaluating the Leader

The degree to which people will respond to leadership depends upon their perceptions of their leaders. In the last years of Lyndon Johnson's Presidency, many Americans, whether justifiably or not, lost faith in Johnson and in the honesty of his administration. This was an enormous handicap to the President and added complications to his attempts to get programs that he favored passed by the Congress. Richard Nixon in 1968 had to overcome several widely held conceptions about himself. His first problem was to eradicate his image as a political loser, particularly the image which had been created by his farewell speech after he lost the gubernatorial election in California in 1962. This could only be achieved by a series of convincing primary victories. Next he sought to erase his reputation as a partisan fighter. To do this, he conducted a relatively low-keyed campaign and emphasized a statesmanlike position. He strove to create the image of a man in control of himself, a man capable of controlling the nation's problems.

Part of the great popularity and leadership ability of Dwight Eisenhower resulted from the immensely favorable perceptions which the country had of him. He was an unusual combination. He had all the records of the great military hero but did not appear harsh or forbidding. Rather Eisenhower had the reputation of being humane, kind, and even modest. He was the personification of the benevolent and

FIGURE 7-2
REINFORCEMENT AND CHANGE OF ATTITUDES

	Consonant Situations				Dissonant Situations			
	(1)	(2)	(3)	(4)	(5)	(6)	(7)	(8)
Your evaluation of the source	+	+	−	−	+	+	−	−
Source position on issue	+	−	+	−	+	−	+	−
Your own position	+	−	−	+	−	+	+	−

Source: Robert E. Lane and David O. Sears, *Public Opinion,* © 1964. Adapted by permission of Prentice-Hall, Inc., Englewood Cliffs, N. J.

trustworthy leader. It was precisely these attributes which gave him great electoral strength and allowed him to withstand all complaints about his lack of accomplishments in the Presidency.

A leader must consider his constituents' estimation of him in all political situations. If we look at Figure 7-2, we can see the impact on manipulation of opinions which a leader's favorable or unfavorable image can have. Figure 7-2, divides conflicts into consonant and dissonant situations. A consonant situation exists where all of a person's perceptions agree. In such situations his original opinions are reinforced, and consequently he need not reevaluate his thinking. A dissonant situation, on the other hand, occurs where one of his evaluations conflicts with the other two. In such cases he is forced to reevaluate his position.[10]

THE CONSONANT SITUATION.   Let us look at case 1 in the figure which is a consonant situation. Your source or leader, is positively evaluated; he is trusted, admired, or respected. He takes a positive stand on a particular issue, and your own position agrees with his. There is therefore no disagreement among attitudes. Similarly, where the source is positively evaluated and his position on the issue is nega-

---

[10] The theory of cognitive dissonance is closely associated with Leon Festinger. See his "A Theory of Social Comparison Processes," **Human Relations,** vol. VII (1954); also see Robert Lane and David Sears, **Public Opinion,** Englewood Cliffs, N.J.: Prentice-Hall, 1964, chap. 8, "The Problem of Conformity."

tive as is your own position (case 2), there is again no attitudinal conflict. In case 3, on the other hand, you have a negative opinion of the source; you distrust or dislike him. Here his attitude toward the issue is positive, but your attitude is negative. Again there is no conflict. It is interesting that people are often disturbed to find themselves in agreement with someone they strongly dislike or with whom they almost always disagree. In this case, the lack of agreement is a reinforcement of both your own opinion of the issue and your opinion of the leader. Similar forces are at work in case 4, where again your evaluation of the source is negative, but this time his position of the issues is negative and your own is positive.

THE DISSONANT SITUATION. In the dissonant situation, on the other hand, one of your three perceptions conflicts with the other two. In case 5, for example, you respect your leader and his position on an issue is positive, yet your own position on the same issue is negative. This creates an attitudinal conflict—one which is not always resolved. If the conflict between perceptions is significant, you may be forced to change one of your three perceptions. Perhaps you will change your mind on the issue. "If this person whom I respect so much is for this proposal, I am probably wrong in being opposed." Alternatively you reevaluate the source and decide that if he can take this position on this issue, you must have overestimated him. He must be stupid, or at least not as good as you thought he was. The fact that finding ourselves in opposition to a respected leader can cause us to reevaluate our own position gives an indication of the potential strength of leadership. In dissonant situations where the source is very positively evaluated, a shrewd leader, by proper invocation of symbols, can move many people to his particular position and way of thinking. Good leadership depends upon a leader's being able to reinforce the beliefs of his supporters and, at the same time, to win over some of those originally on the other side. Thus in case 6, where his opinion on an issue was negative and your own was positive, a very strong leader may persuade you to change your mind.

The last two dissonant situations illustrate an interesting psychological quandary. In both cases 7 and 8 you dislike or distrust the leader and yet agree with him on the particular issue. People are often upset when they find themselves agreeing with people whom they hold in particularly low esteem. Again they may reevaluate either the source or their own position. A disarming statement by a public official aimed at a constituency which is normally hostile may even bring about a positive reevaluation of that official by the audience.[11]

Types of Leadership

Note that "political leadership" refers not only to those we normally think of as leaders. Within every social strata people lead in many different ways. Some people may be interested in political office, while others function as political opinion leaders within their respective peer groups. Especially during election campaigns, people often are guided by those of their friends who are best informed or most knowledgeable on political issues. Such persons are the medium through which the speeches or statements of candidates are interpreted and presented. In many respects these people serve roles similar to those of newspapers and television. When we depend on newspapers for accounts of political activity we are reading synopses. We are depending on the newspaper to report accurately the important things which a particular candidate or official said. To the extent that reporters and editors exercise judgment as to what to include and what to exclude, they present interpreted information. Similarly, the person who is politically attuned and is a source of information for his friends provides interpreted information. Those who respect this person will tend to accept the information he relays, while those who suspect his credibility may discount it. To the extent that he is believed and followed, he is a leader and, on his own, is an important link in the communications process.[12]

Personal influence, no matter how dispersed, can be a decisive factor in the political process. For example, people who wait until late in a campaign to decide how they will vote tend to be less politically motivated than those who make up their minds early in the campaign. These late deciders often stress that the most important factor in their ultimate decision was personal influence and personal interactions.[13] In such cases, they are usually influenced by someone on approximately their own social level.

---

[11] For an interesting discussion of the impact of sources on attitudes see Carl I. Hovland and Walter Weiss, "The Influence of Source Credibility on Communications Effectiveness," **Public Opinion Quarterly,** vol. XV (Winter, 1951—1952).

[12] Elihu Katz, "The Two-Step Flow of Communication: An Up-to-Date Report on an Hypothesis," **Public Opinion Quarterly,** vol. XXI (Spring, 1957).

[13] Bernard R. Berelson, Paul F. Lazarsfeld, and William McPhee, **Voting,** Chicago: University of Chicago Press, 1954, pp. 174 ff.

FIGURE 7-3
THE VARIETY OF LEADERSHIP RELATIONS

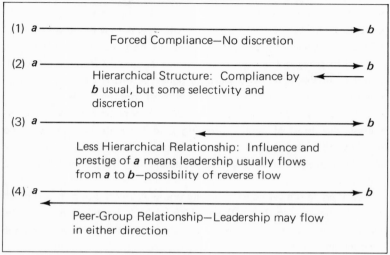

(1) *a* ⟶ *b*
Forced Compliance—No discretion

(2) *a* ⟶ *b*
Hierarchical Structure: Compliance by ⟵
b usual, but some selectivity and
discretion

(3) *a* ⟶ *b*
⟵
Less Hierarchical Relationship: Influence and
prestige of *a* means leadership usually flows
from *a* to *b*—possibility of reverse flow

(4) *a* ⟶ *b*
⟵
Peer-Group Relationship—Leadership may flow
in either direction

Types of Leadership Situations

It is useful to classify the varieties of leadership which may exist in terms of the relative positions of persons with respect to each other. In some situations verbal persuasion is a major element which can be used, while in others leadership depends not upon persuading someone to do something willingly but on the sanctions which leaders can levy for noncompliance.

THE HIERARCHICAL RELATIONSHIP. Figure 7-3 gives us a clearer idea of the various types of leadership situations which are possible. The first relationship is perhaps only hypothetical, for it presumes complete authority of **a** over **b**. It suggests that the relationship is strictly hierarchical. The subordinate is not allowed any discretion as to which of the orders he will follow, or, indeed, as to how he will carry those orders out. A highly structured organization such as the army perhaps most closely approximates this. Yet even here there is some level of maneuverability left to the subordinate. Nevertheless, the relationship of noncommissioned officers and enlisted men to commissioned officers allows for very little interpretation or questioning of orders by subordinates.

Even in the tightest organizations, however, isn't something left to the individual conscience? After World War II the Nuremberg trials questioned both superior and lesser officers about some of the barbaric orders which they had carried out. The officers replied that they were carrying out the orders of higher officials and that was their duty as members of the army. Their role was not to question orders, merely to execute them. Of course, this is a gross overstatement of army discipline. Even some of the German Generals had raised objections and refused to carry out certain orders which emanated from Hitler. Commanders in the field, who were at some distance from Berlin, often ignored orders. Von Choltiz was capable of ignoring Hitler's demands that he sack and burn Paris to the ground before he retreated. Nevertheless, the thrust of military training is to inculcate in men the need to obey all orders issued by their superiors. They are usually taught to neither interpret nor to use any discretionary judgment in carrying out orders.

Yet, there is almost never a totally one-way relationship. It is difficult to force someone to do anything which he finds morally reprehensible. Furthermore, leaders are always to some extent dependent upon the amount and quality of information gathered for them by their subordinates for any order they may issue. They can only make decisions and draft orders insofar as they know that a problem exists. To this extent, no leadership relationship is ever entirely unidirectional. To the degree that subordinates may structure the information which a superior receives, to the extent that they may decide what shall be passed up and what shall not, the decisions of leaders are structured by the following relationships:

SUBORDINATE-SUPERORDINATE RELATIONSHIP: AUTHORITY LIMITED.   The second situation shown in Figure 7-3 occurs when a subordinate-superordinate relationship clearly exists, but the range of authority of the leader is limited. For example, an employer has authority over his employees, yet the range of orders he can expect compliance to is limited by the nature of the job. His authority is limited further by the state of the employment market; if jobs are plentiful and he demands too much from his employees, they may decide to work elsewhere. Here the subordinate has some discretion; he can decide that the request of his superior is beyond what can rightfully be asked of an employee and refuse to comply. He may then have to change jobs, but the employer's sanctions usually do not extend beyond the particular situation. Clearly leadership is structured but its scope is limited. The follower or subordinate exercises more discretion or selectivity in responding to orders than he could in our first example.

SUPERORDINATE-SUBORDINATE RELATIONSHIP: UNCLEAR LINES OF AUTHORITY. The third situation shown in Figure 7-3 is that of a superordinate-subordinate relationship where the lines of authority are not entirely clear. Consider a President dealing with various members of his party. The President can use certain resources to try to gain compliance from members. He can use his authority as leader of the party, threaten to withhold favors, or even threaten to publicly rebuke dissidents. Thus his authority as President and party leader allows him to influence his own party members in several ways. Nevertheless, this leadership is limited. Congressmen, for example, from the President's party vary as to how much heed they pay the President. In cases where they come from "safe" districts, where they are reasonably sure of being reelected no matter what their voting record, they are relatively free to follow or not to follow the President as they choose. Alternatively, should the congressmen feel that he will jeopardize his chances for reelection if he does not follow Presidential leadership, he is likely to listen very closely to his President's advice.

Even for him, however, there is far more freedom than there was in the two previous situations. A President cannot threaten with physical force nor can he fire a congressman. Furthermore, the actions and desires of congressmen often influence the plans and programs of the President. Leadership is no longer unidimensional: Both parties influence each other, even though leadership is more likely to come from the President.

PEER-GROUP RELATIONSHIP. The fourth category in Figure 7-3 illustrates leadership among equals. There is no clear superordinate-subordinate relationship among the participants. We might be talking about a group of friends, a group of senators, or any sort of peer group. In this case, the relationship among the participants does not structure a leadership situation. We cannot presume in which direction leadership will flow. Instead we are likely to find great discretion among individual persons in accepting leadership. Influence is likely to become a two-way process, and who exerts leadership may vary from one circumstance to another.

In each of these four examples, the relationship among persons dictates what forms of leadership will be appropriate in any given setting. Certainly both the institutional and structural relations among people will affect both who shall be leader and what leadership skills or traits will be most useful in any particular setting.

ATTITUDE CHANGE: LEADERSHIP, COMMUNICATIONS, AND SYMBOLS

A fascinating although extreme example of conflict which illustrates the interrelationship among symbols, communication, and leadership was the brainwashing of American prisoners during the Korean War. Here the conflict was between captor and captive. Through brainwashing, the Communists sought to change the value structure of their prisoners; they were introducing a conflict between different value systems. Brainwashing, in that it attempts to change very basic and deeply held beliefs, is an example of very severe attitudinal conflict. What is interesting about the North Korean experiments is the way in which the Communists manipulated the environment in order to break down the resistance of the prisoners and bring about basic change in attitudes.[14]

The Communist brainwashing techniques employed both physical and psychological deprivations. Physically the prisoners were made as uncomfortable as possible. They were crowded together and moved continually from place to place. At the same time they were prevented from establishing meaningful relationships with fellow prisoners. Physical deprivation was linked to psychological isolation.

There were reasons for these deprivations. As we have suggested people depend upon each other for reinforcement of their beliefs. When you isolate people, their source of reinforcement is gone and they have no way of validating their impressions or beliefs. This is most strongly exemplified in conformist behavior where one feels an incessant need to seek approval of actions, to make sure that behavior will be satisfactory and not offensive. All of us to some extent depend upon each other for confirmation of our impressions and opinions. A common experiment familiar to students of social psychology is often used to exemplify this dependency. Suppose ten people are to participate in the experiment. Each of the ten is to look at a series of three drawings and indicate the relative size of the items in each group. Nine of the ten, however, have been told in advance to respond by saying that all three drawings are the same size. The drawings are not the same size; one is slightly but noticeably larger than the others. How will the tenth person respond? As the subjects give their answers, the experimenter seeks to determine the frequency with which the tenth person, lacking

---

[14] Much of the following discussion of brainwashing is based on the research done by Edgar Schein on repatriated prisoners of war. See his "The Chinese Indoctrination Program for Prisoners of War," **Psychiatry,** vol. XVIX (May, 1956).

support or reinforcement from other members of the group, will maintain his independent position. Will the tenth person deny his own sensory perceptions in deference to the judgment of the other people in the room, not one of which agrees with him? With alarming frequency he will indeed change his opinion and accept the position of the others in the group.[15]

This breaking down of sources of reinforcement was a significant aspect of the brainwashing campaign. It was hoped that psychological isolation from others who might have supportive beliefs and exposure only to the Communist viewpoint would bring some of the prisoners over to the Communist side. To accomplish this isolation, the Communists sought to break down all normal communications patterns. Outside mail was censored; no news except that unfavorable to the Americans was allowed to reach the prisoner concerning the war or the peace negotiations. The only source of information was the Communists. Likewise personal letters were delivered only when they contained bad news. An attempt was made to undermine all personal contacts. Spies were planted and rumors were spread about prisoners' defecting. All of these factors made it dangerous to talk to any other member of the camp since no one was ever sure whether he was talking to a friend or to a Communist agent or collaborator.

The Communists also sought to eliminate all leadership among the prisoners. The men were strictly segregated by rank. Segregation by rank was often followed by increased rates of collaboration with the enemy by younger enlisted men who no longer could refer to or take their cues from senior officers. This tactic was designed to remove the traditional source of leadership. Likewise the rumors and spies were used to prevent any new, more informal leadership structure from emerging.

The sense of emotional and social isolation was heightened by the removal of leadership. There was now no reliable source to approve or disapprove of behavior or to reinforce attitudes and beliefs. It was at this moment that the Communists would begin a heavy ideological

---

[15] There are several factors which affect the ability of the group to bring about conformity. See Leon Festinger and John Thibaut, "Interpersonal Communications in Small Groups," **Journal of Abnormal and Social Psychology,** vol. XLVI (January, 1951); Dorwin Cartwright, "Achieving Change in People: Some Applications of Group Dynamics Theory," **Human Relations,** vol. IV (1951); Harold H. Kelley and Edmund Volkart, "The Resistance to Change of Group-Anchored Attitudes," **American Sociological Review,** vol. XVII (August, 1952).

attack on the prisoners' basic beliefs. Several techniques were used. First the prisoners faced what seemed like interminable propaganda sessions consisting of lectures, films, and recorded statements from prisoners who had already defected. The use of defectors was to create a sense of legitimacy to the defection process. Informal techniques, such as group discussions, were also used. The men were forced to publicly read statements condemning what they believed in. There were severe penalties for failure to read the statements. If any mistakes were made, the entire process was repeated not only for the offender but for the entire group. Two forces were operative in this process. One was the power of repetition; continuously repeating statements which they initially did not believe might eventually cause the men to accept some of the propaganda or at least to question some of the facts or ideas which they had always accepted before. The second force was group pressure. If one's own peers could be pitted against offenders, they might be far more willing to go along with the Communists and say what they wanted. Thus the prisoner who committed errors in these discussion sessions not only had to face his own punishment but also inflicted punishment on all the others in his group. Given the normal reaction of mentally and physically exhausted prisoners to a person who provoked even more punishment for them, it is easy to see why the notion of collective guilt was a strong factor going for the captors.

Interestingly enough, the morale of most of the prisoners remained high so long as they presented a totally united front to the Communists. As long as no one broke, it was possible to maintain morale and withstand every propaganda onslaught. Just one defection, however, was enough to lower morale seriously and to set the stage for further defections and collaborations. Unanimity provided some source of reinforcement, and when this broke down it often broke the last elements of group resistance.

While an unusual and extreme form of conflict, these brainwashing techniques illustrate the factors that are operative in the process of conflict, particularly in the activation stage. When two groups oppose each other, they tend to create their own communications systems to give reinforcement to their supporters. This chain of reinforcement is necessary if one expects to keep his supporters. Leadership emerges according to the situation and the relationships of the parties to the conflict. Casting doubt on traditional sources of leadership or the absence of any effective leadership can do much to erode the position and strength of either side to a dispute. Finally, the brainwashing experiments also illustrate the difficulty in bringing about substantial and deep-seated attitudinal change. Such a basic change can only be made first by breaking down the existing patterns of belief and then by constructing a new system. The difficulties which the Communists faced indicate the degree to which our attitude and beliefs constrain our actions and, therefore, the potency of these same beliefs in activating conflict.

SUGGESTED READINGS

Arnold, Thurman, **The Symbols of Government,** New Haven, Conn.: Yale University Press, 1935.

Cartwright, Dorwin, and Alvin Zander (eds.), **Group Dynamics,** 2nd ed., New York: Harper & Row, 1960.

Coleman, James S., **Community Conflict,** New York: Free Press, 1957, chaps. 2 and 3.

Edelman, Murray, **The Symbolic Uses of Politics,** Urbana: University of Illinois Press, 1964.

Edinger, Lewis (ed.), **Political Leadership in Industrialized Societies,** New York: Wiley, 1967.

George, Alexander and Juliette, **Woodrow Wilson and Colonel House,** New York: Dover, 1964.

Hovland, Carl I., Irving L. Janis, and Harold H. Kelley, **Communication and Persuasion,** New Haven, Conn.: Yale University Press, 1953.

Katz, Daniel, Dorwin Cartwright, Samuel Eldersveld, and Alfred M. Lee (eds.), **Public Opinion and Propaganda,** New York: Holt, Rinehart & Winston, 1954.

Katz, Elihu, and Paul F. Lazarsfeld, **Personal Influence,** New York: Free Press, 1955.

Lane, Robert E., **Political Thinking and Consciousness,** Chicago: Markham, 1969.

Rokeach, Milton, **The Open and Closed Mind,** New York: Basic Books, 1960.

Verba, Sidney, **Small Groups and Political Behavior,** Princeton, N.J.: Princeton University Press, 1961.

Chapter 8

*Political
Parties:
Coalition
Formation*

The activation and politicization of demands and issues are a significant part of the political process. It is in this period that the agenda of politics is set. From the multitude of conflicts which may exist within a society, only a small segment at any given time will become part of the political agenda and even a smaller segment will be acted upon. In many societies political parties play the principal role in determining which issues will be considered in the decision-making phase by government elites.

THE DEVELOPMENT OF PARTIES

Political parties as we know them are a relatively recent phenomenon. Organized parties are at most 100 to 200 years old. This is not to say that factions did not compete for political office and rewards prior to this, but rather that large-scale organizations that have as their primary focus the nomination of candidates and the contesting of political office are relatively new. Some political scientists have designated the Federalist party and the Jeffersonian Republican party in this country as the first modern political parties.[1] The growth of parties tended to parallel the emergence of the nation-state and the growth of universal suffrage and parliamentary supremacy. As the size of the electorate increased, parties became vehicles for the expression of choice and the means by which like-minded individuals could express their individual choices with greater force. Parties allowed people to come together and pool their resources for the achievement of political goals.

The movement toward national states in Europe ultimately brought with it the development of political parties. As the monarchy and the aristocracy began to decline as a source of political power, elected institutions such as parliaments assumed greater importance as elements of the political process. In some countries where development was slow and gradual, such as England, political parties took shape after the establishment of parliamentary supremacy and the development of a strong nation-state. Although the Whigs and Tories were called parties, they were little more than rival gentlemen's clubs. They drew their membership from similar socioeconomic strata and members were capable of shifting freely from one party to the other without feeling any significant change in atmosphere or policy preferences. In other countries, such as Germany, political parties emerged concurrently with formation of the nation-state. Germany did not achieve final unification until 1871, after the successful conclusion of the Franco-Prussian War. Consequently, the parties there were relatively sharply defined, represented specific segments of society, and had far less interchangeable memberships than was true of English parties.

More recently, parties have often developed prior to the formation of the nation-state. In many formerly colonial areas the political parties which exist today had their origins in the struggle for independence against the colonial powers. The Congress party in India achieved prominence in the 1930s and included in its membership all of the leaders of the independence movement. After the British partitioned the

[1] William N. Chambers, "Party Development and the American Mainstream," in William N. Chambers and Walter D. Burnham (eds.), **The American Party Systems,** New York: Oxford University Press, 1967, p. 4.

subcontinent, creating India and Pakistan as independent nations, the Congress party became the dominant political party in India and has remained so to the present, although it faces severe internal splits. This pattern has been prevalent in other formerly colonial territories as well. In Ghana, Nkrumah's preeminent position had been due to his leadership in the independence movement which later became the dominant postindependence political party. The downfall of Nkrumah (he was deposed by a coup) and the current problems of the Congress party in India suggest that independence leaders may have difficulty in holding on to power after the departure of the colonial authority.

THE ROLES OF POLITICAL PARTIES

The circumstances which surround the emergence of political parties are likely to vary greatly from society to society as does the degree to which membership within the parties is broadly or narrowly based. Parties are similar from country to country, however, in terms of some of the roles which they perform. Although we will concern ourselves primarily with the roles of parties in democratic societies, we shall also note some of the functions which parties perform in nondemocratic systems as well.

As we indicated in Chapter 5, the output or result of the political process is the formation of public policy and the administration of government. Political systems may be incapable of governing or determining policy because the conflicts in the society are too great, because the actors cannot form meaningful coalitions, or because the rules and procedures of the political system preclude certain segments of the society from full political participation. Such situations occur periodically in various societies, and when they do, the normal process of politics breaks down. Parties are mechanisms which help forestall such breakdowns by providing channels through which conflicts can be articulated, coalitions formed, and proposals for public policy enunciated. Parties are in many respects the vehicles which societies develop both to channel and contain political conflict and to prevent the breakdown of the normal political process.

Parties, then, are agents for forming coalitions, instruments for representing interests, and mechanisms for recruiting leaders. As we indicated in the previous chapter, there are various methods by which leadership and political authority can be transferred. Elections, especially since the extension of the suffrage, provide democratic systems with a peaceful and regular procedure to handle the problem of leadership succession. The legitimacy or acceptance of democratic systems by their populations has rested on the ability of democratic methods through the electoral process to foster competition, provide mechanisms for the resolution of conflict, and to place minimal restraints on the presentation of alternative policies or leaders.

Parties and Democracy

Robert Dahl, in his discussion of **polyarchy** (which can be said to represent an ideal form of democracy), lays down a set of conditions or rules which should govern the politics of such a society. The basic postulate of his formulation is that elections are the means through which alternatives or choices are presented in the political process. Winning is determined by elections; the alternative receiving the highest number of votes wins. The election results are binding and the victorious party is allowed to take office. There are additional limitations and rules which Dahl sets out for a polyarchy, but these do not concern us here.[2]

The basic thrust of his argument is that democracy, in its stress on the electoral process, provides more than a means of selecting leaders by majority vote. It also allows for both the control of leaders by nonleaders and the presentation of alternatives and choices. Indeed, it is this presentation of choice which permits such control. The range of alternatives which are represented at elections in part reflects the divisions within the society. As we discussed earlier, those countries with longstanding conflicts and cleavages along several dimensions tend to exhibit multiparty systems.[3]

Within the United States the two-party system was established at an early point and parties have sought to embrace as wide a coalition as possible. This has not meant that the United States has not had third-party movements. In times of particular stress or where divisions in the country were particularly salient, third parties have developed and have enjoyed varying degrees of success. Some have been unsuccessful, while others, such as the Populists or the candidacy of George Wallace on the American Independence party ticket in 1968, have received

---

[2] Robert A. Dahl, **A Preface to Democratic Theory,** Chicago: University of Chicago Press, 1956, chap. 3, "Polyarchal Democracy."
[3] See Chapter 1.

relatively high percentages of the vote. Nevertheless, in most elections there have been only two significant parties vying for power.

Within any democracy a competitive party system offers, at a minimum, a choice of leadership personnel. Elections at regular intervals provide citizens with an opportunity to select from among competing claimants to political office. Beyond the minimal requirement of offering competing candidates, parties may present voters with alternatives ranging from minor policy disagreements to major differences of philosophy of government or the appropriate nature and shape of political institutions. Parties are the means through which democratic societies seek to institutionalize the most salient elements of political conflict.

If there is to be an effective choice, of course, more than one party must be able to compete for office. It is not logically impossible for a one-party system to present basic conflicts and alternatives to the citizens of a country. To the degree, however, that such conflicts are settled within the single-party organization, the internal mechanisms of that party would have to be structured in such a way as to provide open debate and the raising of alternatives. This usually is not the case. In the United States, for example, past history confirms that even with a primary system, one-party areas, such as the South, tend to have a more limited range of choice than is the case in the more competitive regions. Competition in primaries has not proved to be a satisfactory alternative to competition in the general election.[4]

Yet it is unrealistic to assume that the range of alternatives presented by a competitive party system will parallel the range of desired or preferred alternatives which exist within the population. The range of preferred alternatives within the population may be too broad to be fully represented by political parties. Parties tend to aggregate preferences and offer alternatives on those issues which are of concern to the largest number of voters. This is the only realistic form of behavior, but beyond that it is also socially useful. No political system could act upon all the conflicts and divergences of opinions which are presented to it. Parties perform an economizing function for society by filtering out the most important sources of political conflict and present-

[4] Julius Turner, "Primary Elections as the Alternative to Party Competition in 'Safe' Districts," **Journal of Politics**, vol. XV (1953); Allan P. Sindler, "Bifactional Rivalry as an Alternative to Two-Party Competition in Louisiana," **American Political Science Review**, vol. XLIX, no. 3 (September, 1955).

ing only these to the population in the form of policy statements, party platforms, and so on. This decision by party leaders to focus on only the most important sources of conflict is similar to the way in which individuals limit their attention to important problems. We all have a large number of goals that we desire, and we all prefer some goals to others. Often we consciously sacrifice action on a less desired goal in order to get favorable action on something we value more highly. Parties form coalitions and seek support for those issues which will give them the largest possible share of the total vote. If the goal of the individual person is to try to gain favorable action on those issues of most concern, the goal of the party (or more correctly those running on the party label) is to be elected.

Parties and Nondemocratic Systems

In nondemocratic and noncompetitive systems, parties obviously perform much more limited functions than those that we have been discussing. The role of parties is not to present alternative sets of leaders, nor is it to present alternative policy choices to the voter. The party exists to reinforce the present ruling elites. It is important to note, however, that no elite can rule for a long period of time without paying some attention to the conflicts which do exist within the society and to the demands and aspirations of the citizenry. Disregard of the populace usually means that increasingly coercive and violent tactics are needed just to stay in power. Such tactics may be very costly. This is why such nondemocratic systems often do have a political party. In such systems, the party minimally performs a twofold role. First, it must provide a source of information and feedback as to the state of opinion within the society and the sources of discontent. The party usually has its own hierarchy throughout the country paralleling that of the formal bureaucracy and this structure serves as an additional source of information to the political leaders and also as a check on the bureaucracy. Second, the party through its recruitment and promotion of promising party members can provide a continuing source of leaders for the regime.

A third and related characteristic of parties is common to both democratic and nondemocratic regimes. Parties provide a focus for political participation. They supply an outlet for those who have political ambitions and desire for political office. Even more broadly, parties stimulate interest in politics and generate a certain degree of participation. Obviously, in one-party dictatorial regimes the nature of the participation is far more orchestrated and controlled than it is in competitive political systems. Nevertheless, rulers in one-party systems often have regular elections and plebiscites in order to channel political participation and demonstrate the solidarity of regime and citizenry. Because elections in one-party systems are a way of showing solidarity, these regimes often impose penalties for nonvoting and nonparticipation.

THE GOALS OF PARTIES

Elections represent structured conflict situations. In these situations parties compete with each other to achieve as large a percentage of the vote share as possible. The goal of the participants in the party organization is the desire to win elections.[5] We can analyze an election as a zero-sum game. The number of elective offices is constant; therefore the gains of one party must equal the losses of the other party. In the case of multiparty systems, the payoffs are still limited but cooperative strategies often become possible. Since more than two parties are competing for office, the results of the election may not be decisive for determining who shall control the government. By this we mean that in multiparty systems where no party is capable of achieving a parliamentary majority by itself, the government will be formed as a result of the bargains and negotiations which are reached among the parties after the votes are in and counted. In this situation not only do possibilities exist for cooperative strategies in the electoral arena, but cooperative strategies are essential in the legislature in order to form a governing coalition. Nevertheless, all parties will at least try to get as large a share of the vote as possible.

PARTIES AND THE DISTRIBUTION OF OPINION

While the goal of parties is to achieve a majority of the vote, they are also concerned with avoiding an erosion of what has been their normal vote in past elections. Parties are faced with a difficult problem. Indeed, this conflict may significantly affect the types of issues which parties raise and place on the political agenda. If we look at Figure 8-1 we can see a distribution of opinion within a country (in terms of a liberal-

---

[5] Anthony Downs, **An Economic Theory of Democracy,** New York: Harper & Row, 1957, paperback ed., pp. 28 ff.

FIGURE 8-1
PARTY POSITION IN A UNIMODAL DISTRIBUTION

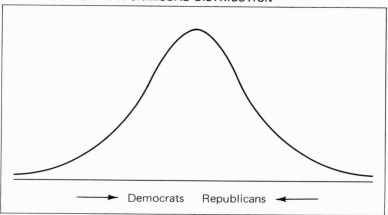

Democrats   Republicans

conservative dimension) which is statistically normal. That is, most people are clustered in the center. In a two-party system there is a tendency for the great bulk of the population to be clustered in the middle of the distribution and for the policies of the parties to converge. Nevertheless, there is a limit to the degree of convergence which is possible. This limit falls at the point at which attempts to maximize support begin to threaten the existing bases of support.

Let us retrace this reasoning. Since most voters are clustered in the center, the two parties should seek to gear their platforms to that group. It would be silly to try to outflank a party. What would happen, for example, if the Republicans tried to outflank the Democrats on the left? Such a maneuver might allow the Democrats to move their position slightly to the right and pick up a much greater share of the vote than the Republicans would pick up on the Democrats' left. We can see how the parties move together if we look at a state such as New York. New Yorkers have traditionally given support to liberal candidates. Therefore, both the Republican and Democratic parties tend to nominate liberal candidates. However, this liberal movement of the Republicans has posed a threat to their electoral position. A Conservative party has emerged to challenge the Republican party on the right. If such a movement becomes truly successful in blocking Republican success, one can assume that the Republican party will move slightly to the right. In a unimodal distribution of opinions, like that shown in Figure 8-1, it is not necessary to pay too much attention to the groups at

FIGURE 8-2
PARTY POSITION IN A BIMODAL DISTRIBUTION

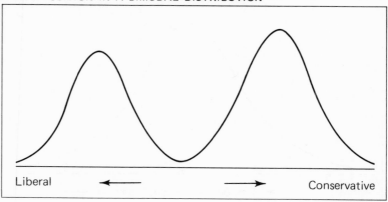

Liberal   ←——————   ——————→   Conservative

the ends of the curve simply because the votes represented there are minimal.

Alternatively, what would happen if the distribution of opinions on conservative-liberal dimensions looked like that in Figure 8-2? The strategies of the parties would be quite different from our earlier illustration. In this distribution the society is polarized and the middle ground is occupied by relatively few voters. Consequently, attempts to move toward each other on the part of either party would be self-defeating since the number of votes which could be gained is small and the potential of splinter parties forming to correspond to such a move is great. One could suggest that this distribution would indicate the breakdown of a political system where polarization has become almost complete.

Our last example is an extreme distribution of opinions. More interesting, in terms of its impact on party behavior, is various polymodal distributions. Italy represents a political system which can be characterized as being polymodal. We have represented this in Figure 8-3. Given such a distribution, there are dynamics operating which tend to keep the parties separate and distinct in the electoral arena and make it difficult for parties to merge. In Italy the Socialist party is but one of the left-of-center parties. In addition there is the Social Democrats, the Communists, and a splinter Socialist group. In the 1960s the Socialists, under the leadership of Pietro Nenni, decided to enter a coalition government with the Christian Democrats and to merge with the Social Democrats. The decision provoked a split in the party and

FIGURE 8-3

THE PROBLEM OF PARTY POSITION IN THE POLYMODAL DISTRIBUTION

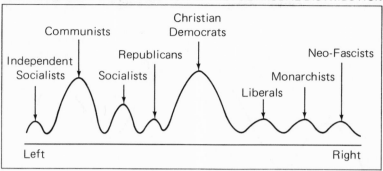

indicated the difficulty that parties in this type of distribution have in moving toward each other. Some who felt that the Socialist entry into the government represented a betrayal found that the existence of a viable alternative to the left of the Socialists, the Communists, allowed them to leave the party and vote Communist. Some of the more radical Socialists left the party and formed a new extreme Socialist party which was Maoist in philosophy. One of the reasons that the Socialists later withdrew from the coalition was that as a result of their participation in the coalition they had been the most significant electoral losers. Their share of the vote and the number of seats which they held in the Italian Chamber of Deputies dropped. This type of distribution makes movement among the parties difficult because for every movement either to the left or right there is another party which is ready to capture some supporters. This can perhaps be even more graphically illustrated in terms of the difficulty of the center party in a trimodal distribution. If we look at the above figure we can see that there are three dominant ideological positions which are represented. The strategic decisions of the parties will be influenced by the size of each mode. Let us assume that the center mode is the largest one in the distribution. As an example of this case, we can look at the electoral situation in Sweden during the early 1960s. The Socialist or Labor party was the dominant party in the country. On the right of the Socialists were a collection of middle-class parties, each one of which was small but who collectively represented a reasonably large segment of the Swedish electorate. On the left of the Socialists were the Communists, who traditionally had been a very small and electorally

FIGURE 8-4
THE TRIMODAL DISTRIBUTION AND THE CENTER PARTY PROBLEM

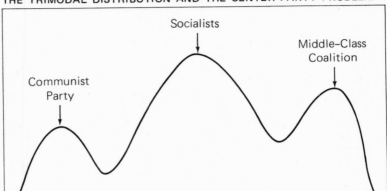

insignificant party. The division on the right and the small size of the Communists on the left had placed the Socialist party in an enviable position. Several events took place, however, which jeopardized that position. The Communist party underwent a leadership change when the old-line leaders were replaced. The new leadership sought to emulate the pattern of the Italian Communist party: to present the party as a realistic and legitimate alternative to the present government. This meant toning down the rhetoric of revolution and stressing the parliamentary nature of the party. This had proved successful in Italy where the Communists had become the second-largest political party.

For the first time in years, the Swedish Socialists were faced with the threat of a viable alternative on the left. At the same time the middle-class parties on the right were forming a temporary electoral alliance for the communal (local) elections. This left the Socialists facing a threat on the left and the right. Theirs was the classic dilemma of the center party. Any move to the right to maintain their support and meet the threat of the newly unified coalition would be met by an attempt by the Communists to take over the left wing of the Socialist vote. Any move to the left to counter the Communist challenge would be met by a movement of the middle-class parties to capture the right wing of the Socialist vote. The Socialists were strategically in a bind and as a result were the major losers in the election.

In any situation where there is a center party and viable alternatives on both the left and the right, there tends to be a squeeze on the center. This in electoral battles is consistent with the general model we have set up for political conflict. As the conflict increases in severity or salience, there is a tendency for the middle position to become eroded. Center parties, because they have the least maneuverability, often feel most the growing conflicts within a society.

What parties are then faced with, as organizations which reflect conflict in a society, is the need to maximize support while avoiding the erosion of existing support. The question of how much support should be maximized is crucial. Game theorists have maintained that the optimal strategy for parties is to secure the minimum winning coalition.[6] The party expends resources and forms coalitions around interests only until it secures that coalition which will allow it to win. Additional expenditures to gain any more votes represents a waste of resources. We can illustrate this point by considering the following hypothetical (and illegal) situation. Suppose you want to win an election and you engage in vote buying. There are one hundred people eligible to vote, so it is necessary to buy or secure 51 votes in order to win. If party A already has bought 51 votes, and we assume that there is honor among thieves (those 51 bought votes will remain bought), what is the utility of spending any more resources to buy the fifty-second or fifty-third vote? Obviously in this case there is no necessity for buying more than the minimum number necessary to win. Anything more than that would be wasteful. Let us note, however, that our reasoning has been based on certain assumptions. The primary one is that the party has all the information it needs to determine whether people whose vote has already been committed will honor those commitments. If a party were not certain of this, then obviously it would need to buy more than 51 votes. While 51 votes still assures victory, the party no longer is certain that all the votes it secured will be delivered. In the light of this uncertainty it will buy more votes as a form of insurance policy. Party A makes a calculation as to how many of the voters are untrustworthy and, on the basis of that calculation, determines how many votes beyond 51 it needs to buy. Obviously, calculations as to the rate of defection among voters are difficult to

[6] William Riker, **The Theory of Political Coalitions,** New Haven, Conn.: Yale University Press, 1962.

make and subject to error. Once you relax the assumption of complete information or certainty, it becomes clear that it is necessary for parties to seek larger than minimum winning coalitions.

In the United States both major parties seek to form broad, large-based coalitions. Vote buying is illegal, so the parties must use other methods, such as raising issues, as a means of attracting support. The parties always work under conditions of uncertainty and imperfect information, and therefore they seek to build as broad a base of electoral support as possible. Even here, however, the nature of the conflicts in the society puts a limit on the degree to which parties will maximize support before such maximizing tactics have counterproductive results. In the South, for example, the Democratic party enjoyed such an overwhelmingly dominant position in the past that the probability of a Democrat winning any given election there was about 85 to 95 percent. The chances of Republican victory were negligible. Nevertheless, there are significant political issues in the South. It might be possible for the southern Democrat to raise his percentage of the vote from 75 to perhaps 85 percent. To do so, however, might require an unjustifiable expenditure of effort in the form of raising additional issues. If the goal is to win, it does not matter much whether the victor wins by a one-vote margin or a landslide. The outcome in either case is the same, and therefore the additional effort is not worth the additional expenditure of resources. That is why most campaign efforts in the South were centered on the Democratic primary. The winner of the primary could sit back and count on his voters' traditional loyalty to the Democratic party; therefore new expenditures for the general election would be wasteful.

Other factors also limit the degree to which parties maximize support. Let us turn again to the Democratic party in the South. The voting rights acts which served to bring pressure on the southern states to enroll more black voters has changed or may change the nature of politics in that region. Previously, the ratio of registered voters to eligible citizens was lower in the South than anywhere else in the country. In part this low rate of registration reflected the lack of competition in the general election. There was no spur to registration; most people are eager to vote only when they feel that their vote may make a difference in the outcome of an election. When you live in a region where the result of the general election is a foregone conclusion, however, the stimulus to register and vote is gone. On top of this, the restrictive registration laws, in the form of literacy tests and poll taxes, cut down the size of the electorate. Indeed, many laws designed to keep black voting down to a minimum also did the same for white voting.

In this situation, as we have indicated, there was little incentive for the candidate to campaign actively in the general election; indeed, there was every reason for him not to campaign. As the electorate has increased, it has become even more dangerous for a Democrat to seek to maximize his support. Given a resurgent Republican party in the South, Democrats tread carefully in order not to risk losing more voters to the Republicans than they could gain by broadening the basis of their appeal. Table 8-1 gives us some idea of how much a threat the

TABLE 8-1

REPUBLICAN OFFICEHOLDERS IN THE SOUTH[a]

OFFICE	1960	1962	1964	1966	1968
Representatives	9	14	18	28	31
Governors	0	1	1	3[b]	5[c]
Senators	2	3	3	5[d]	7

[a] States included are Alabama, Arkansas, Florida, Georgia, Kentucky, Louisiana, Mississippi, North Carolina, Oklahoma, South Carolina, Tennessee, Texas, Virginia.
[b] Includes Nunn of Kentucky elected in 1967. [c] Includes Holton of Virginia elected in 1969. [d] Includes Strom Thurmond of South Carolina who switched party affiliation.

Republican party has become. The Democrats' strategic problem is (1) to avoid allowing the Republicans any further inroads and (2) at the same time to expand their own base of support. For example, Democrats who wish to take a liberal position on race issues have to fear, first, that they will be challenged in their own party's primary, and second, that in appealing for black votes they will lose an even greater number of white votes.

Thus, while all parties seek to win, and in the process to achieve as broad a base of support as possible, they often will hit snags in trying to form a maximum coalition. Even beyond the problem of decreasing marginal utility for additional votes, they must face the possibility that some of their supporters will defect from them as they try to broaden their base of support. This helps explain why parties raise only limited numbers of issues. Just as governments can break down when the amount of conflict becomes greater than the ability of the government to handle it, so too political parties can disintegrate when the number of issues raised is so great that it overstrains the loyalty of the various members of the party coalitions.

We can understand this last point better when we recall the recent history of the Democratic party. Since the New Deal period, the Democrats have drawn support from very diverse segments of the society and have always had difficulty in maintaining their uneasy coalition. The coalition contains both southern support, which is rurally based and highly resistant to any attempts at civil rights legislation or poverty programs, and urban votes, particularly votes from ethnic groups, blue-collar workers, and blacks. To these near opposites can be added the professors and the intellectuals who, while small in numbers, have had a significant impact on the party. As the great economic upheaval of the Depression began to ease, however, the coalition started to weaken. Support for Roosevelt's economic and domestic policies was gradually decreasing in the South. Although World War II temporarily interrupted this process, shortly after the war the strains grew even more apparent. The first major open break occurred at the Democratic national convention in 1948. When the attempt to write a strong civil rights plank into the party platform was successful, the southern states walked out of the convention. Soon thereafter, Strom Thurmond of South Carolina agreed to head a splinter ticket based on states rights and opposition to the platform proposals of the national Democratic party. While his effort was fairly successful in the South, it did not prevent the Democrats from capturing the Presidency, because the rest of the coalition held together quite strongly.[7] Nevertheless, it did make the election much closer than it might ordinarily have been.

In 1968 the strains of conflict were so numerous and diverse that they placed perhaps an insuperable strain on the Democratic party. First there was the usual conflict between the northern and southern wings of the party over the question of race relations and civil rights. This had been brought to a head before the convention by the active candidacy of George Wallace for the Presidency. Wallace was likely to gain many traditionally Democratic votes in the South. Indeed, the growth of Republican strength and the defections which would be caused by Wallace's candidacy did not make it look as if the Democrats could capture many southern states. In addition to this problem, the urban unrest and riots of the 60s had placed new strains on the coalition. The mixture of labor union groups and blacks became increasingly volatile as many blue-collar workers began to feel that the gains and demands

---

[7] Bernard R. Berelson, Paul F. Lazarsfeld, and William N. McPhee, **Voting,** Chicago: University of Chicago Press, 1954; also Angus Campbell, Philip E. Converse, Warren E. Miller, and Donald E. Stokes, **The American Voter,** New York: Wiley, 1960.

of blacks represented a threat to their own position and status within the society. The demands of blacks for entry into the predominantly white construction unions had alienated many labor leaders and workers. This was another source of conflict. A third source, of course, and the most divisive issue of all, was the war in Vietnam. Younger Democrats and the intellectual wing of the party were in open revolt against Lyndon Johnson's Vietnam policy and called for an end to American involvement there. This was in sharp contrast to the labor segment of the party which had given staunch support to Johnson's foreign policy. The South had also taken a relatively hawkish stand on the war and was not in favor of compromise on this issue. The party was split early in the year by the candidacy of Eugene McCarthy of Minnesota for the Democratic Presidential nomination. His strong showing in New Hampshire emphasized the divisions in the party, and the candidacy of Robert Kennedy only underlined them still more. Although McCarthy did not win in New Hampshire, he made a very strong showing which was all the more impressive because he was challenging an incumbent President within his own party. At the end of March, 1968, Lyndon Johnson dramatically removed himself from the struggle for the nomination. It was left to Hubert Humphrey, with none of the advantages of the Presidency and all the disadvantages of the Vice-Presidency and his close association with the administration's Vietnam policy, to try to pick up the nomination and somehow hold together the coalition which had been so remarkably successful from 1932 through 1964.

It was not an easy task. The assassination of Martin Luther King and later that spring the assassination of Robert Kennedy gave the most graphic and dramatic indications of the depth of conflict which faced the country. While these were two isolated acts of violence, they were symptomatic of the larger violence and malaise which had been gripping the country. The street fights and riots in Chicago during the course of the Democratic convention divided the party and left it in a very difficult position to fight an election campaign. That the election was as close as it was can only be regarded as a testimony to the indefatigability of Hubert Humphrey and his running mate, Senator Edmund Muskie of Maine. Nevertheless, the Democratic party lost support throughout the country. The number of conflicts which had been fed into the party and on which the party was supposed to take a stand were just too numerous and too divisive.

In 1968 the Republicans were in the politically more enviable position.

They did not have to answer for what was becoming a very unpopular administration. They were able to absorb and capitalize on the dissatisfaction with the Johnson administration which was felt in many quarters. After the bloodletting of 1964, the Republicans also seemed intent on a quiet convention and effectively maneuvered the platform and nominating process to a conclusion without any strong show of disunity. They profited, of course, from the fact that most of the action was directed, by the protesters, at the Democratic party.

COALITION BUILDING

As we have indicated, the role of parties is to engage in the political process, to select those issues of greatest concern, and to form the coalition which is most likely to succeed and which involves the least possible organizational costs. Any coalition is limited by the amount of resources which are available to those forming it and by the costs associated with maintaining it. Larger coalitions are more expensive to maintain.[8] Nevertheless, most parties seek, within certain limits, to form as large a coalition as their resources will permit. In the United States the coalitions which affect public policy are formed within the electoral arena. Both the Democrats and the Republicans put together coalitions of different groups who have varying demands. This is in contrast to many multiparty systems where the coalitions are formed primarily in the parliamentary arena. In multiparty systems each party tends to represent a specific and relatively homogeneous segment of the population. Often no one party is capable of achieving an electoral majority, and therefore the formation of the government requires negotiation and bargaining among the various parties as to how governmental positions will be allocated. In this sense, the coalitions are formed after rather than prior to the election.

There are several factors which influence whether coalitions are formed and what sort of bargains are struck among the various segments of the parties. Parties and interest-group leaders may engage in an exchange relationship in which the party agrees to lend its support to the group's demands in return for a commitment from the group either in terms of votes, monetary contributions, manpower, or any of various other services. Not only does the party offer promises of support for

---

[8] For a discussion of the relationship of the size of a coalition to costs, see Chapter 9.

the desires of individuals and groups, it can promise to make certain that such groups have access to decision makers. The nature of this relationship is complex, but for purposes of our analysis it can be noted that there is justification for group leaders to be active participants in the party process.

The problem of the party which builds broad coalitions, then, is one of providing a delicate balance of rewards and benefits to the various members of the coalition.[9] This tends to be a difficult task to achieve when the members of the coalition have contradictory or mutually exclusive goals. In part, one can say that the only reason that the southern Democrats have remained a significant element in the Democratic coalition is that the federal system in this country gives the local and statewide party great autonomy. While there are great conflicts among the wings of the party, the interaction required of the groups is minimal. The national convention brings all sectors of the party together in a situation in which they must reach a joint decision. Aside from this, however, it is completely possible for any segment of the party to pursue its activities in complete isolation from each other—and it is even possible to pursue contradictory policy preferences. Extended one-party dominance in the South has long allowed southern Democrats the luxury of using the Democratic party label even while disowning the national party. This is far more difficult to do in competitive regions or in regions where the national party position is likely to have an impact on local voting patterns. The strains that are difficult to handle are those which arise in the context of the integrated party (as at the national convention) or those which arise in competitive situations (as in many of the large states) when various minority groups compete for limited rewards.

In part, then, the size of the coalition can be determined not only by the available resources but also by such structural factors as how much autonomy can be given to its constituent units. Because the United States is organized as a federal system which gives considerable autonomy to both local and state governments, parties are organized on the local and state level. The national coalition may look like a strange and highly unstable congeries of forces; however, given the fact that the interaction of these forces is minimal, the coalition can remain intact.

---

[9] Samuel Eldersveld, **Political Parties,** Skokie, Ill.: Rand McNally, 1964, chap. 13, "The Party as a Task Group."

PARTY AND CONSTITUENCY

Again the physical size and the structural characteristics of the United States have made it strategically more sensible to work within the basis of broadly based parties. Joseph Schlesinger has developed a typology of constituencies in this country. He notes that constituencies may be **congruent;** that is, the boundaries for one office are exactly the same as the boundaries for other offices. For example, the county sheriff and the county judge share the same constituency. Or they may be **disjoint** in the sense that the boundaries for one constituency do not coincide or intersect with those of another constituency, for example, governors running for reelection in different states. Or constituencies may be **enclaved;** that is, one constituency is a part of and completely enclosed within another.[10]

In a sense all constituencies are enclaved if we consider them in relation to the Presidency. Every electoral constituency is a part of the Presidential constituency, the nation. If the federal nature of the political system allows for large and often antagonistic coalitions to be built because many of the constituencies are disjoint with relation to each other, the fact that constituencies are also enclaved requires that there be some mechanism which unites the various factions or parties which compete on the state and local levels. The existence of national and local party organizations allows groups to exercise influence within the local party organization and also allows the same or different groups to bargain and try to achieve satisfaction within the party at the national level.

If parties were only regional they would have great difficulty in affecting national policy, since their regional concentration would give them no organization through which to reach the rest of the country or to capture the Presidency. Similarly, narrowly based parties which tried to compete in all states would find it difficult to organize enough support to affect national priorities. To win national office one must have a base organization in all or most of the states, and this is an expensive and difficult organizational task. Unless an organization is capable of winning elections at more than the local level, it will be unable to

[10] Joseph A. Schlesinger, "Political Party Organization," in James G. March (ed.), **The Handbook of Organizations,** Skokie, Ill.: Rand McNally, 1965, pp. 787 ff.

maintain a viable organization for more than a short period of time. Local candidates will recognize that this type of party offers them little chance for satisfying their political ambitions and will likely switch to one or the other of the major parties. Indeed, since the resolution of conflict often requires concerted effort at the local, state, and national levels, only broadly based coalitions will have the organization through which conflict can be resolved and members will be satisfied.

PARTIES AND ELECTORAL LAWS

There is one further factor which has encouraged the existence of broadly based political parties in the United States: this is the existence of a single-member district winner-take-all electoral system. In the United States the vote for Congress, for example, takes place in districts each of which elects a single member to Congress. In each of the 435 House districts the winner is the candidate with the largest number of votes. There is no fractional division of a seat; the one with the most votes gets the seat whether he won by one vote or by thousands of votes. In proportional systems of representation, on the other hand, members are often elected to the legislature on an "at large" system; that is, they are elected from multimember districts. Suppose, for example, that a country has one hundred members in its national legislature. Members are not elected from districts; instead they compete for votes within the total national electorate. Each party puts up a slate of one hundred candidates. Under a system of proportional representation, the party which wins the most votes does not get all one hundred seats but instead receives a number of seats roughly equivalent to the percentage of the total vote which the party received in the election. In the case of pure proportional representation, the party receiving 40 percent of the vote would receive 40 percent of the seats in the legislature, the party receiving 50 percent of the vote would receive 50 percent of the seats, and so on. Thus the party receiving 10 percent of the vote would get ten seats in the legislature. In actuality, of course, no electoral system represents such perfect equality between vote share and seat share because of problems with fractional percentages and fractions of seats. Indeed, it has been demonstrated that all electoral systems are skewed to some degree or another in favor of the largest parties. The degree to which the systems

skew the results may vary, but all to some extent distort the seat allocation from the vote percentages.[11]

Given a single-member district system, however, there is little payoff
to the smaller parties. A minor party cannot receive any seats unless
it achieves a plurality of the vote in specific districts. Votes for small
parties therefore tend to be wasted insofar as the smaller party has no
real chance of gaining office. Unless there are certain very specific
reasons for voting for a minor party, it usually is not sensible to do so.
George Wallace in 1968 tried to counter the often-expressed feeling
that a vote for him would be a wasted vote. He emphasized that it was
possible, by voting for him, to prevent any candidate from clearly winning. If this were the case, Wallace suggested he would then be in a
strong bargaining position to gain concessions for his supporters, concessions which would be impossible unless he could prevent either of
the two major candidates from achieving victory in the electoral college.
The electoral college is the peculiar method of indirect Presidential election which we use in the United States. In order to win, a candidate must
get an absolute majority of the electoral votes. These votes are apportioned among the states on the basis of population. The candidate who
receives a plurality of the votes in each state, receives all of that
state's electoral votes. This, of course, means that Presidential elections
are contested state by state and winning is determined by amassing
a majority of electoral votes. The problem that the minor party candidate raises is that in a close election he may be able to withhold
enough states from either candidate to prevent anyone from achieving
a majority in the electoral college. When that occurs, the election is
thrown into the House of Representatives where each state casts its
vote as a unit and every state has only one vote. If there is a stalemate
in the electoral college, there is room for negotiation among the candidates, and the candidate of the minor party may be in a position to
control the outcome of the deliberations in the House. In any event,
under a single-member district system of elections, votes for minor
parties usually are wasted. Under such a system larger parties, which are
broadly based, are likely to be heavily rewarded. For example, under
such a system it is possible for a party to receive 51 percent of the
vote in every district and therefore receive 100 percent of the seats.

---

[11]For an excellent account of the impact of various electoral systems, see Douglas
Rae, **The Political Consequences of Electoral Laws**, New Haven, Conn.: Yale University Press, 1967.

PARTIES AND CAMPAIGNS

Parties present candidates for elections because they wish to win. This premise is as crucial as it appears simplistic. For the purposes of our discussion we shall make a second assumption: that a sizable proportion of the total electorate is already predisposed toward voting for one or the other of the parties. This is not an unrealistic assumption to make; the empirical evidence shows that large numbers of people vote in accordance with their partisan affiliations or predispositions. Furthermore, these predispositions are formed at a relatively early age and tend to be durable.[12]

The campaign itself represents an attempt by each of the parties to mobilize the predispositions of its supporters. This requires some means of cuing its voters: of getting them interested in the campaign and willing to vote. This is an **activation phase.** Each party will direct its rhetoric and symbols to those groups already predisposed to support it. For example, throughout the campaign the present party platform and candidates will be linked to the heritage of the party. Democrats, who forged their majority coalition during the Depression, will stress the lineage of the party from Franklin Delano Roosevelt and the programs of the New Deal. This is symbolic invocation. It is an attempt to use symbols which have favorable connotations among the Democratic segment of the population in order to increase solidarity and elicit commitment. Voters will be gently but consistently reminded of what the Democratic party has done for them over the course of the years.

For the Republicans the towering figure of Lincoln and the prestige of Eisenhower present analogous sources of symbolic cohesion. In addition, Republicans tend to emphasize their moderateness, their responsibility, and their greater maturity with respect to foreign affairs. Appeals to audiences which already have these predispositions are highly partisan in tone. They are intended to evoke feelings of partisan loyalty in order to "get out the vote."

Beyond the committed or relatively committed voters, a second segment of the population leans slightly toward one or the other of the parties. Appeals to the partisan loyalty of these voters are of limited value because the commitment to the party is weak. A new and different

---

[12] Campbell, Converse, Miller, and Stokes, **The American Voter,** New York: Wiley, 1960, chap. 7, "The Development of Party Identification."

set of tactics must be developed for this group. For them greater attention is directed to the candidate and the issues of the campaign. The
parties will try to sell their candidate or to portray his opponent as
being inept or ill-equipped to handle the problems which confront the
country. Appeals directed to this audience may emphasize the statesmanlike character of the candidate. Or they may attempt to isolate
those issues which transcend party lines. In 1968 the question of law
and order, the fears generated by the urban riots of the past summers
and the student unrest on the campuses, was an issue which transcended
party lines and which was used (more by the Republicans, since they
were campaigning against the record of the Democrats) to gain support. George Wallace's campaign in many respects can be characterized
as one which, in seeking to break traditional partisan loyalties, played
on the fears of the population and sought to emphasize those issues
unrelated to the traditional platforms of the two major parties.

An additional and difficult strategic situation faces the minority party
in a campaign. In terms of registration figures, the Republican party
has been the national minority party for a long period of time. In order
for the Republicans to win the Presidency, they must be able to hold on
to well over 90 percent of the traditional Republican vote, capture a
large percentage of the independent vote, and make inroads among
Democratic supporters. Without defections from the Democratic party,
Republicans cannot win. This poses a strategic conflict. In the election
campaign, the two parties are pitted against each other in a zero-sum
game.[13] One of the requirements of the conflict is that the parties activate their supporters. This often requires highly partisan appeals which
extol the virtues of one's own party and deprecate the policies and
record of the other party. Yet at the same time, the minority party has
to phrase appeals so as to attract support from members of the other
party. Partisan appeals are likely to dissuade potential converts from
the majority party. Indeed, they may arouse hostility. Somehow the
minority party must pursue at least two strategies simultaneously; it
must make the partisan appeals that will activate its own supporters
and at the same time present essentially nonpartisan appeals to members of the opposition party. This type of strategy is often used by the
Republicans in mayoral elections in large cities. In most large cities
Republican registration percentages seldom go above 40 percent. Obviously, since they are a small minority, an election campaign designed

---

[13] See chapter 2 for a discussion of the qualities of the zero-sum game.

to elicit support only from registered Republicans would be doomed to failure. Assuming that the party wants to win more than it wishes to preserve its doctrinal purity, it must strive for a more broadly based coalition. John Lindsay in his first New York City mayoralty campaign in 1965 emphasized a nonpartisan style and downplayed his Republican affiliation. This was a completely sensible strategy. It was a strategy, however, which alienated him from his own party. Republican regulars felt that he had deserted his own party. This in part accounts for Lindsay's failure to win the Republican primary and endorsement for mayor in 1969. Their lack of endorsement did not prove to be a crippling blow, but it did illustrate the difficulty of having to play a two-edged strategy. Failure to appeal to both sides can pose problems, indeed, although for the minority party in urban mayoral contests failure to develop the nonpartisan strategy can be even more damaging to victory than not appealing to one's own party members.

COMPETITION: THE CRUCIAL VARIABLE

As we know, one of the crucial roles parties perform is to present alternatives within democratic societies. They provide channels through which individual citizens or groups may raise issues or conflicting demands. The effectiveness of this role, however, depends in part upon the presentation of alternatives and therefore on the degree to which interparty competition is present. Wherever one party is overwhelmingly dominant, other parties find it difficult to be viewed as viable means for presenting either alternative policies or alternative leaders. We need only recall our example of the Democratic South to remind ourselves of this problem.

Competition, then, is a crucial variable which determines in part how effectively parties will be able to perform their role. Unfortunately, competition is not an easy concept to measure. We can talk broadly of a competitive political situation as one in which parties compete rather evenly for the contested offices, or more precisely, as one where party A has approximately the same chance of winning an election as party B. The assignment of probabilities to various parties for specific offices is quite difficult. If we assume that each election is independent of all others, past and present, we can simplify the procedure somewhat. We could then assume that party registration figures are meaningful and assign probabilities of winning to each party on the basis of its varying percentage of the registered electorate, making corrections for those who are registered but who have not expressed a partisan preference. This exercise would be relatively simple, but it would ignore the impact of past elections as well as the relationship between voting for one office and voting for another at the same time. All evidence would indicate that to ignore such interrelationships is to miss much of the intricacy and complexity of party and voting behavior. These two factors, however, make the problems of measuring competition much more difficult.

The extremely noncompetitive area, of course, is easy to identify. Where one party has consistently won all elections by a fairly wide margin, we can describe that area as noncompetitive. Within the United States such areas have become relatively few. Before the 1960s (see Table 8-1) the South probably fit this category best; today there is no large region which consistently fits this definition.

In discussing competition in most elections, then, shall we consider past elections and rates of competition? If so, how long a period of time should we consider? For example, if we are looking at the competition for the Presidency in the United States, it makes a great deal of difference how long a time span we use. Using too short a time span may lead us to place undue emphasis on what may be short-run deviations from a long-term trend. Thus, in considering short-term results, we may fail to relate present situations to past ones. On the other hand, what happens if we analyze too long a period of time? Then we are far too likely to ignore or severely discount the most recent events. Given a long enough span of time, there is a tendency in analyzing any phenomenon to note cyclical effects. This too often has a tendency to lead to very mechanistic and deterministic theories which are based on the assumption that what has happened in the past must inevitably repeat itself. Unfortunately, no matter what time span we choose, however, it will provide some distortion for our analysis. Perhaps we can avoid most of the pitfalls by studying relatively long periods of time but adding some corrective factor which allows us to weight the most recent elections more heavily than those in the distant past. With this system, if changes are occurring at the end of the period, they will show up in the calculations as changes in the relative competitiveness among the parties.[14]

---

[14] David B. Meltz, "Competition and Cohesion: A Model of Legislative Majority Party Bargaining," unpublished Ph.D. thesis, The University of Rochester, 1970. Meltz has developed a very useful measure of competition which avoids many of the problems of using long time spans.

There are additional problems in discussing competitiveness. If we agree on a specific time period, what factors within it will be used as a measure of competition? Shall we look at the number of years which each party has controlled the office or set of offices under consideration? For example, if we look at the number of years the Democrats and the Republicans have controlled the Presidency from 1900 to 1972, we find that both parties have been in power for thirty-six years. This can be seen in Table 8-2.

Let us, however, look at Table 8-2 a little more closely. While it is

TABLE 8-2

PRESIDENTIAL ELECTION RESULTS FROM 1900 TO 1972

TERM	REPUBLICANS	DEMOCRATS
1901–1905	X	
1905–1909	X	
1909–1913	X	
1913–1917		X
1917–1921		X
1921–1925	X	
1925–1929	X	
1929–1933	X	
1933–1937		X
1937–1941		X
1941–1945		X
1945–1949		X
1949–1953		X
1953–1957	X	
1957–1961	X	
1961–1965		X
1965–1969		X
1969–1973	X	

true that each party has held the office for thirty-six years, it is equally clear that during this period of time there were cycles of one-party dominance. An additional criterion is necessary—the frequency with which the office alternates from one party to another.[15] Looking at Table 8-2, we can note that within our seventy-two-year period, the Presidency changed party control six times. If it had changed parties

[15] Joseph A. Schlesinger, "A Two-Dimensional Scheme for Classifying the States According to Degree of Inter-Party Competition," **American Political Science Review**, vol. XLIX, no. 4 (December, 1955).

at every election, perfect alternation, this figure would have been seventeen. It would seem that the closer the probabilities of either party's winning are to those of the other (the closer the competition), the greater is the likelihood of frequent alternations. Thus, in a non-competitive area, party control would be likely to change not at all or very few times, while in a perfectly competitive region it might change nearly as many times as there have been elections. In this sense (1) the number of alternations and (2) the number of years each party has controlled the particular office give you a relatively good idea of how competitive elections for a particular office are likely to be.

While this type of measure can tell us whether competition tends to be high or low for a given office, it cannot indicate whether a given election is more or less competitive than one in the past, how competitive elections are for any other office, or the degree to which voting for one particular office is related to voting for other offices. This requires additional measures and calculations. The degree to which parties offer alternatives can be best ascertained only on a state-by-state or office-by-office basis. In a country like the United States, where elections take place on numerous government levels, the structure of competition is likely to vary from office to office and from place to place.

Indeed, within the United States, history tells us that the range of competition has varied according to time and place. Between 1900 and 1932 the Republican party dominated the Presidency. The two elections which the Democrats won during this period were deviations caused in 1912 by the independent candidacy of Theodore Roosevelt and in 1916 by the advantages of incumbency which Woodrow Wilson enjoyed in his campaign for reelection. Yet even with all the advantages that an incumbent President has in seeking reelection, Wilson barely won in 1916. In the period from 1932 to 1968, on the other hand, the Democrats dominated the Presidency and the two Republican victories can be attributed to the attractiveness of Dwight Eisenhower and to the fact that he was considered by many to be more of a nonpartisan candidate than a Republican. The significance as to whether Richard Nixon's election in 1968 constitutes a deviation from this Democratic dominance or indicates perhaps the start of a Republican cycle is still difficult to determine.

One of the factors which allows the minority party to survive during long periods of one-party dominance of the Presidency is the existence of independent state and local elections. While the Democrats were in control of the Presidency, the Republicans were still able to hold on to a solid core of seats in the Senate and in the House and a few times had a majority in both Houses. They were also able to capture many governorships. The ability of the party to remain strong and viable on lower levels provides the basis for its capacity to sustain the conflict on the national level, even in the face of repeated losses. In a non-federal system, repeated losses at the national level may quickly bring about the demise of the party.

PARTIES: AN OVERVIEW

In seeking to summarize some of the statements we have made about parties, we can note that they are unique organizations which direct the conflicts that exist in society into formal political channels. Parties seek to win elections, and, in so doing form coalitions. The basis of the coalitions is the understanding that the party will seek to further the varied interest of its members. Nevertheless, parties in seeking to win operate under conditions of incomplete information and relative uncertainty. This forces them to try to make larger coalitions than would be necessary if information were complete. However, the size of coalitions is limited to some degree by the distribution of attitudes among the population and by the fact that attempts to gain more votes may have decreasing marginal utility or, in fact, may be absolutely counterproductive. The campaign is the arena in which parties raise issues and seek to activate and solidify their supporters. A political party will often engage in multiple strategies in order to win the largest possible vote. The major factor determining the effectiveness with which parties can channel conflict is their competitive position with respect to each other. In a country such as the United States, the degree of competition is not easy to measure and varies from setting to setting. Nevertheless, the amount of competition present helps determine whether or not parties can function as institutions for the effective channeling of political conflict.

SUGGESTED READINGS
Alford, Robert, **Party and Society,** Skokie, Ill.: Rand McNally, 1963.
Barnes, Samuel H., **Party Democracy,** New Haven, Conn.: Yale University Press, 1967.

Berelson, Bernard R., Paul F. Lazarsfeld, and William N. McPhee, **Voting,** Chicago: University of Chicago Press, 1954.

Campbell, Angus, Philip E. Converse, Warren E. Miller, and Donald E. Stokes, **The American Voter,** New York: Wiley, 1960.

Chambers, William N., **Political Parties in a New Nation,** New York: Oxford University Press, 1963.

Dahl, Robert A. (ed.), **Political Oppositions in Western Democracies,** New Haven, Conn.: Yale University Press, 1966.

Downs, Anthony, **An Economic Theory of Democracy,** New York: Harper & Row, 1957.

Duverger, Maurice, **Political Parties,** New York: Wiley, 1963 ed.

Eldersveld, Samuel, **Political Parties,** Skokie, Ill.: Rand McNally, 1964.

Key, V.O., **American State Politics,** New York: Knopf, 1956.

LaPalombara, Joseph, and Myron Weiner (eds.), **Political Parties and Political Development,** Princeton, N.J.: Princeton University Press, 1966.

Leuthold, David, **Electioneering in a Democracy,** New York: Wiley, 1968.

Ordeshook, Peter, "Extensions to a Model of the Electoral Process and Implications for the Theory of Responsible Parties," **Midwest Journal of Political Science,** vol. XIV, no. 1 (February, 1970).

Rae, Douglas, **The Political Consequences of Electoral Laws,** New Haven, Conn.: Yale University Press, 1967.

Riker, William, and Peter Ordeshook, "A Theory of the Calculus of Voting," **American Political Science Review,** vol. LXII, no. 1 (March, 1968).

Schattschneider, E. E., **Party Government,** New York: Holt, Rinehart & Winston, 1942.

Schlesinger, Joseph A., **Ambition and Politics,** Skokie, Ill.: Rand McNally, 1966.

Schlesinger, Joseph A., "Political Party Organization," in James G. March (ed.), **The Handbook of Organizations,** Skokie, Ill.: Rand McNally, 1965.

Schlesinger, Joseph A., "The Structure of Competition for Office in the American States," **Behavioral Science,** vol. V, no. 3 (July, 1960).

Schlesinger, Joseph A., "A Two-Dimensional Scheme for Classifying the States According to Degree of Inter-Party Competition," **American Political Science Review,** vol. XLIX, no. 4 (December, 1955).

Chapter 9

$\mathcal{S}$ome
$\mathcal{T}$heoretical
$\mathcal{C}$onsiderations

In Chapter 5 we presented a model of the political process. We broke the process down into three major stages: (1) activation, (2) decision making, and (3) execution and integration. These stages were, of course, more clear-cut and sharply defined in our analysis than they are in reality; nevertheless they are useful in helping us to understand the role of conflict within the politicial process. In the past few chapters we have focused on the activation phase. Let us now turn to decision making itself. Are there rules governing decision making? What methods of reaching decisions are possible? What are the implications of these methods? In this chapter we shall concentrate on theoretical considerations involved in the decision making process. We shall then apply this theory to actual decision making situations in Chapters 10 and 11.

THE NATURE OF DECISIONS

To make a decision is to choose one from among several possibilities or forms of action. Even choosing not to act is a decision. Each day we are faced with many decisions, both in our personal lives and as members of society. Some take a great deal of thought and time; some hardly seem to be decisions at all. The ease with which we are able to choose from competing alternatives depends in part on our previous training and thus on the rules we live with, our modes of behavior, and of course, our preferences. Thus the small child constantly faces decisions which the adult answers out of habit and almost unconsciously. Since the child has not yet formed habits or routine patterns of thinking, nearly all decisions assume equal weight in his mind. Should he eat now or continue playing? Does he want to play inside or outside, wear white socks or blue socks? Should he trust or fear you? These are all important decisions to him, and until he has had to answer them often enough, he will rethink them anew each time. The world seems very large and very strange, and it is filled with as many choices and important problems for him as it is for any President.

As we grow older, we form habits and learn to answer many questions routinely. For example, we tend to form certain eating patterns. Few of us decide anew every time we are going to eat; we have a fairly regular plan for meals and no longer have to make a conscious decision about them. Similarly, whether we are going to get up each morning and whether or not we will go to work have become routine decisions. If we have a job, we assume that it requires our daily presence at a specific location; without even questioning our actions we arise and stumble off to work. Indeed, the great bulk of our daily activities become habitual; they fall into a routine which makes much of our decision-making an easy, almost automatic process.

Maturation also involves a second type of learning which eases the decision-making process: learning to discriminate between important and unimportant decisions. Choosing from among competing alternatives always costs us something—whether it be time, money, or any of several resources. Making an important decision may even cost us a friend or ally. Consequently, we tend to rank decisions in order of importance; and the more important the decision, the more we are willing to spend in order to make it.

Thus, as we mature, the range of our decision making both expands and contracts. It contracts, in a sense, as we develop habits and a daily routine and in so doing choose automatically what we once chose consciously. On the other hand, the scope of our decision making expands as we learn to rank problems in their order of importance. We learn to balance the costs of making a decision against the decision itself, and in so doing we learn to devote more and more of our resources to the most important problems.

In any society individuals are faced with sets of costs. One set of costs is **external. External costs are those imposed on us by the actions of others.** These costs arise from the increased interaction and interdependence of individuals in complex societies. Many of the actions which an individual takes have an impact on the life-style of others. Urbanization, for example, is a phenomenon which occurs as large segments of a population move from sparsely settled areas and concentrate in a particular locality. As the number of inhabitants living in a particular locale increases, this imposes costs on the other inhabitants or the older inhabitants. The problem of pestilence and disease which exists in overcrowded areas may require greater expenditures for health facilities. Increased population may increase the probability of crime and therefore raise the costs of providing security to inhabitants of urban areas. The decision by others to move to urban areas is something over which you may have no control. Yet it imposes a cost on you. The move may necessitate higher and more extensive levels of services. It may also have an enormous impact on the life-style of the community in which you live.

Obviously, not every action which an individual can take will have an impact on others. There are whole ranges of decisions and actions which are in no way capable of imposing external costs on others. However, as societies become more complex and interdependent, the range of actions which one can take that are purely private—that is, that have no external effects on others—becomes increasingly limited.

Given the fact that we live in a world where the actions of others may impose costs on us, produces or generates a second set of costs. We make decisions in part to counter the possibility of others imposing costs on us. Yet, as we indicated, no decision is costless. Decision-making costs are those costs which arise from the necessity of at least two people reaching agreement on a particular course of action.[1] These decision

---

[1] James M. Buchanan and Gordon Tullock, **The Calculus of Consent,** Ann Arbor: University of Michigan Press, 1962, paperback ed. p. 45.

FIGURE 9-1
INTERNAL COST AS A LINEAR RELATIONSHIP TO THE
NUMBER OF PARTICIPANTS

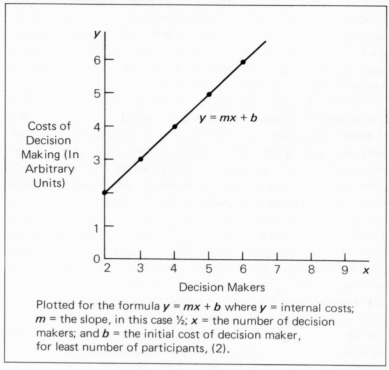

Costs of Decision Making (In Arbitrary Units)

$y = mx + b$

Decision Makers

Plotted for the formula $y = mx + b$ where y = internal costs; m = the slope, in this case ½; x = the number of decision makers; and b = the initial cost of decision maker, for least number of participants, (2).

making costs are the costs which arise from reaching agreement with others as to how best to meet the external costs which living in society can create. We are eliminating from our discussion decisions which the individual can reach by himself without consulting others.

DECISION MAKING COSTS

Decision making costs are the costs of organized activity. One of the most significant factors affecting these costs is the number of people whose agreement is necessary to take action. Can two people make a decision or does it require the consent of five or fifty people? The larger the number of decision makers involved, the higher the costs of decision making are likely to be. While we cannot say, with any security, what the cost of each additional decision maker will be in every situation, we can suggest at least three ways in which decision making costs may

FIGURE 9-2
DECISION MAKING COST AS AN EXPONENTIAL RELATION TO
THE NUMBER OF DECISION MAKERS

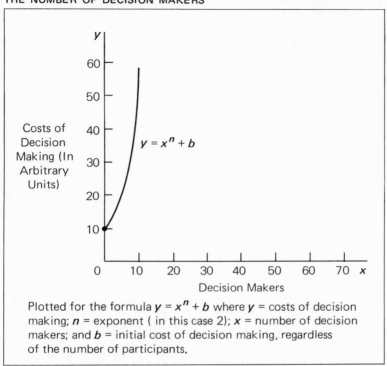

Plotted for the formula $y = x^n + b$ where y = costs of decision
making; n = exponent (in this case 2); x = number of decision
makers; and b = initial cost of decision making, regardless
of the number of participants.

vary as a function of the number of participants to a decision. The
three examples we will use are situations in which costs are related to
number of decision makers in a linear, exponential, or logarithmic relationship (see Figures 9-1, 9-2, and 9-3). In all three cases, however,
the costs rise as more and more people become involved.

Figure 9-1 represents a linear relationship between the number of
individuals and the costs of decision making. It stipulates that for each
additional individual there is a fixed increment by which costs rise. We
can also note that in our figures we postulate that there is in each situation a fixed level of overhead costs. If our base point is the costs for
two people to make a decision and we are comparing how much the
addition of other individuals raises the costs, it is important to note that
even at the lowest point there are certain costs which are basic to the
decision making process. In Figure 9-2 we can see how much difference
each individual makes if costs are related in an exponential way to the

FIGURE 9-3
DECISION MAKING COST AS A LOGARITHMIC RELATION
TO THE NUMBER OF DECISION MAKERS

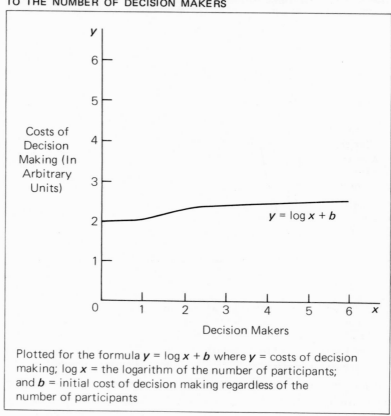

Plotted for the formula $y = \log x + b$ where y = costs of decision
making; $\log x$ = the logarithm of the number of participants;
and b = initial cost of decision making regardless of the
number of participants

number of individuals involved. Here the increments of cost increase at
an exponential rate with each additional number. We can note that in
situations which resemble this type of function, a requirement that large
numbers of people interact to reach a decision would make the costs
of decisions quite prohibitive. On the other hand, if we look at the
logarithmic relationship shown in Figure 9-3, we can note that here
while each individual raises the costs of decision making, the increments
become increasingly smaller for each individual. In this case, large
numbers of decision makers would not raise the costs very quickly or
dramatically. Obviously, the number of people who will be involved in
a decision will be limited by the costs of sustaining that involvement.

There is an added subtlety to the relationship between decision
making costs and the number of decision makers. This involves the

method of decision making or the decision making rule: the number of people whose consent is required in order to take action. Let us assume that a family of five is looking for a new car. All five of them will consult on what kind of car to buy, and this will impose costs such as the time involved in talking to everybody. Consider the time involved if all five must reach unanimous agreement. What would happen if you only needed final agreement among two of the five members of the family? The chances are that you would be able to make a decision in less time; thus the costs would be lower. As soon as two members agreed, the decision would be made. In both cases we are considering the costs for consultation among all five family members. The difference in costs relates to the number of the total body whose agreement is necessary for the decision to be made.

The Decision Making Rule

Decision making rules are arbitrary by definition. Any percentage of a total group can be required to obtain action on a given decision. In most democratic electoral systems, we think of the operative rule as being the majority. In the United States, for example, the rule for electing the President is that the winning candidate must have an absolute majority of the votes in the electoral college.[2] Nevertheless, for most other legislative and executive offices, we apply the rule of the plurality. If in a congressional district there are more than two candidates running, the only stipulation is that there can be no tie. A candidate need only get more votes than any other candidate; he is not required to have a majority of all votes cast in order to win.

Some countries use alternative decision making rules within one election. In France, for example, two rules are applicable in the parliamentary elections. On the first ballot, a candidate must have a majority of all votes cast in order to win a seat. If no one candidate receives a majority, a second election is held and the winner is determined on the basis of the plurality rule. Countries use several variations of these decision rules in the electoral arena. Most Americans, used to a two-party system where a plurality often is also a majority, tend to think that there is something automatic or mystically correct about a majority decision making rule. Few Americans would even question the principle that the majority should win. Yet logically this designation is as arbitrary

---

[2] An absolute majority is 50 percent plus 1 of the total votes which can be cast. A simple majority would be 50 percent plus 1 of the actual votes cast; and a plurality is, of course, the alternative receiving the highest number of votes.

as any other; much of its strength stems simply from tradition. There may be moral reasons or it may seem to some people ethically superior that the wishes of the many should take precedence over the wishes of the few, but one could still ask why the figure should be set at 50 percent plus one instead of at 60 percent or some similarly arbitrary point. If there are one hundred voters, why are fifty-one intrinsically better than fifty-two or fifty-three at making decisions?

Whatever the accepted rule, it does affect the costs of decision making. The larger the number of voters necessary to reach agreement, the greater the costs involved. This is true both on a percentage basis and as a function of the absolute number of people involved. Two groups may both stipulate that a majority is necessary for the transaction of business. Group A has a membership of 100, and group B has a membership of 500. While both employ the majority-rule principle, in group A all that is required is agreement among 51 people. In group B the number required to take action is 251. Obviously the costs will be greater where 251 people must agree. Thus the decision rule and the size of the organization operate together to determine the decision making costs.

Phrased differently, the decision making rule stipulates what the minimum coalition is, expressed as a percentage. We do not know exactly how many people will vote, and winning is a function of gathering the most votes cast. While we may not know the absolute number, in a majority system we know what the winning percentage must be. In a plurality system, however, we must guess at what probably will be a sufficient percentage of the vote to secure victory. This fact helps to explain again why parties in elections often seek to build greater than minimum winning coalitions. The smaller the group, the greater the likelihood that there will be information available concerning the preferences and expected behavior of each member. Where information is fairly complete, the minimum winning coalition probably will be formed relatively frequently, since larger coalitions will be wasteful. Where information is less complete, decision makers will not be able to determine how large the winning number must be and factions or groups will pursue maximizing strategies.

Information Costs

We have suggested that the number of people involved in a decision affects the costs of reaching that decision. One of the costs which the

FIGURE 9-4

DETERMINATION OF THE OPTIMAL AMOUNT OF INFORMATION

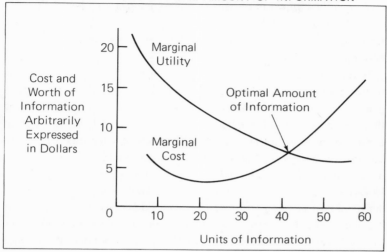

Units of Information

number of people affects is the cost of gathering information. If we assume that decision making involves a series of bargains, negotiations, and compromises through which winning coalitions are formed, then the gathering of information affects both the nature of the negotiations and the costs involved in forming coalitions. Where information is complete and accurate, strategies will differ from situations in which information is sketchy. The making of decisions involves spending resources to gather information. Yet there are limiting factors. At some point in time we will decide that the cost of gaining further information is greater than the worth of that information. We can graphically demonstrate this point by looking at Figure 9-4.

Each additional unit of information obtained will have both **marginal utility** for and **marginal cost** to our decision makers. These quantities are the worth or cost of the last item purchased; thus the marginal utility of the twenty-first piece of information would be the difference between the total worth of 21 and the total worth of 20. Units of information are interchangeable and their worth can be expressed in dollars. The marginal utility of each item tends to diminish and generally can be represented by a downward sloping curve. Thus the very first unit of information is very valuable to decision makers; the second still tells him a lot but perhaps somewhat less than the first. Let us say that the tenth unit is still worth $16 to him. The thirtieth unit, however, doesn't really help him that much; it is only worth $10. The fortieth unit, then, might give him $8 worth of help in campaigning, for example; the 55th unit, $7; and so on. Still, even the sixtieth piece of information does have some worth to him. Should he buy it? What is the optimal amount of information to obtain?

To answer this question, our decision maker must look at the marginal cost of each item. Marginal cost works in much the same way as marginal utility, except that this time we are measuring the **cost of buying** that one last unit of information. At first, marginal cost may diminish as economies of scale set in. Thus the fifth piece of information may cost $5. Having bought it, however, our decision maker has an "in" for gaining more information, and the sixth unit may only cost him $4.80. Nevertheless, information will eventually become more scarce, and the marginal cost will begin to rise with each additional unit bought. Thus the twentieth unit of information may only cost our decision maker $3, but by the time he reaches the thirtieth unit, information will be twice as difficult to come by, and he will have to pay $6 additional to buy it. The fortieth unit may cost $8 more, and the sixtieth unit as much as $17.

How many units of information should our decision maker buy? Let us look again at Figure 9-4. At the fortieth unit of information the marginal cost and the marginal utility are equal. The last unit is worth $8 to our decision maker, and he must pay $8 to buy it. This, then, is the optimal amount of information for him. If he obtains less, he will be losing out on information which is worth more to him than he will have to pay for it. If he buys more, he will be paying more for the additional information than it is worth to him. At forty units, his marginal utility exactly equals his marginal cost and he is maximizing his resources.

Let us look at two actual examples of the decreasing marginal utility for information in the decision-making process. In 1968 George Romney announced himself a candidate for the Republican Presidential nomination and filed to compete against Richard Nixon in the New Hampshire Presidential primary. Romney's candidacy represented an investment of resources. He had placed his prestige as a vote getter on the line, he had assembled a staff to aid in the campaign, and he had expended money and time in his effort. Romney, like many other candidates, wanted to have information about the degree of voter sentiment in his favor in New Hampshire so that he could gear his campaign accordingly. He hired a public opinion firm to sample public opinion and help determine his strategy. The polls showed him to be trailing Nixon in New Hampshire apparently by an insurmountable margin. Obviously the sampling could not provide complete information. Furthermore, the date of the primary was still a few weeks off, and there may even have been a chance for Romney to win. Additional polls could have been taken to determine where he could pick up support and what type of strategy might improve his position. Nevertheless, Romney decided that on the basis of the information he already had, he had no chance to win. He felt that further information was not likely to provide any additional clues as to how to surmount Nixon's lead. He therefore concluded (perhaps not as consciously or precisely in the way we are stating it) that seeking additional information would not be worth the cost. He therefore decided to cut his losses and he renounced his candidacy.

In 1969, Richard Nixon, now President, announced his choice for Abe Fortas' replacement on the Supreme Court. The President had his advisers scout the list of potential nominees who fitted the criteria that he had outlined. Nixon had clearly stated that he wanted to add balance to the liberal Court by adding conservative judges. He had also made clear that his intention was to pick a conservative judge from the South. Each nominee presumably had been thoroughly screened, and his chances for confirmation had been carefully assessed. When the President nominated Judge Clement Haynsworth of South Carolina, he probably felt sure that the investigation had been adequate and that Haynsworth would be confirmed. It had been customary to accede to the President's wishes in appointments. It is not at all clear whether Nixon's advisers were fully aware of Judge Haynsworth's financial dealings. Certainly they did not have adequate information to judge public and senatorial reaction to the disclosure of his financial interest in companies that had cases brought before his court. Such additional information might have spared the President an embarrassing defeat. Once such information was disclosed it placed Republican senators, who had made an issue of judicial ethics in the Fortas case, in an untenable situation. The decision not to gather further information was extremely costly. The decision that the marginal utility of further information would be insufficient to compensate for the extra cost stemmed in part from the belief that the judge had made a creditable record on the lower court and in part from a strong past history of Presidential appointees being confirmed. In all decision making situations, information gathering must end at some point. Nixon's experience points out that unless information is nearly perfect, we usually will not be able to judge either the exact marginal utility or the exact marginal cost of one last piece of information. As the President discovered, no matter how thorough we think we may have been, there is still margin for error.

EXTERNAL COSTS: PRIVATE OR COLLECTIVE ACTION

We have indicated some of the costs of decision making itself. External costs are those factors which require us to reach decisions. They are the costs we bear as the result of the actions of others over which we have little or no control. External costs are not costs of decision making; rather they are costs imposed on us by virtue of the fact that we live in a complex and interdependent society. The existence of these costs often force us to make decisions as to the most appropriate way to reduce the externalities of modern life. For example, the decision to buy auto-mobile insurance reflects in part a reaction to the possible action of others over which we have no control. Someone may try to steal your car or to break into it. Or someone may crash into you, hurting not only your car but also the passengers. The nature of these costs are such that we arrange for insurance to protect ourselves against possible losses. In this case, the nature of the external costs is such that we usually try to reduce such cost through private rather than collective action. Each person individually arranges for his insurance. However, it is interesting to note that in recent years it has been felt by many that the external costs are not sufficiently reduced through private voluntary action. Many people drive without insurance. Therefore, many states now have compulsory insurance laws or require the payment of high premiums for automobile registration for those motorists who do not carry automobile liability insurance. Our example is useful in illustrating the fact that we respond to external costs in varying ways. Sometimes it is most economical to respond to an external threat by private action. In other cases it is more efficient to arrange for protection through collective processes. At times we may use a combination of the two.

The existence of nuclear weapons poses a potential external cost. As nuclear weapons proliferate, the possibilities rise that other countries can impose great costs on our country through the use of such weapons. We may wish to stockpile more weapons or deploy more missiles to compensate for the arms buildup in other countries. We have no control over their defense policy and yet we are obliged to respond to it. In this case the response to external costs is to reduce those costs through collective governmental action. National defense is a collective good which can most efficiently and best be produced as a result of governmental action. There is no way the individual can privately arrange for his defense from foreign enemies. A bombing attack affects all inhabitants of the target area equally. In this case the cost of providing defense is most efficiently handled by government through revenues raised as a result of taxation.

As we noted earlier, if all human beings were totally self-sufficient and able to avoid interacting with each other, there would be no external costs and therefore no need for government. The existence of external costs makes government imperative for the reduction of costs in those cases where private action is either impossible or uneconomical.

Police protection arises largely from our fear that others, over whom we individually have no control, may harm us. We may decide that the probability of such external costs being imposed on us are not sufficiently high to justify police protection. If so, we would be declaring that the utility of police protection, the degree to which it would save us from the actions of others, would be less than the cost for such protection. While there is no logical impossibility in our reaching this decision, it is unlikely that anyone living in a complex society would be willing to forego the police services performed every day. However, it is possible that people might decide that the threat of external costs should or could be most appropriately met through private rather than governmental means. If we assume that police protection is not a collective service provided by government, then any person may contract with other persons to provide protection for himself, family, and his property. Obviously, the degree of protection which people have will then vary according to the amount they can afford to spend and their estimate of how much they need to be protected. We can suggest that such a system would be inefficient and would not substantially lower the external costs. Individuals will vary in their degree of police protection. Since, for example, Mr. Jones has no way of controlling the amount of protection which Mr. Johnson has, he cannot with impunity, visit Johnson or make use of Johnson's property without some degree of uncertainty as to his safety. The uncertainty concerning basic protection and the costs resulting from that uncertainty would be prohibitive. Such a system would also be inefficient since there would be great overlap in services within a community and probably more men providing services than would be necessary if the services were provided on a collective basis. These are some of the reasons why police protection is provided as a collective service by all governments, no matter what their structure. The nature of the external costs makes this procedure most efficient. Public police protection avoids the uncertainties which would arise from any alternative system.

On the other hand, public policing does not mean people do not hire private protection agencies. They do so, however, when their demands for protection are above normal and therefore greater than the public is willing to provide from collective revenues. While it is economical to provide a level of police service which is demanded by the great bulk of the population, it would be uneconomical to publicly provide services which are only of benefit to very limited segments of the community. Those segments that desire greater than the collective level of service should be required to privately contract for such service. For example, it would be extremely expensive for a large city to place a policeman in each bank and bank branch; but the public police do promise that in case of robbery, their services will be available. If the bank feels that it needs a guard on duty at all times, then it must contract for this protection privately. By doing so it will be supplementing the protection which is provided by the government. By providing a level of police protection as a public service, people can order their lives more regularly, move from place to place, and transact "business as usual." One of the virtues of a collective good or service is that it provides fairly constant, if minimal, levels of operation.

Fire protection is another example of a service which is provided collectively. Fire, when it occurs, does not confine itself very neatly. Unless you have provided for the action or lack of action in others, inadequate protection can be very costly. Imagine what would happen if firemen were not provided by the government, but instead were contracted for purely by private arrangement. We would have all the diseconomies and problems suggested in our example of the police. There is an additional problem which arises when such services are not provided on a collective basis. Suppose we consider Mr. Smith and Mr. Johnson again. Smith has arranged to have equipment and men on call in case his property catches fire. His property is adjacent to Johnson. Johnson is a cagey and miserly character. He has decided that fire protection is unnecessary because he knows that if fire breaks out in his home,

Smith could not stand by and do nothing. The fire on Johnson's property represents a threat to his own. If he allows the fire to go unchecked, it could spread to his own home. Therefore, he almost certainly will use his men and equipment to bring Johnson's fire under control, if only to minimize the threat to his own property. Indeed, this is the selfish reasoning behind Johnson's decision not to have fire protection. As long as one person can be convinced to take out fire protection, it may be unnecessary for his neighbors to arrange for it too. However, the extent of coverage will vary from area to area, and there may be neighborhoods where no one is capable of providing protection. The provision of fire protection by governments achieves some assurance of equity (minimum coverage), predictability, and coverage at lower costs than could be arranged through private action. Often communities have volunteer (as opposed to permanent salaried) fire departments. Yet here, too, protection is offered to all people as a collective good. Such volunteer departments tend to spring up in small communities where it would be impractical to establish a full-time service. Nevertheless, here as much as in the largest city the threat of fire hangs over the entire community. There is no way to allow one house to burn down without jeopardizing others.

THE DILEMMA OF RISING COSTS

As the need for both public police and public fire protections makes abundantly clear, external costs help determine areas of governmental action. We have discussed how each political structure establishes channels for the raising and resolving of conflicts; distributes goods and services; and, in general, provides stability and the guidelines for interaction within its society. External costs determine whether a conflict will be solved privately or through governmental action. If we could assume that the costs of decision-making would be negligible, then in most situations where there are external costs, it would make sense to opt for collective solutions.

Here, however, we encounter the dilemma which faces so many modern governments. We know that external costs are the costs of interdependence and interaction and that such costs rise as societies become more complex and heterogeneous. As a result, the external costs which one can expect to be imposed upon him by the activity of others must also grow, and governments are called upon to solve more and more problems and provide more goods and services on a collective basis. This would pose no problem if we could assume that the decision making costs remained constant or were negligible at the same time that external costs were rising. Unfortunately, the very same factors which raise external costs tend to multiply decision making costs as well. As the population of a country increases, no matter what decision making rule is accepted, the costs of decision making must also rise. As a nation becomes more heterogeneous and as opinions and interests grow more diverse, new bargaining and new negotiations will be needed. Precisely the same factors which impel societies toward collective decisions make those decisions difficult or costly to obtain. This helps explain why most governments do not try to deal with every source of conflict in the society. As both external and decision-making costs spiral, political institutions must learn to deal with the many existing conflicts selectively. Within this context it is interesting to note how a society limits the role of government or how it sets a premium on being able to change ground rules and expand the nature of governmental activity. Within this context it is useful to look at the criteria which societies establish for winning in particular political situations.

WINNING

In any decision-making setting, when has the final decision been made? We have discussed the decision-making rule, the rule which indicates what percentage of the total group must agree before a decision can be made. The criteria for decisions vary from place to place and time to time. Thus in the United States, as we mentioned, we are used to the principle of majority rule, and yet we often require only a plurality of votes to win in any given election. For our most crucial decisions, however, we tend to require concurrence among even more than a majority of the decision making strata.

For example, in the United States, as in most countries, amendment of the Constitution requires a greater degree of consensus than do more minor decisions. All federal laws go into effect when passed by majorities in both Houses of Congress and signed into law by the President. Constitutional amendments, however, require higher levels of agreement. Article V of the Constitution stipulates that

> The Congress, whenever two thirds of both Houses shall deem it necessary, shall propose amendments to this Constitution, or,

on the application of the legislatures of two thirds of the several
States, shall call a convention for proposing amendments which,
in either case, shall be valid to all intents and purposes, as part
of this Constitution, when ratified by the legislatures of three
fourths of the several States, or by conventions in three fourths
thereof, as the one or the other mode of ratification may be
proposed by the Congress; . . .

The passage actually applies three different decision-making rules:
two-thirds approval, three-quarters approval, and majority rule. A
constitutional convention cannot even be called except by two-thirds
vote of both the Senate and the House, or by a majority vote in two-
thirds of the state legislatures. Yet even after the delegates have con-
vened or an amendment has been submitted, it must then be approved
by majority vote in three fourths of the states. Of course, it is easy to
see why constitutional questions apply a more stringent decision-making
rule than do other types of decisions. Constitutions specify the ground
rules under which all further decisions are made. In essence, constitutions set out the rules of the game and therefore define many of the
costs of decision making.

In their economic analysis of political decision-making, Buchanan
and Tullock emphasize that from the point of view of the individual
citizen constitutional decisions would best be made only by the rule
of unanimity.[3] Since a constitution specifies what the range of governmental action should be, any change in it may also change both the
external and decision-making costs. For example, if a government is
not allowed to set maximum income laws, then individual earnings
theoretically will be settled by the supply of and demand for labor.
Should the Constitution be changed to permit such laws so that I, as an
individual citizen, will have new external costs imposed on me? After
such a constitutional change, a majority of elected representatives over
whom I have little control can impose new costs on me and state that I
may only earn a certain amount of money in any given year. Anything
above that amount goes to the government treasury. Therefore, the
most sensible or economic strategy that I can pursue is to demand that
all basic decisions relating to the scope of governmental activity be
subject to unanimous consent. In this case I can exercise a veto over

[3] James M. Buchanan and Gordon Tullock, **The Calculus of Consent**, Ann Arbor:
University of Michigan Press, 1962.

such actions which are likely to be contrary to what I consider to be my own best interests.

Obviously a unanimity rule on votes would make agreement impossible on most programs except those clearly perceived by all to be best handled on a collective basis. Such a rule, even for constitutional decisions, would likely result in an extremely limited government. As we indicated earlier, the greater the number of people who must participate in the decision-making process and who must agree to a decision, the higher the costs and the smaller the likelihood of achieving action. Because the stakes are higher in constitutional questions, people are less likely to agree to change here than they are in lesser decisions. They are willing to assume the greater decision-making cost in order to decrease the potential for higher external costs.

An example from nineteenth-century America will give us some idea of the importance of the constitutional decision-making rule. John C. Calhoun propounded his theory of the concurrent majority in **A Disquisition on Government,** originally published in 1853. The theory of the **concurrent majority** was based on Calhoun's assumptions that the different regions of the country had varying needs and desires. He felt that under a strict majority system, one region would be able to consistently impose its views on the others. Calhoun basically distrusted centralized political power and felt that the excesses of power could only be checked by the existence of alternative centers of power. Calhoun noted a distinction between the numerical majority and the concurrent majority. A numerical majority "considers the whole community as a unit having but one common interest throughout, and collects the sense of the greater number of the whole as that of the community."[4] The concurrent majority, on the other hand, "regards interests as well as numbers—considering the community as made up of different and conflicting interests, as far as the action of the government is concerned —and takes the sense of each through its majority or appropriate organ, and the united sense of all as the sense of the entire community."[5] If Calhoun's theory had been applied, then any action would require a majority in each of the regions and therefore any region could exercise a veto. His theory stemmed from the friction between the North and the South over the slavery issue. Positive action would only be possible

---

[4] John C. Calhoun, **A Disquisition on Government and Selections from the Discourses,** C. Gordon Post (ed.), Indianapolis: Bobbs-Merrill, 1953, p. 22.
[5] Ibid., p. 23.

on those issues on which there was a clear consensus. The practical effects of Calhoun's proposal would be to raise the decision-making costs by raising the level required for winning.

An interesting dilemma along these lines is raised by Buchanan and Tullock.[6] Small homogeneous communities are places where the rule of unanimity could be used without fear of paralyzing government action. However, the rule is seldom used or necessary in such communities. In heterogeneous communities, where the unanimity rule would effectively bar almost any action, on the other hand, more complex and stringent decision rules tend to be adopted. Thus, as long as there was substantial agreement within Congress, no one disputed majority rule. When conflict developed and one region felt itself threatened, however, demands arose for more strict safeguards and therefore a more stringent decision making rule.

STYLES OF DECISION MAKING

We have seen how, as a result of both external and decision making costs, some issues become foci for governmental action and others are settled privately. We know that in both public and private negotiations the greater the number of decision makers which are required for final agreement, the more difficult it is to act. Increasing the number needed for concurrence is likely to lessen the scope of possible action. Furthermore, we can assume that all decision makers are protagonists or at least interested participants in each political conflict or decision that is reached. All parties to a decision seek to achieve a solution that will in no way harm them. Even an impartial member may feel a commitment not to the particular decision but to his position or office. His goal will be to see that the decision making does not endanger his position as arbiter or judge; indeed, if possible, he will try to enhance that position.

There are basically two decision making approaches: **comprehensive** and **incremental**. We discussed these in a somewhat different context in Chapter 5; perhaps you may remember that actual decisions tend to be of varying gradations between the two extremes (see the comprehensive-incremental continuum, p. 72). Both approaches involve cer-

---

[6] James H. Buchanan and Gordon Tullock, **The Calculus of Consent,** Ann Arbor: University of Michigan Press, 1962, chap. 5, is an excellent discussion of some of the advantages and dilemmas of the unanimity rule.

tain costs and build some sort of bias into the political system. In fact, no political system relies completely on either one. Nevertheless, certain governmental structures tend to allow for greater use of one approach or the other. Let us focus on both approaches and on the political structures where we are most likely to find them.

Comprehensive Decision Making

Comprehensive decision making involves the process of solving or responding to conflicts in a total perspective and engaging in action which may imply large-scale changes in the scope or range of governmental activity. Unfortunately, the term has often been used as a straw man. Many scholars claim that it is impossible to arrive at decisions in a truly comprehensive manner. No group of decision makers can possess sufficient time or complete information to consider all the implications of any decision. Used in this sense, comprehensive decision making is impossible. The distinction, however, is trivial. It merely implies that all decisions are made from less than total information and that at some point those charged with making a choice must stop gathering information and refuse to consider any additional evidence. We have already indicated, in the Haynsworth case, that all decisions made by men are subject to error. We can gather too little information or fail to evaluate it sufficiently. Our present concern, however, is not with the comprehensiveness of information gathering. It is with the comprehensiveness of the decision itself and of the change involved. Comprehensive change refers to a political system's capacity to make large-scale change, not to its ability to make decisions comprehensively.

By now we perceive how much the ability of a society to make comprehensive decisions is determined by the prevalent decision-making rule. Societies which require extensive agreement are far less likely to make comprehensive changes quickly than are societies which need the consensus of just a few. Oligarchies and dictatorships can engage in comprehensive decision making more readily than democracies. This does not mean that oligarchies and dictatorships are more innovative than democracies; it does mean that they can make large-scale changes more easily. Imagine two countries, both characterized by capitalist economies. Country A is a dictatorship, while country B is a democracy. Both countries are considering nationalizing the transportation industries. In Country A the decision can be made by a group of ten leaders of the country. In country B a representative assembly will first consult with the various corporations and stockholders who would be affected by such nationalization, and then perhaps pass legislation which must in turn be approved by the executive. Obviously country A will be able to nationalize its railroads much more quickly and easily than country B. This does not mean that the decision, once made, would encounter no opposition in country A; we are only suggesting the decision could be made more expeditiously there.

In Nazi Germany during the prewar period it was relatively easy for the government to make decisions which rewarded some types of economic activity and punished others. The work force could be moved about and priorities could be changed with very little consultation or advance notice. It was even possible to pursue a policy for a while and then change it abruptly without having to consult with or secure the consent of those affected by such actions. Similarly in the 1920s it was possible for the Soviet Union to depart from Marxist orthodoxy long enough to implement the New Economic Policy, a plan which represented partial return to private ownership. The policy resulted from practical recognition that, until suitable replacements could be trained, the Communists had to have the supervisory abilities of the former middle class. Yet at the end of the same decade, the nation was able to change that policy just as abruptly and force collectivization in both the argicultural and the industrial sectors of the economy.

Imagine the difficulties which our democracy, with its requirements for broader-based agreement, would have implementing policies such as those outlined above. Yet if speed is an asset, these same examples also hint at the cost of requiring the consent of relatively few people to basic decisions. Certainly centralization of decision making implies a corresponding centralization of information gathering. When people are excluded from the decision making process, they tend also to be overlooked when information is being gathered and opinions are being solicited. Consequently, centralized decision-making precludes extensive information about probable reactions to decisions. This can be an important factor, especially when we realize that each decision, to the extent that it redistributes or maintains the present distribution of goods within a society, will affect much of the population. These people will be vitally interested in such decisions and, of course, will react to them. Failure to assess their reactions adequately can be disastrous. If, for example, a society were to prohibit alcohol (as the United States did from 1920 to 1933) and the probable reactions to this prohibition had not been carefully studied, the new restraint could throw the entire country into turmoil. In the United States the decision-making process requires great consultation and prohibition was enacted through constitutional amendment. Yet many of the popular reactions and consequences still were unforeseen. How much more dangerous could the consequences be had almost no consultation taken place? Centralized leaders easily could promulgate comprehensive programs only to find that, as a consequence, the nation was on the verge of a revolt. Yet to have sought more information would have been to extend the decision-making process. The internal costs (the time and money required for information gathering) would have been greater and would have delayed the decision that much longer.

There is a corollary to the problem of insufficient information. Centralized decision making may overlook the views of nondecision makers and may be equally susceptible to overlooking alternative forms of action. Comprehensive action involves a significant departure from the status quo. Therefore before deciding to act, the decision maker, at least theoretically, should be aware of as many alternatives as possible. In centralized systems, the range of options considered will be smaller than if information were solicited on a broader basis. Some alternative may be considered which would be tossed aside were adequate information available. Similarly some of the best plans may not be considered or even conceived by the decision makers.

Perhaps the greatest cost of centralized decision making, however, is the tendency toward frequent and rapid shifts of policies and priorities. The economic gyrations during the first decade of Communist rule in Russia were one example of this. Such flux need not go hand in hand with centralized decision making, but it is more common here than in countries where the authority is highly decentralized or fragmented. Indeed such shifts can be so rapid that they will catch an entire population by surprise. During the rise of the Fascist movements of the 1920s and 1930s there were repeated clashes between Communists and Fascists. Each portrayed the other as the mortal enemy and spoke of the ultimate and inevitable clash between the two systems. All western Communist parties adopted the policy emanating from Moscow, of cooperating with the other political parties against the common Fascist enemy. They called for common front or popular front governments to meet this threat. Indeed, in the middle and late 1930s such a front was formed in France under the leadership of the socialist Leon Blum. The rationale of the popular front, in France and elsewhere, was that only by unifying progressive democratic forces would it be possible to tackle the basic problems and sources of discontent and thereby forestall a Fascist takeover. It was a sensible policy for the Communists, particularly the Soviet Union. A powerful, rearmed, and increasingly militant Germany threatened, and past history suggested that the threat could not be ignored. Thus Soviet foreign policy under the direction of Foreign Minister Maxim Litvinov was to establish informal alliances against Germany with the western powers. The subsequent decision to abandon that policy coincided with Litvinov's replacement by Vyacheslav Molotov in May, 1939. Until then, however, popular-front governments and consulation with the West were the means of sustaining Soviet security. Molotov, once in power, began secret negotiations with the German Foreign Minister, von Ribbentrop. As a result, to the astonishment of most of the West as well as the western Communist parties, the Soviet Union and Nazi Germany signed a mutual nonagression pact in August, 1939. The pact specified that any move into Poland by Hitler would not be opposed by Stalin and, further, that certain Polish territories would be reincorporated into the Soviet Union. There were further agreements concerning the disposition of the Baltic states, and territorial rights in Rumania and other countries.

Such a sudden about-face in foreign policy would have been very difficult to achieve in a more decentralized political system. Both the Germans and the Russians, however, had small centralized leadership groups, and the change was quick and dramatic. On the other hand, it caught many of the Communist parties in other countries completely off guard. They were still either participating in popular-front governments or calling for their formation. Yet overnight the Fascists had become allies. The change was so rapid and extreme that they could not predict it, nor was it easy to support it.

Several arguments have been offered which make the Soviet decision more understandable although still reprehensible. The Soviets felt that they faced a probable attack from Germany. Their hope for security lay in forming some accord with the western powers which would clearly indicate that if Hitler attacked Russia he would be fighting a two-front war since he would be attacked on his western flank. The fact that the Nazis did later fight a two-front war contributed in no small measure to their ultimate defeat. Yet the refusal of the western powers, notably Britain and France, to take action against German rearmament, the passiveness of the French to the German take-over and remilitarization of the Rhineland, the acceptance of the

Anschluss (union) with Austria, and the eventual complicity of England and France in the dismemberment of Czechoslovakia were hardly convincing demonstrations of the willingness of the West to honor its treaty obligations. Both western powers had an obligation to support Poland if attacked. Stalin felt that given the past record there was no guarantee that the British and French would attack Germany. If they did not, the way would be paved for a continued German onslaught into Russia. Whatever we may say about the ethics of the pact or its ultimate practicality, at the time it may have offered the only chance for Soviet security. It at least bought the Russians time to strengthen their defense and prepare for the actual German attack.

Soviet history provides us with examples of another cost of centralized decision making. Frequent and rapid shifts of priorities tend to bring with them dislocations and, ultimately, waste of resources. A decision to place high priority on agricultural development implies a certain commitment of resources and talent to that project. A shift of priorities to the heavy industrial sector two or three years later would involve severe dislocations of those resources and some inefficiency in further deployment of material and labor. A farmer does not cheerfully become a skilled laborer overnight. Even beyond the immediate dislocations, the possibility of more rapid shifts in priorities creates an atmosphere of uncertainty and makes routine difficult. In many dictatorial or authoritarian regimes, the rules of appropriate conduct may be changed quite frequently and with little warning so that what was permissible today might be a punishable offense tomorrow. Thus in 1956 Nikita Khrushchev made his famous "secret" speech before the Communist Party Congress. In that speech he denounced Stalin for crimes against the people and for the development of a "cult of personality." Stalin was to blame, according to Khrushchev for most of the ills which plagued Soviet society. The startling character of the denunciation is difficult to imagine, particularly in countries where we are used to voicing criticism of elected officials or other leaders. Prior to the speech Stalin had been revered as the Communist saint who had developed the country under communism, protected it from foreign enemies, and rid it of counterrevolutionary forces. Cities and towns had been named for him. After the speech this changed. Many of Stalin's former associates began to join the chorus and list the many crimes and deviations from communism which were the fault of Stalin. Cities and towns changed back to their original names and close association with Stalin in the past became a cause for suspicion and even banishment. Molotov, Malenkov, and others were quietly and unceremoniously removed from their offices.

The subsequent ouster of Khrushchev and statements by his successors, Brezhnev and Kosygin, give us further proof of the precarious position of one man in a society where power is so centralized that policy shifts swiftly and dramatically. Today Khrushchev is accused of many of the same crimes as Stalin, particularly of fostering a cult of personality. Stalin has been partially rehabilitated under the new leaders and the trend of internal liberalization, begun under Khrushchev has in many cases been slowed down or reversed. Under Khrushchev a certain degree of liberalism had been tolerated. Today less divergence is permitted. Each set of new leaders tends to bring new policies and priorities.

One last cost of rapidly changing policies stems from the nature of comprehensive decision-making itself. We know that there are few decision makers; they are likely to gather too little information and therefore may fail to consider the consequences that certain strategic choices will have. As a result, a decision once made may have to be changed several times before the proper alternative is found. In this sense a centralized decision-making structure may even raise decision-making costs. Indeed, all comprehensive decisions are susceptible to such reevaluation. Each time a decision is rescinded all options which had been discarded or set aside again become subjects for discussion. The remaking of decisions is expensive and leads once more to all the vacillations and shifts that we have already described.

Incremental Decision Making

We have termed our second major category **incremental decisions.** By incremental decision making we mean that individuals operate from the premise that the parameters of action are set and that decisions basically involve modifications of existing policies. They need not consider the entire range of considerations which are necessary in comprehensive decision making. Most incremental decision making is change at the margins of a society and does not involve the asking or resolving of basic value questions.[7] These types of decisions are made

---

[7] For an interesting and enthusiastic defense of incremental decision making, see David Braybrooke and Charles E. Lindblom, **A Strategy of Decision,** New York: Free Press, 1963, chap. 5; and Charles E. Lindblom, **The Intelligence of Democracy,** New York: Free Press, 1965.

frequently and undramatically. Perhaps this is because the incremental procedure often results from requiring a considerable degree of consensus. Where the number of participants in the decision making process is high and the number required for action is also high, the style of decision making tends to be incremental. We have discussed some of the reasons for these limitations earlier in this chapter.

Incremental decision making is therefore most common in relatively decentralized political systems. Decentralized decision making tends to take into account persons and groups in a variety of settings. In a heterogeneous or highly complex society, decision makers usually represent a wide variety of interests. This is another way of saying that their interests diverge and they will often disagree. Not only is it difficult to elicit agreement on large-scale change but also it will become increasingly difficult to do so as the size of the decision making unit increases.

In our discussion of decision costs, we noted that the greater the number or heterogeneity of decision makers, the smaller the bargaining range. If we omit the possibility of side payments, trading votes, or the introduction of additional issues, then the area for fruitful bargaining exists only where there are intersections of interests among the political actors. Furthermore, all the participants must attach approximately the same value to these intersections if bargaining is to take place.

In any situation the present state of affairs is a known commodity. All participants to the decision-making process are aware of present policy and, given a certain degree of intelligence and sophistication, can assess its impact on their own positions and interests. Proposed changes cannot be so well understood. Any decision maker knows that information will never be complete and that any new policy is likely to elicit some unanticipated reactions. Given both their uncertainty concerning the implications of change and their widely divergent interests, it is easy to see why decision makers will tend to restrict themselves to small or incremental changes. If they merely alter an existing policy, they will be more certain of its outcomes than they would be should their decision represent a dramatic departure from past procedures. As long as their changes are based upon extensions of existing policies, the implications of their policies will remain relatively clear. The development of minimum-wage and other labor laws in the 1930s was a radical departure for the federal government. The speed with which comprehensive changes were implemented then probably could never have been attained had there not been an unprecedentedly severe depression. Succeeding changes in social welfare programs have been introduced at a much more gradual pace.

Where decisions are made on an incremental basis, the system will have a built in bias to maintain the status quo. Again this is another way of saying that where decision making is decentralized and fragmented, it is nearly impossible to achieve comprehensive change in a short period of time. Thus, where decision making is nearly always of an incremental nature, problems must pyramid almost to a crisis level before the society will agree to take sustained and comprehensive action. For years we have had a health crisis in this country. The supply of medical personnel, the quality and quantity of hospitals, the costs of medical care, have been significant problems. We have periodically responded to the problem with very limited measures. We are now only beginning to respond on a larger scale to these problems because they have become increasingly more glaring. Similarly, the problems of conservation and pollution have been building until now they are of immense significance and can no longer be ignored.

Yet if the inability to make rapid, comprehensive changes is a significant drawback of incremental decision making, such systems have their benefits as well. One such benefit is certainty and stability. As we argued earlier, one function of the political system is to provide laws and patterns for approved behavior so that a citizen can live in reasonable certainty as to what he can and cannot do and what is expected of him. In societies where rules are subject to rapid change, such certainty all but disappears. Indeed we might be looking at the reverse side of the coin from the centralized governments which we discussed before. For example, consider two cases concerning urban renewal. In country A urban renewal can be accomplished by fiat. Thus one fine spring morning the government issues a directive without prior consultation with anybody. It declares that all inhabitants in the affected area must vacate by a specified date. No arrangements are made to aid in securing substitute housing for those displaced. The buildings are razed and new developments are built. There is no consultation about reimbursing property owners. A rate of reimbursement is set and there can be no appeal. Such an example is extreme and might never actually take place, but it represents the state of uncertainty which can exist in a highly centralized system.

In country B a similar urban renewal program is slated. The bill establishing such a program must be debated and approved in a representative legislature. Then the proper housing agency must help arrange adequate housing for all people who will be displaced by the program. It must also negotiate with the existing residents as to how much time they can have before they must move. Then property owners must be compensated for their property on the basis of impartial assessment. Should property owners feel that they are not being sufficiently reimbursed, they may seek court action in the form of an injunction against the government or perhaps a suit challenging the government's estimate of their property's value. Then the government negotiates as to what will replace the razed structures. Public hearings must be held and consideration must be given to the impact of any new building on the total character of the area. Only after all these details have been worked out and contractors, builders, and architects have submitted their bids, will the project actually get under way. Perhaps this sketch is no more than a description of an ideally participatory situation for urban renewal but it does give us an example of what the deliberation and care would be like in a society where decision-making authority is decentralized and widespread consultation is common. The pace of action is slower but the time for negotiation and presentation of interests allows for greater forethought and preparation than would have been possible in country A.

Decentralization, of which federalism is a good example, may mean that certain aspects of programs can be dealt with at the local level and then coordinated with larger aspects of the program at successively higher levels. Such a governmental hierarchy allows for greater flexibility in the development and implementation of programs. Particularly in large and heterogeneous countries, the conditions which exist in one region may be vastly different from those in another. Similar problems may exist in two regions, but because of the demographic or even geographical character of the regions, a solution which is applicable in one case may not be appropriate in the other. Yet these differences can only be ascertained where there are mechanisms to solicit and process information from the different localities. In this respect the increased flow of information characteristic of a decentralized decision-making system nearly always benefits the system. While decentralization may increase the decision-making costs initially, it is likely to decrease the long-run costs by a greater amount.

There is a third important benefit which flows from a decentralized decision-making system. Because such a system precludes, except in special cases, comprehensive changes, the decision maker can restrict his consideration to modifications in existing programs and approaches. This is an economical system of decision making. While it is true that we mentioned that the centralized decision maker is not able to consider all alternatives, this is in part from ignorance or an inadequate information-gathering network. Since he is considering comprehensive changes, such failures can be quite costly. In the decentralized system our decision makers consciously exclude certain alternatives, and since they are not concerned with comprehensive change this is a useful and economical process for them.

There are some interesting paradoxes resulting from a decentralized decision making system. We know that such a system makes it relatively easy for persons or groups to pass on information concerning their desires and priorities. The governmental structures are set up to give information gathering high priority. Yet at the same time that decentralization provides the channels for information and demands to be processed, it also inhibits action on those varied and often mutually exclusive demands. This, we realize, is because of the need to achieve substantial concurrence on every major action and of the difficulty in doing so when interests are so varied and even conflicting. While demands can be raised, it is difficult to get positive action on them. In the centralized decision making system, by contrast, the capacity for quick and positive action is adequate but the ability to receive and process demands and information as to the best course of action often is limited. Because centralized systems do not often allow for local variations and problems, they often have the capacity to innovate quickly and the tendency to be very rigid in their administration.

CONCLUSION

Certainly any form of decision making involves both costs and benefits. The particular structure of decision making and the decision rule which characterize a society will influence what these will be. One of the underlying assumptions of democratic societies is that the political process should be responsive to the population and participation by the people is important. If this is given highest priority, then a decentralized system and a relatively stringent decision rule seem to be the obvious choice. Where rapid comprehensive changes are given priority, then a centralized government will be a more effective alternative. Most political systems are neither totally centralized nor totally decentralized. Neither is there any political system which makes only incremental or only comprehensive decisions. Rather what we have tried to indicate is that in any given society there are tendencies and potentials which indicate whether one form of decision making or the other will predominate or be more common. The structures of a society determine in many ways the costs of decision making and whether conflicts are most economically settled on a collective basis or as the result of private action.

SUGGESTED READINGS

Arrow, Kenneth J., **Social Choice and Individual Values**, New York: Wiley, 1963 ed.

Bauer, Raymond, and Kenneth Gergen (eds.), **The Study of Policy Formation**, New York: Free Press, 1968.

Black, Duncan, **The Theory of Committees and Elections**, Cambridge: Cambridge University Press, 1958.

Braybrooke, David, and Charles E. Lindblom, **A Strategy of Decision**, New York: Free Press, 1963.

Buchanan, James M., "An Individualistic Theory of Political Process," in David Easton (ed.), **Varieties of Political Theory,** Englewood Cliffs, N.J.: Prentice-Hall, 1966.

Buchanan, James M., and Gordon Tullock, **The Calculus of Consent**, Ann Arbor: University of Michigan Press, 1962.

Dahl, Robert A., **A Preface to Democratic Theory**, Chicago: University of Chicago Press, 1956.

Dahl, Robert A., and Charles E. Lindblom, **Politics, Economics and Welfare,** New York: Harper & Row, 1953.

Lindblom, Charles E., **The Intelligence of Democracy**, New York: Free Press, 1965.

Rae, Douglas, "Decision-Rules and Individual Values in Constitutional Choice," **American Political Science Review,** vol. LXIII, no. 1 (March, 1969).

Snyder, Richard C., H. W. Bruck, and Burton Sapin, **Foreign Policy Decision Making**, New York: Free Press, 1962.

Chapter 10

Legislative Conflict Resolution

THE GROWTH OF THE LEGISLATURE

The development of legislative institutions and the growth of their powers as a source of governmental authority has been a long and often difficult process. In England it began as early as 1215 with the Magna Carta and it has been a process which has continued to develop. The growth of the legislature marks the culmination of the battle between executive authority and legislative or representative groups. The Magna Carta in England did not establish representative institutions. What it did do was to limit the power of the king and demand that he consult with the nobles before taking certain actions. This is a far cry from a situation where executive power is balanced by the existence of a popularly elected representative legislature. In England the battle was slow and gradual. First the Lords developed their powers and then the House of Commons gradually grew in influence until today, of course, the House of Lords exerts little real authority, while most governmental authority resides in the House of Commons. In some countries the events leading to the development of a representative legislature occurred at a much faster pace than in England, and in some the victory of the legislature has been far less conclusive. The French Revolution was a reaction against autocratic excess and an attempt to develop representative institutions based on the supremacy of a popularly elected legislature. The demand for power to legislatures represents in many respects a demand for the decentralization of decision-making power, a demand for a greater sharing in the formation of political decisions.

So ingrained is the belief in the representative assembly that almost all countries pay at least lip service to the notion of the legislature. Even highly autocratic societies maintain legislatures even if in a clearly subservient state. In Spain, Franco has maintained the **Cortes** although it has little influence. In the Soviet Union there is a bicameral (two-house) legislature which theoretically exercises great decision-making power in that country. Legislatures tend to be totally abolished under military regimes or as the result of coups. Yet even in this case there is always promise that as soon as "peace and tranquility" return to the land, elections will be held and the legislature reconvened.

The rise of the legislature has been dramatic and in most countries has occurred in a relatively short period of time. While the existence and importance of legislatures is a common phenomenon, the rules and patterns of operation of legislatures vary enormously from country to country. The nature of the legislative rules and the impact of the larger political structure have great consequence for the manner in which conflicts are resolved and the types of conflict to which the legislature will respond. In discussing the impact of such structures we will focus primarily on the United States Congress while using the British Parliament as a useful contrast.

CHALLENGES TO THE MODERN LEGISLATURE

Many of the challenges which face present-day legislatures are a result of the changing legislative role. In many countries the legislature began as a means of providing a counterbalance to the monarch. What occurred over the years is that the necessity for such a counterbalance became less significant as monarchs lost most of their powers.

In many democratic systems executive authority became subservient to the legislature. If the nineteenth century can be said to represent the consolidation of legislative power, the twentieth century has again raised problems which have shifted emphasis from the legislature to the executive as the focus of decision making. As such, new roles and problems of initiation of policy, controlling administration, and the need to ensure responsiveness have become crucial. As societies have become more complex, the demands made on legislators to increase their scope and depth of information on diverse issues and topics became greater. As a result of the demands, legislatures have continued to evolve and have in many respects fundamentally changed in the last century as a result of the challenges of modernization and complexity. Such trends are particularly apparent in the United States Congress and most striking in the United States House of Representatives.

THE UNITED STATES CONGRESS

The Congress is a bicameral legislature consisting of one house, the Senate, based on a territorial form of representation, and another house, the House of Representatives, based on population. In essence the structure was a compromise worked out at the Constitutional Convention between representatives of the large and small states. The larger states wanted a legislature based solely on population, while the smaller states, fearful of domination by the large states, wanted a system of representation which provided equal representation for all states regardless of population. The Congress is a compromise in which both systems of representation are used. All legislation requires the concurrence of both houses of the legislature and thus would ensure that the House, with its large-state bias, would not be able to inflict its will on the Senate where the interests of the smaller states are represented. It was also felt that since the members of the House were directly elected they would tend to be radical and would therefore be checked by the Senate, which was originally based on indirect election; senators were elected by the various state legislatures. The compromise which established a two-house legislature and demanded the concurrence of both houses for the passage of legislation immediately served to set high decision making costs. A majority was necessary in both houses, thereby increasing the number of participants whose concurrence was necessary for action to take place. Each bill had to receive separate consideration in both houses and coalitions of support had to be built separately in each house. The use of two different bases of representation assured that there would be different perspectives represented and thereby served to institutionalize conflict.

Several aspects of the Congressional Rules affect the way in which decisions are reached and conflicts resolved. The legislative function can best be described as the enactment of laws which establish procedures governing conduct in a society. Federal laws determine which categories of activity are criminal and which are not. Laws determine the ways in which a society attacks its problems, distributes its rewards, and enforces its actions. In the United States there is an additional role which the legislature performs by virtue of the system of separation of powers which exists in this country. The founding fathers, fearful of strong executive authority, separated the executive and legislative branches and provided mechanisms by which various branches could check and veto the activities of each other. This institutionalized conflict between the various component branches of the government and required that the legislature function partially as a check on the executive and engage in what has been called the oversight function. This function implies that one of the roles of the legislature is to see that the acts which are passed are fairly and efficiently administered. Additionally, it is also to make sure that the executive authorities do not usurp the rights and responsibilities of the Congress.

Any organization in discharging its responsibilities adopts certain procedures and norms to govern its conduct. Organizations establish such guidelines for the same reasons that people establish governments, to introduce some predictability and certainty into the relations among members and to regularize activity. Each body of the Congress operates under somewhat different rules. The House is particularly complex and has evolved a set of both formal and informal rules which guide conduct in that body. Without debating the virtues or limitations of such rules we can, however, discuss the impact of such rules and their relation to decision making and conflict resolution.

THE HOUSE OF REPRESENTATIVES

The rather staid and ritualized procedure of the House of Representatives today is a relatively recent development. The changes which have occurred in the House are in some respects a response to demands raised in the early part of this century for the need to democratize House procedures and decentralize decision making. Many within the country and within the House felt that the leadership of the body was too conservative and too wedded to business interests in the country. They demanded that the powers of the leadership be broken and that power be decentralized within the House as a means of increasing responsiveness to various other groups and segments within the society. Many felt that the centralization of power in the hands of the Speaker had created a situation where the House was incapable of being responsive to the demands of labor, ethnic groups, farmers, and other segments of society. The rules against which the protests were lodged had evolved over a long period of time. The codification and expansion of many of the rules of the House had been accomplished in 1890 with the adoption of what was called Reed's rules, named after Speaker Reed. Many of the rules which were adopted were designed to regularize House procedures and to deal with the problems of minority obstructionism. Previously, it had been possible for a small determined minority to prevent House action on many major pieces of legislation. The rules which were adopted gave great powers to the Speaker. But by 1910 much resentment had arisen over the use of those powers, particularly in the hands of Speaker Cannon. A successful revolt led by George Norris of Nebraska curtailed many of the Speaker's powers. His power to appoint all standing committees and their chairmen was abolished, as was the Speaker's chairmanship of the Rules Committee.[1] Until these reforms were put into effect, however, the Speaker's power was great and in the appointment of committee chairmen he could pay as little or as much attention to seniority as he wished.

When the rules were changed, seniority became the primary means by which individuals acceded to positions of power and authority in the House. Committee chairmanships were decided upon by length of service of various party members. When one is elected to the House, he receives certain committee assignments. As he accumulates seniority on particular committees, he progresses up the ladder to the chairmanship. The only factors which influence whether or not he becomes a chairman are whether his party remains in control of the House and

---

[1] George B. Galloway, **History of the House of Representatives**, New York: Crowell, 1962, pp. 53 ff.

whether he succeeds in getting reelected. The office of the Speaker itself has become in recent years a culminating point in the seniority system. Whereas in the nineteenth century it was possible for Henry Clay to enter the House as a freshman congressman and be elected Speaker, today such a situation has become impossible. One succeeds to the speakership as a result of longevity of service and a procession through the leadership ranks. This discussion is not meant to imply that prior to 1910 no attention was paid to seniority but rather that the seniority system was not really strictly developed and adhered to until the powers of the Speaker were broken, for with the removal of those powers a new means for distributing influence in the House became necessary. The seniority system has the virtue of being simple and automatic. There is no basis for argument or continual bickering or fighting over who is to become committee chairman. It is a regularized procedure for transferring authority.

The seniority system, as it is set up in the House, results in two separate leadership structures and, therefore, the decentralization of decision making. The chairmen of the various House committees do not owe their positions to any party loyalty or to party discipline. Their sole claim to the chairmanship is their ability to get reelected and serve longer than other members of the House. This means that committee chairmen enjoy a base of power which is independent of the party leadership. This dual structure can be seen in terms of the chairmen of committees composing one set of leaders, and the party leadership— the Speaker, majority leader, and whips—composing another set. There is no necessary overlap between these two groups and indeed the two groups are placed in somewhat antagonistic roles. When the House is controlled by the same party that controls the Presidency, the party leadership in the House acts as floor manager for the President's legislative program. They are supposed to help push the President's program to passage and to secure the loyalty of party members in the House for that program. The committee chairmen, however, are institutionally placed in a different role. As chairmen of the various substantive committees, it is the nature of their work to scrutinize and be skeptical of the President's program. Given the fact that there is no effective means of control that the Speaker or party leadership can exert over committee chairmen, the two groups of leaders often find themselves in opposition.

In 1961 John Kennedy realized that the Rules Committee presented a formidable barrier to the passage of his legislative program. There was a conservative majority on the committee, headed by Chairman Howard Smith of Virginia. The Rules Committee had the power to prevent legislation from reaching the floor for a vote. Because the committee chairman, Smith, had power independent of the party leadership, there were few sanctions which the then Speaker Sam Rayburn could apply to force Smith to be receptive to the Kennedy program. Rayburn, as Kennedy's floor leader in the House, discussed the problem with the President and decided that the most useful strategy would be to try to increase the size of the Rules Committee and thereby add some liberal members, increasing the probability that the President's program could reach the floor of the House for votes. This was a strategy designed to activate the least possible opposition and the one which Rayburn felt had the best chance for success. The issue was decided on the opening day of the session and the question of the size of the committee was put to a vote. With all the prestige and influence which Rayburn had in the House and the years of service he had performed for almost all members of that body he was able to get the rules changed by the barest of margins. It is questionable whether any other Speaker of lesser influence could have achieved even this minor a change. Much of the reluctance to the change came from conservatives opposed to Kennedy's legislative program and also from those who felt that such action would deprive the Rules Committee of its independent function. Much of the opposition was similar to that aroused by Roosevelt's court-packing plan. Many congressmen felt that the change would give the executive undue influence in the legislature, and being jealous of their prerogatives they were anxious to prevent this.

It is interesting to note the impact which the reforms of 1910 have had on the House. Perhaps the most significant, as we have said, is that power is decentralized within the chamber. Success in the House not only requires the support, or at least the nonopposition of the Speaker, but also the support of the appropriate committee chairman and the members of the appropriate committee. This decentralization of decision making requires that all legislation must be widely acceptable. For not only must the legislation have the support of the majority on the floor, it must have sufficient support to pass through the various other phases of legislative decision making, all of which are characterized by **veto points.** Veto points indicate that it is possible at several stages of consideration to block the passage of a bill or even block or prevent a vote on any specific issue. This multiplicity of veto points, which is a characteristic of decentralization, insures that many of the decisions made by the Congress will be incremental in nature.[2] This means that for those who demand that the Congress act quickly and invoke large-scale change, frustration will be a common reaction. The effect of decentralization in the House has been to build a conservative bias into the chamber. It is interesting that the leader of the reform movement in 1910 was the liberal and progressive from the state of Nebraska, George Norris. Norris would have been quite dismayed at the conservative implications his reforms have had. Much of the basis for southern strength within the Congress has stemmed from the strict adherence to the seniority rule. Southern Democrats, coming from basically non-competitive constituencies, could and did accumulate long years of service in the House, and unlike many of their northern colleagues who also came from safe districts, a greater proportion of southern House members seemed willing to make the House their career. This in part is a function of the fact that while northern congressional districts may be noncompetitive, statewide offices often are. Thus there are more rapid turnovers in political office in the North, which creates more advanced political opportunities and makes it attractive for the northern congressman to give up his seat and try for higher political office. In the South the high rates of incumbency of southern senators and the limited opportunity structure for political office which resulted from lack of interparty competition made a House career desirable. As a result, the overwhelming number of committee chairmen in the House of Representatives have come from southern states. We can see this predominance if we look at Table 10-1.

A significant trend of the twentieth century may very well be related to the seniority principle. This is the tendency for more and more congressmen to make their political careers in the House of Representatives. In this century the average number of new congressmen entering each Congress has steadily declined. The average age of congressmen and of committee chairmen has increased. Perhaps adherence to the seniority principle has simplified the path to leadership positions. When promotion to leadership positions was dependent upon maintaining the good will of the Speaker, the House was perhaps far less promising as

---

[2] See Chapter 9 for a discussion of incremental decision-making.

TABLE 10-1

DEMOCRATIC HOUSE CHAIRMEN: 1947–1970

AGRICULTURE	
Cooley	North Carolina
Poage	Texas

APPROPRIATIONS	
Cannon	Missouri
Mahon	Texas

ARMED SERVICES	
Vinson	Georgia
Rivers	South Carolina

DISTRICT OF COLUMBIA	
McMillan	South Carolina

BANKING AND CURRENCY	
Spence	Kentucky
Patman	Texas

EDUCATION AND LABOR	
Lesinski	Michigan
Barden	North Carolina
Powell	New York
Perkins	Kentucky

FOREIGN AFFAIRS	
Kee	West Virginia
Richards	South Carolina
Gordon	Illinois
Morgan	Pennsylvania

GOVERNMENT OPERATIONS	
Hoffman	Michigan
Dawson	Illinois

HOUSE ADMINISTRATION	
Norton	New Jersey
Stanley	Virginia
Burleson	Texas
Friedel	Maryland

INTERIOR AND INSULAR AFFAIRS	
Crosser	Ohio
Priest	Tennessee
Harris	Arkansas
Staggers	West Virginia

JUDICIARY	
Celler	New York

MERCHANT MARINE AND FISHERIES	
Bland	Virginia
Hart	New Jersey
Bonner	North Carolina
Garmatz	Maryland

POST OFFICE AND CIVIL SERVICE	
Murray	Tennessee
Dulski	New York

PUBLIC WORKS	
Whittington	Mississippi
Buckley	New York
Fallon	Maryland

RULES	
Sabath	Illinois
Smith	Virginia
Colmer	Mississippi

SCIENCE AND ASTRONAUTICS	
McCormack	Massachusetts
Brooks	Louisiana
Miller	California

UN-AMERICAN ACTIVITIES	
Wood	Georgia
Walter	Pennsylvania
Willis	Louisiana
Ichord	Missouri

VETERANS AFFAIRS	
Rankin	Mississippi
Teague	Texas

WAYS AND MEANS	
Doughton	North Carolina
Cooper	Tennessee
Mills	Arkansas

SELECT SMALL BUSINESS	
Patman	Texas
Evins	Tennessee

a career in the sense that leadership positions were always somewhat unstable and success depended upon maintaining the Speaker's confidence and loyalty. Now leadership depends simply upon getting re-elected.

The impact of many of the rules changes has been to institutionalize procedures in the House.[3] In many respects the reforms represented an attempt to internally democratize the House. Liberals felt that such democratization was essential for getting liberal programs through. However, what many liberal reformers forgot is that getting consistent policies through a legislature is dependent upon some means of securing compliance from party members. The liberal as well as the conservative Speaker can only get a legislative program through to the extent that he has rewards and sanctions which he can use to generate support among members of his party. Any movement toward decentralization inevitably diffuses authority and thereby reduces the resources which any single leader can bring to bear in gaining support from his followers. In the House the development of chairmen as independent sources of power from the Speaker meant that the resources of the party leadership in pursuing consistent policies or in creating a more ideological program for the party were limited because of the decreased powers at the leadership's disposal. Decentralization itself of necessity does not lead to a conservative or a liberal coalition, but it does imply that many of the decisions and the decision making style will be incremental rather than comprehensive. Similarly, were powers again centralized in the House in the Speaker, there is no guarantee that such a change would result in greater chances of success for liberal programs or greater success for conservatives. Much would depend upon who holds leadership positions at any give time and what their political preferences are like. An example of how significantly power is decentralized in the House can be seen if we look at the operations of the Rules Committee in that body.

The Powers of the Rules Committee: The Impact of Decentralization

The United States House of Representatives has a mechanism for scheduling legislation and avoiding an overload at any particular

---

[3] See Nelson W. Polsby, "The Institutionalization of the U.S. House of Representatives," **American Political Science Review**, vol. LXII, no. 1 (March, 1968); also see Nelson W. Polsby, Miriam Gallaher, and Barry S. Rundquist, "The Growth of the Seniority System in the U.S. House of Representatives," **American Political Science Review**, vol. LXIII, no. 3 (September, 1969).

time in the chamber. This mechanism is the Rules Committee. Prior to the changes of 1910, the Rules Committee was an arm of the Speaker. As the committee which decides which bills shall reach the floor of the House for discussion and vote and what the terms of the debate on such bills will be, it provided him with enormous power. The reforms took the chairmanship of the committee away from the Speaker and removed his power to appoint the members of the committee. One of the chief powers which party leaders can use is their ability to control the calendar of the legislative chamber. Taking this power away creates in many respects a chairman whose powers are in some measure coequal with those of the Speaker. The Rules Committee chairman, like other chairmen, however, does not owe his position to his being in good standing with the party leadership. Rather the position is the result of the automatic operation of the seniority principle. There may be bills which the Speaker and the party leadership desire to bring to the floor for a vote. However, they have little influence beyond the power of persuasion in getting such legislation out of the Rules Committee if the chairman and a majority of the committee do not want to report the bill out. This is why in our earlier example we noted that Kennedy and Rayburn were concerned about the obstructive potential of the Rules Committee.[4] The Rules Committee may be able to extract concessions as its price for reporting bills out. For example, those who desire a particular piece of legislation to reach the floor may have to modify such legislation before it can come up for a vote. The committee chairman can often let the word out that only if certain sections are removed from a bill will he allow that bill to be voted on. This is considerable leverage and often means that bills which represent sharp departures from previous governmental policy will find it difficult to reach the House floor for debate and vote.

There is one further power of the Rules Committee which is significant. Not only does the committee determine which bills shall be debated and voted upon, it also has the power to set the terms of the debate. If the committee issues a closed rule, the particular bill must be debated and voted upon and no amendments are possible from the floor. Alternatively, the committee may issue an open rule, which permits amendments to a bill. This is a significant combination of powers.

---

[4] Milton C. Cummings, Jr., and Robert L. Peabody, "The Decision to Enlarge the Committee on Rules," in Robert L. Peabody and Nelson W. Polsby (eds.), **New Perspectives on the House of Representatives,** 2nd ed., Skokie, Ill.: Rand McNally, 1969.

There are procedures for circumventing the Rules Committee but these have generally proved to be too cumbersome to be used very often. The position of the Rules Committee and its combination of powers establish it as a significant arena where proponents of particular legislation must fight and win crucial battles. If you desire a particular piece of legislation to be passed, such legislation must first be approved by one of the House committees, then must be approved in the Rules Committee, and only then does a bill go to the floor of the House. In such a situation the possibilities for obstruction and delay are many. For those who claim that the House is slow and unresponsive in dealing with important legislation, it should be remembered that part of the reason for this is the adoption of liberal rules designed to decentralize decision-making authority in the House. As we noted in Chapter 9, the decentralization of decision making allows for delays and the exercise of vetoes because such a system reflects a high decision making rule—consent is required in several arenas before bills can actually be passed.

The Appropriations Committee: Further Decentralization

There is still another aspect of House procedure which increases the scope of the decision-making rule and thereby increases the potential for veto. This has to do with the particular nature of the appropriations process. Every bill which requires the expenditure of funds must first be approved by a subject-matter committee, and then the amount of monies which can be spent for the program must be approved by the appropriations committee. Each bill then requires separate hearings before the subject committee and the appropriations committee. For example, defense expenditures and programs first come up for discussion in the Armed Services Committee. The figure for such programs is decided after hearings in the Appropriations Committee. The House must vote on the report or recommendations of both of these committees. The pivotal role of the Appropriations Committee in the governmental process assures that the committee and its chairman occupy a significant position of power in the chamber.[5]

The Committee System and Legislative Procedures

In general, as we have indicated, the committee system, where

---

[5] Richard F. Fenno, Jr., "The Appropriations Committee as a Political System," in Robert L. Peabody and Nelson W. Polsby (eds.), **New Perspectives on The House of Representatives,** 2nd ed., Skokie, Ill.: Rand McNally, 1969.

such committees are vested with substantial powers, raises the degree of consensus which is necessary in order to get important legislation passed. It increases the probability for incremental decision making. This is again either harmful or beneficial, depending upon the particular goals or values of the individual who is evaluating the procedures. It is difficult to get quick action on pressing issues, but the structure provides that when action is taken it will be done after careful consideration and screening of alternatives and after a consensus has developed that such action is desirable and useful. What this implies is that there is less likelihood that acts passed by one Congress will be repealed by succeeding ones. Since many of the occupants of Congress return with great frequency, the legislative process assumes a high degree of stability.

There are several positive benefits which accrue from the committee system and seniority. The range of subject matter which must be considered by the modern legislature has become increasingly complex and broad in scope. Some division of labor is essential for the smooth functioning of the legislative body. The committee system allows the members of the legislature to divide the work among themselves and to specialize in particular areas. While it would be impossible for the member of any modern legislature to be expert or knowledgeable in all areas of legislation, it is not unrealistic for him to acquire expertise in particular fields. Service on committees allows individual members to build up expertise and to act intelligently on issues in their particular domain of knowledge.

It must be remembered that in the gathering and processing of information, the executive branch has a clear advantage over the legislature. In preparing legislative programs, the executive can draw on the entire bureaucracy for information and technical expertise. The resources of the individual congressman are much more meager. He has a relatively small staff with which to analyze and interpret the mass of information he receives. By limiting attention to specific areas, the congressman can at least be sure of asking the pertinent and at times embarrassing questions in the committee hearings. As various congressmen become expert in particular areas, other members of Congress tend to rely on their judgments and evaluations. The distribution of work allows for a more economical and efficient operation of the legislature.

The seniority system also has some benefits. For one thing it does serve to prevent one-man rule of the House. The existence of a seniority system provides the individual members with a source of independence from the Speaker. Second, it is an orderly procedure, if a somewhat anachronistic one,[6] for transferring positions of authority and leadership within the Congress. Given that progression to positions of leadership is based on seniority, there is little reason to engage in continuous competition over particular ranks and positions on various committees. It is possible that in the absence of seniority, great amounts of time would be spent in building coalitions to depose or maintain existing chairmen. In the absence of seniority, the position of the individual legislator would be far more circumscribed. He would be dependent upon the leadership for support and would be reluctant to publicly challenge that leadership.

Indeed, the most often used criticism of the seniority system is not really a fault of the seniority system itself. Liberals in the United States have long maintained that adherence to the seniority principle means that control of important positions in the Congress will always remain in the hands of conservatives, and particularly southern conservatives. This is not an inevitable result of seniority but rather a reflection of the noncompetitive nature of politics in particular regions of the country. Until recently the number of Republican congressmen elected from the South was very small. In recent years, however, Republicans have shown striking gains[7] in this region and the potential exists for a much greater degree of party competition arising. If this becomes the case, then we can assume that committee chairmanships will begin to be distributed in a more normal distributional pattern. All that the seniority system does is reflect the fact that two-party competition is not uniformly present throughout the country.

Decentralization and Party Cohesion

One of the charges which has been leveled at American parties is that they fail to be consistent in their programs. As we have seen earlier, however, parties are organizations for electoral victory. The factors which exist within the United States favor the development of broad aggregative parties. Beyond this, however, the institutional structures within the Congress itself make party cohesion and the presentation of consistent programs very difficult. The internal democratization of the House has left the party leaders with only meager resources to

---

[6] See Chapter 12 for a discussion of the methods of transferring political power.
[7] See Table 8-1.

bring to bear in insuring party unity or high rates of cohesion for party programs. The political party, which in many ways is the exemplar organization of the activation phase, is uniquely ill-suited to perform as a cohesive decision-making unit in the legislature.

THE SENATE

The Senate is similar to the House in many respects. Both use a seniority system; both have a highly developed committee system. There are, however, some interesting variations. In many respects the Senate extends decentralization even further than the House. It does so through its principle of unlimited debate. The Senate is one of the few parliamentary institutions which still adheres, for all practical purposes, to unlimited debate. Members may speak at any length on any piece of legislation; as a matter of fact the Senate does not require that the individual's speech be germane to the subject under discussion. The only means by which debate can be ended on a particular bill is through the use of Rule 22. This is the Senate's cloture rule. It stipulates that to end debate, two thirds of the senators present and voting must agree to such a limitation. This rule makes it very difficult to end debate and provides a powerful weapon for any minority within the chamber which is opposed to the passage of a particular piece of legislation. If the legislation is controversial, it is difficult to get sufficient support to end debate. In light of the powerful obstructive factor which unlimited debate represents, it is unusual or remarkable that it has been used so sparingly. Filibusters are relatively rare. In recent history they have been most common on civil rights legislation. It has been possible, however, to mobilize support to break such filibusters. When we consider the range of issues which the legislature considers in any given year, one can only be struck by the infrequency with which the filibuster is actually used.

The filibuster, which is the outgrowth of unlimited debate, is not, however, the exclusive province of southern senators to prevent civil rights legislation. It has been used in the past by liberals as well. For example, during the debate over the establishment of the Communications Satellite Corporation, liberals such as Wayne Morse of Oregon tried to filibuster the bill but lacked sufficient support to prevent passage of the legislation. Nevertheless, this action illustrates that the existence of unlimited debate is a tool which can be used by either conservatives

or liberals. Perhaps this explains why it has been difficult to get sufficient support to change Rule 22 so that debate could be ended by a
simple majority vote. The rule's utility to several groups within the
Senate, plus the strong emphasis of tradition in that body, makes it
difficult to change the rule.

The threat of the filibuster, particularly at a busy time in the legislative calendar, may often send a controversial bill to its death through
tabling or may bring about substantial modification of a bill in order
to forestall a filibuster. In many cases the threat of a filibuster may be
more effective than the actual attempt. The requirement of two-thirds
support before debate can be ended raises the decision-making costs
on controversial legislation. It ensures that legislation is likely to represent incremental changes from the present. This is so because any
substantial minority of senators can block any comprehensive change.
This means of course that often a problem has to continue to build
strength until the demands for action are obvious enough to secure
the necessary coalition to ensure passage. The amount of agreement
which was necessary to secure passage of the Civil Rights Act of 1965
was quite high. It was impossible to get the bill passed without the
support of the late Everett Dirksen of Illinois. While supporters of the bill
had more than the majority of votes necessary for passage of the bill,
they were short of the required two-thirds support to break the filibuster
against it. Dirksen provided the key to breaking that filibuster. He
could bring over the crucial few more senators that were necessary.
His price for joining the civil rights coalition was to demand that
certain provisions of the bill be modified. The final bill was not as strong
as some of the proponents had originally wanted, yet it did represent a
stronger civil rights bill than many thought could be passed at all.
In this case the higher decision-making rule required that some concessions be made, and the act was weaker than some desired. Without
the possibility of the filibuster, it is possible that the Senate could have
passed a much stronger bill. However, the margin of victory would have
been narrow. In such a situation it is possible that at succeeding elections
a change of a few seats would enable opponents of civil rights legislation to repeal provisions of the bill. The high degree of consensus
which is brought about by the existence of the two-thirds requirement
may provide a weaker bill but it assures that the base of support for
such action is broad enough so that repeal is unlikely.

For those who seek to exert leadership in the Senate, the path is not

TABLE 10-2

DEMOCRATIC SENATE COMMITTEE CHAIRMAN: 1947–1970

AERONAUTICAL AND SPACE SCIENCE	
Johnson	Texas
Kerr	Oklahoma
Anderson	New Mexico

AGRICULTURE AND FORESTRY	
Thomas	Oklahoma
Ellender	Louisiana

APPROPRIATIONS	
McKellar	Tennessee
Hayden	Arizona
Russell	Georgia

ARMED SERVICES	
Tydings	Maryland
Russell	Georgia
Stennis	Mississippi

BANKING AND CURRENCY	
Maybank	South Carolina
Fulbright	Arkansas
Robertson	Virginia
Sparkman	Alabama

COMMERCE	
Johnson	Colorado
Magnuson	Washington

DISTRICT OF COLUMBIA	
McGrath	Rhode Island
Neely	West Virginia
Bible	Nevada
Tydings	Maryland

FINANCE	
George	Georgia
Byrd	Virginia
Long	Louisiana

FOREIGN RELATIONS	
Connally	Texas
George	Georgia
Green	Rhode Island
Fulbright	Arkansas

GOVERNMENT OPERATIONS	
McClellan	Arkansas

INTERIOR AND INSULAR AFFAIRS	
O'Mahoney	Wyoming
Murray	Montana
Anderson	New Mexico
Jackson	Washington

JUDICIARY	
McCarran	Nevada
Kilgore	West Virginia
Eastland	Mississippi

LABOR AND PUBLIC WELFARE	
Thomas	Utah
Murray	Montana
Hill	Alabama
Yarborough	Texas

POST OFFICE AND CIVIL SERVICE	
Johnston	South Carolina
Monroney	Oklahoma
McGee	Wyoming

PUBLIC WORKS	
Chavez	New Mexico
McNamara	Michigan
Randolph	West Virginia

RULES AND ADMINISTRATION	
Hayden	Arizona
Green	Rhode Island
Hennings	Missouri
Mansfield	Montana
Jordan	North Carolina

SELECT COMMITTEE ON SMALL BUSINESS	
Sparkman	Alabama
Smathers	Florida
Bible	Nevada

easy. The body is highly decentralized. The existence of the seniority principle in the Senate creates a dual leadership structure similar to that in the house. However, certain innovations have been made in the seniority principle in the Senate which have given the party leaders greater leverage as they attempt to exert some degree of party discipline.

In 1954 Lyndon Johnson became the majority leader of the Democrats in the Senate. He soon proved to be particularly astute and carefully expanded his powers as majority leader.[8] He introduced a significant modification of the Senate rules of the Democratic party. Because the Senate is a smaller body than the House, senators serve on more than one committee. In the Senate as well as the House, some committees are perceived by members as more desirous than others. In the House, the Ways and Means Committee, the Rules Committee, and the Appropriations Committee are particularly prestigious. In the Senate, the Foreign Relations Committee, Armed Services, and Finance are committees that members aspire to be placed on.

The reform which Johnson got through the Democratic caucus was that no senator could sit on more than one major committee until all Democratic senators had a seat on at least one. The strategic significance of this move can not be underestimated. It opened up a number of seats on major committees as senior senators chose which committee they most preferred to serve on. Freshmen senators then expressed their preferences for committee assignments. Johnson was able to get a great deal of support from the freshman senators who entered each year. These senators owed their positions on major committees to Johnson. Although once on the committee Johnson could not throw them off, the initial debt was there and was subject to recall. Additionally, while all members were placed on a major committee, that committee assignment might not represent their first choice. Movement from committee to committee was dependent upon remaining in the good graces of the majority leader. For example, Senator Joseph Clark of Pennsylvania had long coveted a seat on the Foreign Relations Committee. Every time a vacancy occurred on that committee, Johnson was always able to find a freshmen senator or some other senator to take that position. Many felt that this was because of Clark's refusal to go

[8] Ralph Huitt, "Democratic Party Leadership in the Senate," reprinted in Ralph Huitt and Robert Peabody (eds.), **Congress: Two Decades of Analysis**, New York: Harper & Row, 1969.

along with Johnson on several issues. Such behavior on the part of the majority leader was a clear indication that he was willing to use his influence to reward his friends and punish his enemies. The movement away from a strict seniority principle placed great leverage in the hands of the leadership, and the Democrats were relatively cohesive under Johnson's leadership. Whether such cohesion is beneficial or not depends upon one's perceptions of the leadership and the degree of agreement or disagreement you may have with the goals and priorities of the incumbents of such leadership positions.

What we have suggested is that the internal rules and structures of a legislative body affect the manner in which it will respond to issues and the nature of the decisions which will result. Cohesiveness of the legislative party is a prerequisite to comprehensive decision making and this can take place where party leaders have sanctions at their disposal to enforce party discipline. The dispersion of influence is likely to be characterized by a more incremental style of decision making and in less cohesiveness in party voting as leaders possess few sanctions to enforce discipline. The structure and rules of the United States Congress tend to reflect this decentralization. In part this is a reflection of the existence of a federal system of government which is already decentralized and in part it is a reflection of the norms which the Congress has itself adopted.

There is another significant set of actions which affect the decision-making style. In part the norms which a legislative body adopts are a way of reacting to the structures of the institution. Because of the decentralized nature of the Congress, sets of internal norms of conduct have evolved which facilitate the transaction of business and influence the decision making process.

THE CONGRESS AND INTERNAL NORMS OF BEHAVIOR

Both the House and the Senate have evolved specific norms of conduct but these are much more elaborate and highly developed in the Senate. It is here that we will focus our attention. Sometimes to the outside observer the rules and rituals of the United States Senate seem ludicrous or overdone. Yet there are important reasons for adherence to these norms. In the Senate a largely unwritten code of conduct is a set of behavioral rules that regularize the procedures governing the interactions of members and assure a certain predictability of behavior.

The existence of a code of behavior also fosters an esprit de corps among the members and is an important factor in reducing friction in the chamber.[9]

A significant aspect of the norms of the Senate is the emphasis on courtesy. Members are expected to refrain from personal insult or invective toward colleagues. This is not a norm which is universally adhered to in all legislatures. In many legislatures invective and even fighting among members is not uncommon. This is extremely rare in the Senate. Similarly in the House of Commons in England, personal vituperation is often great among members, but the Speaker of the House of Commons usually sees to it that during the course of debate the invective does not get out of hand.

One can see this norm of courtesy manifested in the sometimes elaborate manner in which senators address one another. It is common to refer to one's colleague as the distinguished and admirable Senior Senator from the state of . . . There is no necessary correlation between the number of favorable adjectives which one senator uses in addressing another and the degree of friendship or mutual respect between the senators. In some cases the relationship of favorable adjectives and respect may be negatively related. If this is the case, why such an elaborate and at times seemingly hypocritical procedure? This can best be explained by the fact that the Senate is a continuing body whose members interact and must continue to interact with each other on a day-to-day basis in committees, subcommittees, on the floor of the Senate, and at the numerous social gatherings which bring political figures together in Washington.

Senators occupy a desirable political position and most of them wish to maintain those positions. Given the fact that the Senate term of office, six years, is a long one and the rate of reelection for senators is high, most members can anticipate a rather long period of association with each other. The size of the body, one hundred members, makes it a relatively intimate body with frequent and close association among members. While the norm of courtesy may lead to flowery oratory, it does prevent or remove a great deal of abrasiveness or hostility which might arise from long hours of legislative sessions where feelings and tempers may run quite high. Most of us can probably remember being

---

[9] Much of this discussion draws on the work of Donald Matthews. See his **U.S. Senators and Their World,** Chapel Hill: University of North Carolina Press, 1960.

involved in arguments with friends or close relations when, in the heat of the moment, we have made a statement or used a term in describing somebody that we later wish we had not used. Courtesy as a norm of behavior in the Senate serves the same purpose that good manners do in other settings, it allows individuals who disagree with each other on one particular issue to still maintain their ability to work together on other issues. The coalitions that are built on one legislative issue may be quite different from the coalition of support which forms on another. It is almost impossible to accurately gauge whether a present opponent might not at some future time become an ally. In part this is the result of the fact that party cohesion is not strictly developed in the Congress. On almost any vote, Republicans and Democrats are on both sides of an issue. There is some basic degree of unity in the voting patterns of Republicans and Democrats in the legislature, yet there is enough deviation that on any given issue it may be necessary to extract support from members of the opposite party. For example, the defeat of President Nixon's nomination of Clement Haynsworth and G. Harrold Carswell for the Supreme Court was accomplished by a coalition of Democrats and Republicans. Despite the fact that the Democrats control the Senate, there were sufficient defections from their ranks that Republican support was necessary to defeat the nominees. On many issues coalitions form and cut across party lines and these coalitions change from issue to issue.

This is not a peculiar or unusual occurrence. The varied nature of constituencies in this country and the broad base of the parties would indicate that there would be a frequent amount of interparty coalition formation. This is not true of the British House of Commons. Although rules of courtesy are adhered to in the British Parliament, there is usually very little likelihood of interparty coalitions being formed, except in periods of the most severe crisis. In Britain there is a high degree of party unity on important issues. This party unity and discipline is strongly maintained. The adherence to norms of courtesy is much more important in legislatures where coalitions are likely to cross party lines and shift in composition from issue to issue. In part the elaborate ritual of courtesy is a function of uncertainty. In the absence of strong party discipline, one is not always positive where support can be secured at any given time.

There is a further aspect of the courtesy rule. All senators extend to each other the right of vetoing any appointment from their own state.

It is an unwritten custom that no Presidential appointment shall be made in a state without the consultation of the senator or senators of the President's party from that state. There are sensible reasons for such a system. The President counts on and needs the support of senators of his own party. Senators are concerned about maintaining their position within their states and preventing their opponents within the party from building a base to challenge them. There is a vested interest, common to all senators, in preventing Presidents from appointing political enemies. Such a nomination if allowed to go unchallenged would or might possibly erode the senator's support in his own state. As a result, all senators extend to each other the courtesy of denying nomination to any appointee who is considered to be personally obnoxious to the affected senator. For example, Judge Haynsworth would not have been nominated if Senator Thurmond of South Carolina had opposed him. This is because Nixon and Thurmond are both Republicans and Haynsworth is from the state of South Carolina. The objection of Senator Birch Bayh of Indiana, however, was not in and of itself sufficient to kill the nomination. The defeat required the building of a large and difficult coalition. Often a President is faced with a situation in which there are two senators from his party in a given state. An appointment has become vacant, but since the two senators are from different factions of the party it may be difficult to reach agreement. Senators extend this courtesy of approval on appointments in recognition that each must of necessity protect others while seeking to preserve his own political base.

The norms of the Senate and indeed those of many legislative bodies are complex. Often rewards go to those who adapt to those rules and are most efficient in using those norms. Often, in the Senate, the most powerful figures are not those whose names often appear in the headlines, but are rather those senators who have mastered the rules of the body and know how to use them most effectively.

There are several norms which exist and are adhered to but it is not necessary to enumerate them all. What is necessary to note is that the rules of a body such as the Senate allow a group of one hundred legislators charged with very important responsibilities to work together and discharge those responsibilities in an atmosphere that is conducive to achievement. The basic system of legislative behavior is based on bargaining. Senators and congressmen have various interests and causes. Some of these interests are determined by the nature of the legislator's constituency. Others are a function of the development and peculiar interests of the legislator himself. The way in which favorable action is achieved in a legislature is through compromise and bargaining, and for these functions these internal norms of behavior play a crucial role.

COMPROMISE, BARGAINING, AND LEGISLATIVE DECISION MAKING

We can assume that among the various issues which may come up or which may be important in any legislative session, each legislator has certain preferences concerning the importance of each particular issue and the outcome he desires. It would be unrealistic to assume that in as diverse a society as the United States there exists in a legislature a majority of individuals whose preference rankings and whose utility for various legislative outcomes is identical over a wide range of issues. Two legislators opposed to each other on environmental control bills may find themselves allied on aid to education programs. Because of the unlikelihood of a consistent majority formed across all issues, a certain amount of bargaining is necessary among legislators in order for many of them to achieve at least partial satisfaction of their preferences.

If we assume that during the course of a legislative session five pieces of major legislation will be considered, we can begin to see what is involved in the bargaining and decision-making process. We have further assumed that each of the senators has a specific position on each of these five issues, and, for the moment, we will assume that each senator can rank his preferences in terms of the intensity of his feeling on each issue. Realistically the legislator will know that it is unlikely that he will win on all five issues. Therefore, he may rank his preferences in terms of those issues he most strongly favors, those issues on which he is strongly opposed, and those issues where his preferences are not intensely held. The area where preferences are not intense represents the bargaining area for most of the legislators. That is, they are willing to engage in logrolling, to trade support on those issues where they have no intense preference for support on those issues where their preferences are quite strong. This has long been the basis of support for many of the coalitions which have existed in the Congress. In part the Southern Democratic-Conservative Republican coalition has

been formed on the basis of such logrolling. By agreeing to give support
to conservative Republicans on those issues which are of little concern
to them, the Southerners have extracted, if not outright, at least the
passive support of conservative Republicans on such issues as civil
rights and states rights.

Of the five legislative issues which our hypothetical legislature has
to consider, we can conceive of various ways in which the legislators
might array their preferences. For illustrative purposes we will list the
preferences of some six legislators in Table 10-3. We will assume that

TABLE 10-3

PREFERENCE RANKINGS AND COALITION POSSIBILITIES

LEGISLATOR	ORDER OF PREFERENCE				
	1	2	3	4	5
A	1	4	5	3	2
B	5	1	3	2	4
C	5	4	1	2	3
D	4	5	1	3	2
E	2	3	1	4	5
F	2	3	4	5	1

the first and last preference orderings reflect the highest level of intensity for the legislators. That is, the first preference is the one which
the legislator most intensely desires to see enacted and the last
reflects the issue he most wants defeated. We are assuming that each
legislative player is trying to form the coalition which gives him positive
results on the greatest number of issues and minimizes his losses. Certainly he is not going to form a coalition with other legislators if the
cost of that coalition exceeds his anticipated gains or involves a greater
expenditure of resources than he is willing to pay. As we can see from
looking at Table 10-3, legislators A and D can easily bargain as can
legislators E and F. While it is possible for legislator B to form a
coalition with E on issues 1 and 3, this would be unlikely, since B can
form a coalition with A and C and secure his first two preferences.
There are several aspects of the coalition strategy in the legislature
which differ from the electoral strategy.

Legislative rules, as we have indicated, are established to assure
some predictability in behavior and to routinize procedure. The stages
which are preparatory to the actual voting in the legislature are infor-

mation-gathering sessions. Members become aware of bills and try to form coalitions of support to pass or block specific pieces of legislation. The rules which are adopted in the Congress reflect the continuing nature of the coalition-building process and coalitions are formed, discarded, and new alignments emerge. This information-gathering process goes on among a relatively small group of individual legislators. When compared to the electorate, which is necessarily large and somewhat amorphous, the chances for complete information are much greater in the legislature than in other decision-making arenas. Because voting is usually open and recorded, members can check whether others have kept their word. Since the formation of coalitions is constantly repeated, individual legislators have a stake in keeping their bargains when they form coalitions. They can perhaps double-cross their partners once. After that they will not be trusted and will have little influence in the legislature. The cost of breaking one's word is very high and precludes the possibility of exerting influence on other pieces of legislation or advancing within the legislative body. It is important for legislatures to make the penalties high for not keeping one's word. Without such penalties the predictability of the process is shattered and the ability to form coalitions becomes a game of chance where the highest rewards would go to the most convincing liar. This is not a situation which most legislators desire or seek to structure.

Because information can approximate completeness, it is theoretically possible to form only the minimum winning coalition. In practice, however, coalition sizes often exceed the minimum. There is good reason for this. Legislatures are constantly passing and considering bills, and participants are usually interested in building coalitions over several issues. Therefore, while the size of the coalition may be more than minimal for issue 1, it may represent the minimal size for positive action on issues 1, 2, and 3. Because legislative coalitions often form not around a particular issue but around clusters of issues, it may be necessary to form larger coalitions than would be necessary for each individual issue. However, the costs of forming a coalition once for several issues will probably be less than forming minimal coalitions for each issue.

If we look again at our table we can see that the bargaining range for legislators A through D consists of those issues on which they are indifferent. A is willing to give support to B, C, and D on issue 5 in return for their support on issue 1. A can also bargain with C and

D with relation to issue 4 but this might cause the defection of B who is violently opposed to the passage of 4. The most profitable coalition would be one of A, C, and D. However, if B's vote is necessary, some concession might have to be made in order to get B's support for issues 1 and 5.

We do not mean this to sound unduly complex. Legislators will simply try to form those coalitions which will ensure them success on the largest range of issues. Rewards and side payments will be made by the players in order to bring members into the coalitions. It is useful to note, however, that while it is in the self-interest of the actors to gain information about intentions and preferences, it is also in their self-interest to withhold information from others. We cannot assume that all actors will be equally compensated for their membership in a coalition. As the time for voting on a particular issue approaches, the number of uncommitted legislators becomes increasingly small. If neither side is sure that it has sufficient votes to win, the value of the final uncommitted members becomes quite high. Initially we can say that individual A wants to form a coalition to promote high agricultural subsidies for corn growers. He needs 51 votes to secure passage of the legislation. He can assume he has support of other legislators from corn growing states so that he does not have to negotiate with them. Let us assume that the legislators desiring corn subsidies have 30 definite votes, with 25 votes lined up against them. That means that they must pick up 21 more votes out of a possible 45 as yet uncommitted legislators. They can do this by offering side payments and transfers of support on other issues. Note, however, that as the pool of potential votes drops, each additional supporter can continue to demand a higher price for joining the coalition. Since we can assume that the remaining pool of uncommitted legislators are relatively indifferent to the outcome of this struggle, they can negotiate with both sides to see who is willing to make the best offer. The price, therefore, that is paid to later members of the coalition is often higher than the price paid to the early joiners. They disguise their vote intentions and withhold any information which would commit them to one side or the other until they are ready to strike their bargains. By withholding information about vote intentions they raise the costs of information gathering and coalition building. This again explains why often larger than minimal coalitions are formed. It is much more economical to gather information and make side payments over a range of issues. Coalition size will not be minimal with relation to a particular issue but rather with respect to a range of issues.

Players who seek to withhold information about vote intentions in order to maximize their payoffs do run a risk. They can withhold support or information for too long a period of time and find themselves not able to extract a price from either side. This can sometimes be seen to happen at the national nominating conventions of the American parties. The convention is in many ways similar to a legislature. It is a voting body which adopts the rules for the national party organization and selects the Presidential nominee of the party. At the convention, information is often at a premium. Various candidates and leaders are interested in assessing the preferences and commitments of the delegates. Often leaders of state delegations seek to bring those delegations to the convention uncommitted to any candidate. This is done in order to maximize the benefits which can be gained from going with one candidate or the other. In 1960 at the Democratic National Convention several state delegations came uncommitted to any candidate. They were prepared to either join a move to block John Kennedy or to extract a price for being the delegation which could put John Kennedy over the top. The New Jersey delegation, led by then Governor Robert Meyner, was an excellent example. It was not fated to be successful however; Kennedy picked up support elsewhere and had enough votes without the support of New Jersey. He therefore refused to bargain with or make any concessions to Meyner.

Similarly, in 1968 Governor James Rhodes of Ohio probably overestimated the strength of the stop-Nixon movement. Uncommitted to either Nixon or Rockefeller before the convention, Rhodes hoped to strike a bargain that would enhance his position within the party. Many maintained that Rhodes had his eye on the Vice Presidential nomination. Nixon's strength was sufficient without the Ohio delegation, however, and Rhodes' holdout did him no good. Withholding information or support until the strategic moment is a sensible strategy to follow but the success of that strategy, as is the case in many other situations, depends upon more accurate timing and planning than either Meyner or Rhodes displayed.

We have assumed that because of information-gathering costs and the desire among some legislators to withhold information, coalitions will form around clusters of issues. Remember, though, that our original table presented a highly simplified representation of reality. Legislators consider far more than five issues in any given session. Countless appropriations bills must be considered with the submission of the yearly budget. These are in addition to any new programs which may be proposed in any given session.

While ultimately every legislative issue boils down to the yea or no vote, there is also a great deal of maneuverability concerning the final contents of legislation before it reaches the floor of the legislature. The possibilities for trades of support exist not only on the final vote but also within the terms of the bill itself. It may cost less to gain support by modifying certain sections of proposed legislation than by using resources to try to get the bill passed as it is. These two approaches, bargaining based on modification and compromises in the bill itself, and bargaining based on logrolling are the common ways in which legislative coalitions are formed. Trading occurs at the margins of the coalition, where uncommitted or indifferent legislators are induced to join. The use of logrolling or compromise will depend upon the resources available to the participants and on the degree to which sections of the proposed legislation can be modified without causing defections.

As the number of legislative issues increases, the chances for forming coalitions over a wide range of issues also increase. The larger number of issues means that probably no one person can hope to maximize his preferences without coordinated efforts with others. The need for coalition formation is imperative.

THE BRITISH HOUSE OF COMMONS

We can perhaps best understand the cumulative effect of internal norms, structures, and rules as they affect the United States Congress if we briefly compare the American system to another legislature, the British Parliament. For all practical purposes, today's British legislature is unicameral. While Parliament consists of the House of Lords and the House of Commons, over the years the power of the Lords has gradually declined. At the moment the most that the Lords can do is delay action on legislation to which they are opposed, and even this power is sharply limited. Consequently, Parliament has become synonomous with the House of Commons. As opposed to the past, when many prime ministers and cabinet members were from the House of Lords, all recent leaders have either been members of the House of Commons or have resigned their hereditary title, as in the case of the former Earl of Home, who denied his title to assume the post of Prime Minister. In the nineteenth century it was not at all uncommon for members of the hereditary aristocracy to serve as Prime Minister. In the twentieth century, however, this has become impossible. A member of the House of Lords must delegate to someone else the task of being party leader in the House of Commons. Since power has shifted almost completely to the Commons, this would mean that an aristocratic leader would not be able to exercise daily control over his followers in the legislative chamber.

The Unified Executive and Legislature

Within Britain there is no separation between the executive and legislative branch. In theory the executive head of state is the monarch. In fact, the Prime Minister used to be the King's representative in Parliament. As the power of the monarchy has waned, however, the Prime Minister has become, if not in law at least in practice, the head of the British government. The King or Queen no longer chooses the Prime Minister; rather the choice is predetermined by the election results: The Prime Minister is always the head of the majority party. Today the only time that Queen Elizabeth has any discretion is when there is no clear party leader. This was the case when Anthony Eden resigned as Prime Minister after the Suez Canal fiasco of 1956. At the time of Eden's resignation there were two contenders for the Conservative party leadership, R. A. Butler and Harold Macmillan. The Queen, after consultation with Conservative party leaders and elder statesmen, chose Harold Macmillan. Nevertheless, this is a rare occurrence caused by the resignation of the leader of the party in power. The leadership of the country is placed in the hands of the leader of the House of Commons who retains his seat in the legislature while he is Prime Minister. This, of course, is quite different from the United States where the President and his cabinet are not members of the legislature. All of the leaders of Britain, the cabinet, and junior cabinet ministers, are members of Parliament. Because the executive authority springs from the legislature, there is a much greater coordination between legislation and administration than in the United States. The executive leaders are in the legislature to exert the pressure of party discipline on a daily and face-to-face basis.

If the nineteenth century in Britain can be characterized as the century of the House of Commons, the twentieth century can be described as the age of the rise of the cabinet and the decline in influence of Commons. In Britain, as in other countries, increasing complexity and the rapidity of events have given an ever-larger scope to executive authority. As the need for quick executive action has grown, the great debates of Parliament have similarly declined. In the United States legislators have developed the committee system to a fine art and instituted the principle of seniority as a means of developing bases of authority not subject to and indeed autonomous of the executive leadership.

That a similarly powerful committee system has not developed in Britain is a prime factor in explaining the decreasing significance of parliamentary debate. Again, in Britain, in the nineteenth century it was not unusual for governments to fall and political crises to be precipitated because of breaks in party unity which brought down the government. Such an occurrence would be almost unthinkable in this century. In Britain this occurs because the individual MP has no independent base of power from which he can challenge the party leadership.

The British Parliament has had no incentive to adopt a seniority system similar to the one in use in the United States because committees in the House of Commons have no real power to be coveted. The American committee chairman deals with specific subject matter and over the course of years can acquire expertise and establish very effective liaisons within his fields. For example, the power of Wilbur Mills in the House of Representatives stems not from his being a committee chairman, but from his being the chairman of the Ways and Means Committee. This means that all legislation dealing with raising of government revenue and all changes and modifications in tax laws and social security benefits and deductions must pass Mr. Mills' scrutiny. All committee chairmen in the United States Congress are not so important. The truly important men are those who chair key committees such as Ways and Means, Rules, and Appropriations. Their importance is a function of the importance of their committees. In Britain, however, committees are not functionally specific. Most are just labeled alphabetically. Bills are assigned to committees on more or less of a random basis. Sometimes committee A will get appropriations bills to consider; at other times it may get education bills or bills dealing with the merchant marine. Consequently, committee members have no chance to develop great skill or power in a particular subject area. Those members who do achieve expertise in specific areas are the members of the cabinet or junior ministers and, as such, their influence or power derives from their being part of the executive structure rather than from their legislative seat. In such a system all the sources of influence and information are concentrated in the cabinet. Individual members of Parliament have very meager resources with which to challenge the cabinet or exercise a truly independent role. The cabinet, which represents the party leadership, of course, is not chosen on the basis of seniority. While it usually is necessary for a politician to have served a certain amount of time in Commons before achieving a cabinet posision, the positions themselves are not distributed according to any particular system other than that of trying to achieve a balance among the various factions within the party. Because the party leadership holds all the positions of authority and influence within Parliament, advancement for the individual member depends upon the evaluation which the leaders of his party make of him. If the evaluation is positive, a junior ministry may be in the offing. If it is negative, he probably is doomed to an obscure career in Parliament. Party discipline is much easier to enforce because of these structures in Britain than in the United States. In the U.S. Congress, as we have seen, being reelected to office a sufficient number of times determines a legislator's influence or importance. If a member can continue to be reelected, he may disagree with the party leadership and still achieve a position of influence. This would be inconceivable in Britain. Because the leadership of the House of Commons also comprises the executive for the country, there usually is no problem in securing rather rapid passage of the government's program—unlike this country, where the President in trying to get approval for his legislative program finds that he must use all his influence and persuasion in dealing with individuals whose base of power is independent of the President as leader of his party. The British Prime Minister usually can count on much quicker and unamended approval of his program. He must negotiate with his cabinet ministers and get their support for his program, but for a strong Prime Minister this is not an insuperable barrier and, after this stage of consultation is over, passage of his program is assured.

Both the British and American systems have had rather admirable records. Each has its own benefits and costs. The British system seems particularly geared to coordinated decision making. It is possible to organize a legislative program in order to achieve certain goals and to be relatively sure of the enactment of that program. The cabinet and junior ministers have a monopoly on information and other resources, and there is no basis for building autonomous centers of power. This assures a relatively centralized decision-making process and, of course, increases the political system's ability to respond to demands for comprehensive or rapid change. On the other hand, the United States Congress is a relatively decentralized system. The development and refinement of the committee system and seniority have produced centers of power and influence in Congress which are independent of party leadership. This imposes a higher decision-making rule in Congress than in the British Parliament. Passage of controversial legislation requires the building of large coalitions and a high degree of consensus that action is needed and the legislation under consideration is the appropriate response to the need for action. The separation of powers between the executive and legislative branches builds in certain institutional jealousies between the two branches of government. The legislative system embodied in the Congress is one of multiple arenas and is therefore one in which vetoes or blocking action can be successfully achieved in any of several places. Yet while this system extracts a price, it also has its benefits. It develops an independent arm of government which can challenge the executive. The opposition to the Vietnam War in the Democratic party during the Johnson Presidency and the Republican opposition to Nixon's policies would be inconceivable under the British system. Yet for Johnson the opposition from his own party had such significance that it influenced his decision not to seek reelection. The basis for such action arises in the independent positions of influence which members of Congress have with respect to the President. While this may involve costs, it also offers a benefit in providing additional channels for the raising and articulation of alternative positions and demands.

LEGISLATIVE DECISION MAKING: AN OVERVIEW

Legislative decision making is a complex phenomenon. The structure of the legislature and rules both formal and informal affect the manner in which conflicts will be raised and resolved. In the United States a decentralized legislative structure provides alternative channels and arenas for raising and articulating positions. It also indicates that the decision making style of the legislature is incremental. These rules are in part an attempt to regularize and routinize legislative business. The rules determine what activities are likely to lead to beneficial payoffs for the individual members of the legislature and what types of strategies are most successful for both maximizing personal influence in the legislature and securing passage of those bills that the individual most desires. As our brief comparison with the British system demonstrated, there are variations in these rules and structures and these variations affect the style of politics. Both the British and American systems have specific benefits as well as costs. In each society the nature of its legislative structure affects the capacity of the political system to respond to conflicts.

SUGGESTED READINGS

Beer, Samuel H., **British Politics in the Collectivist Age,** New York: Knopf, 1965.

Bolling, Richard, **House Out of Order,** New York: Dutton, 1965.

Burns, James M., **The Deadlock of Democracy,** Englewood Cliffs, N.J.: Prentice-Hall, 1963.

Clark, Joseph S. (ed.), **Congressional Reform,** New York: Crowell, 1965.

Cummings, Milton C., Jr., **Congressmen and the Electorate,** New York: Free Press, 1966.

Fenno, Richard F., Jr., **The Power of the Purse,** Boston: Atlantic-Little, Brown, 1966.

Galloway, George B., **History of the House of Representatives,** New York: Crowell, 1962.

Huitt, Ralph K., and Robert L. Peabody (eds.), **Congress: Two Decades of Analysis,** New York: Harper & Row, 1969.

Jewell, Malcolm E., and Samuel C. Patterson, **The Legislative Process in the United States,** New York: Random House, 1966.

King, Anthony, **British Politics,** Lexington, Mass.: Raytheon/Heath, 1966.

Luce, R. Duncan, and Arnold A. Rogow, "A Game Theoretic Analysis of Congressional Power Distributions for a Stable Two-Party System," **Behavioral Science,** vol. I (1956).

Mayhew, David, **Party Loyalty Among Congressmen,** Cambridge, Mass.: Harvard University Press, 1966.

Miller, Clem, **Member of the House,** New York: Scribner's, 1962.

Peabody, Robert L., and Nelson W. Polsby (eds.), **New Perspectives on the House of Representatives,** 2nd ed., Skokie, Ill.: Rand McNally, 1969.

Polsby, Nelson W., **Congress and the Presidency,** Englewood Cliffs, N.J.: Prentice-Hall, 1964.

Polsby, Nelson W., Miriam Gallaher, and Barry S. Rundquist, "The Growth of the Seniority System in the U.S. House of Representatives," **American Political Science Review,** vol. LXIII, no. 3 (September, 1969).

Polsby, Nelson W., "The Institutionalization of the U.S. House of Representatives," **American Political Science Review,** vol. LXII, no. 1 (March, 1968).

Riker, William H., and Donald Niemi, "Stability of Coalitions on Roll Call Votes in the House of Representatives," **American Political Science Review,** vol. LVI, no. 1 (March, 1962).

Ripley, Randall B., **Majority Party Leadership in Congress,** Boston: Atlantic-Little, Brown, 1969.

Robinson, James A., **The House Rules Committee,** Indianapolis: Bobbs-Merrill, 1963.

Rose, Richard, **Politics in England,** Boston: Atlantic-Little, Brown, 1964.

Sampson, Anthony, **Anatomy of Britain Today,** London: Hodder and Stoughton, 1965.

Truman, David B. (ed.), **The Congress and America's Future,** Englewood Cliffs, N.J.: Prentice-Hall, 1965.

Chapter 11

Administrative Decision Making

Throughout most of history, political decision making has been the product of autocratic rule. Monarchs governed absolutely and often arbitrarily. With the industrial revolution, however, "subjects" became "workers" and "entrepreneurs"; and they strove to gain some say in the decision-making process. Their principal instrument of power was the elected legislature. Through the legislature they could control the actions of hereditary rulers and contain or remove some of the excesses of autocracy. In several countries, such as England, their fight for power was gradual and eventually complete. In others, it was more revolutionary and sometimes also less conclusive. Thus the French revolutionists overthrew the monarchy only to pave the way for the rise of Napoleon. Yet in almost all countries the legislature became increasingly active and powerful. It broadened the political base; it added a new voice to the process of conflict resolution and a new arena where demands could be raised. With a representative legislature the costs of decision making grew, but so did the democratic nature of society. More and more people were able to participate in the decision-making process.

During the nineteenth century, legislatures continued to expand in power while executive authority shrank. In the twentieth century, however, this process seems to have reversed itself. Individual leaders, complete with a growing retinue of administrative agencies, reasserted themselves as life became more complex and sophisticated. Many of the challenges of the twentieth century seemed to shake people's belief in the wisdom of legislative supremacy, and indeed, in the virtue or usefulness of democratic principles. World War I brought an end to nineteenth-century thinking far more conclusively and dramatically than the turn of the century had done. That struggle among nations changed the nature of warfare, obliterated the optimism of the Victorian period, and set into motion forces which would change the nature of life throughout the world. Wars were no longer confined or glorious, as they once had been pictured. The staggering number of deaths, the extensive destruction of property, were such that a return to prewar life was inconceivable. The very map of Europe changed drastically. The ancient Turkish and the Austro-Hungarian empires were dismembered, and new nations were created or old nations resurrected. The age of imperialist conquest drew to a close and the concept of self-determination took hold: Ineluctably, natives in colonies began to call for independence. At the same time there were many technological changes resulting from the war. The development of the airplane meant that in all future wars enemies would be able to transcend national boundaries and geographical barriers. In peacetime the airplane implied the end of physical isolation. Then the Russian Revolution set in motion forces which would be felt throughout the world for years to come. Indeed, the reverberations are still being felt.

These changes and many others, such as the development of mass communications and of the internal combustion engine, brought with them new questions and conflicts. Legislative problems mushroomed. Even technological changes greatly increased the scope of governmental activity. In some countries political authorities were set up to run the mass media facilities as government monopolies; in other countries the communications industry developed as a private enterprise, but was subject to governmental regulation and control. The rapid rate of advances in these and related fields created new economic imbalances, fostered conflict, and led to a spiraling of political demands. In every respect, life had lost its leisurely pace. Governments were faced with rapid changes which they were forced to deal with ever more quickly, even as the problems increased in complexity.

Meanwhile the world witnessed the birth of a new form of political system. The Russian Revolution brought with it the first triumph of Marxist ideology. It was a strange victory because communism triumphed first in a relatively backward almost semifeudal society rather than in highly industrialized countries such as Germany. This was the opposite of what Marx had predicted. Nevertheless, the revolution came and the Communists quickly succeeded in gaining control. Partly as a result of the changes in the twentieth century the Communists, particularly under Stalin, developed executive authority and central control that earlier monarchs could only have wished for. Furthermore, modern technology, while it meant new problems, also provided new and powerful weapons for those in the political elite who could use them. The weapons were peculiarly suited to executive use, and particularly to strong central authority such as that emerging in Russia. Many Americans, including many who were not Communists, traveled to the Soviet Union in the 1920s and 1930s to see the changes that had been brought about by Communist rule. Many, although upset by the secrecy of the regime and as yet unaware of many of the excesses of the rulers, were impressed by the obvious and rapid changes. After years of inept rule under the czars, Russia seemed to be progressing quickly into the twentieth century.

RISE OF TOTALITARIANISM IN EUROPE

The great worldwide recession which began at the end of the 1920s posed another severe test for democratic political institutions. Although most nations had nearly recovered from World War I, there were still significant soft spots in their economies. For example, in the United States the agricultural sector of the economy continued to be depressed even during the great prosperity of the 1920s. In Europe France's manpower still had not reached its prewar levels in many sectors. Germany, meanwhile, was faced with galloping inflation. During the early 1920s the savings of thousands of German citizens were wiped out in a frenetic inflationary spiral. The shocks of the war, the changes in technology, and finally the economic depression all contributed to a general feeling of skepticism about the ability of democratic institutions as a whole and about the most preeminent of those institutions, the legislature, to meet the challenges and demands of modern times. Indeed, in several countries the democratic institutions simply collapsed. As early as 1921 Benito Mussolini was in control of the Italian government. Mussolini disdained democratic institutions and felt they were anachronistic. What was important in the modern era was leadership, strength, and the ability to take decisive action. He quickly set about consolidating the Fascist hold on the country. Then, in 1923, Adolf Hitler staged his abortive coup in Munich. Though the coup failed, it revealed the precarious nature of the democratic structures of Weimar Germany. As a result of the coup, Hitler was imprisoned for a period of time. It was during this period that he wrote **Mein Kampf.** The Nazis reverted, after 1923, to parliamentary tactics and did not try to overthrow the government. Of course, the Nazi brown shirts still roamed the streets and engaged in terrorist acts. However, the main focus of the Nazi effort was to gain enough support to overthrow the system through the electoral process. Hitler had no respect for parliamentary institutions but felt that this was the best and easiest path for taking over the government. Many of the middle class were still traumatized by the inflationary spiral of the decade; many were still resentful of Germany's defeat in the war; others were upset by the rise of the Communists. These feelings, coupled with the fact that the Republic had never achieved great legitimacy in many sectors of Germany, continually swelled the total of Nazi votes. By 1932 Hitler was in virtual control of Germany. Parliamentary institutions were discarded and the darkness of the Third Reich became Germany's fate.

Meanwhile in Russia, as we have mentioned, the Communists were already in power. When Czar Nicholas II abdicated in 1917 and Alexander Kerensky's brief attempt at democratic socialism failed, the Communists took over complete control. Furthermore several other countries flirted with various forms of dictatorship. In Spain the civil war between Franco and the Republicans ended the Republic and the existence of democratic institutions there. Franco quickly began setting up institutions which emulated those of Mussolini and Hitler, his principal allies during the Civil War. After the close of World War II, Franco began to play down the Fascist elements of his rule. France, although it remained a democracy, was so immobilized by the divisions among its people that it seemed a perfect example of the failure of democratic institutions to cope with complex problems.

What must be remembered is that during this period **democracy** had become a term which was used with derision by many people. Today nearly everybody seeks to portray his actions and goals as being democratic; Communist nations declare that they are the true democracies. During the 1920s and 1930s, however, Fascists and Communists were openly talking about the failure of democracy. To them democracy was a shadow from the past which should be discarded as quickly as possible. Newer governmental forms and autocratic rule were needed to face the challenges and demands of the twentieth century. Even in the United States several political movements arose during the course of the Great Depression which declared that only with an extremely centralized authority could the government of a modern society be viable. The conclusion of World War II saw the defeat of the Fascist powers by the allies. The whole rhetoric had changed and democracy was again a word which had favorable connotations. However, while the Fascist regimes may have died, the problems which led to their rise and the demands for greater executive authority still persist. If fascism was only, one hopes, a temporary insanity, the problems which its rise reflected still pose challenges to democratic systems. It is to these problems and their impact on conflict resolution that we now turn our attention.

THE GROWTH OF BUREAUCRACY

The demands of the twentieth century have made the affairs of goverment more complex. The reaction in most democratic systems has been a growth of the bureaucracy and an increasing reliance on administrative specialization. Both the government itself and the scope and influence of its programs have grown enormously. Yet as governmental activity has multiplied, in many cases the initiative for action has passed from the legislature to the executive branch of government. This does not mean that legislatures have become anachronisms. Rather, legislators tend to draw up broad policy directives and to set the contours of action. The decisions as to the implementation of these policies, however, are left to the administrative staff of the government. It is this area of governmental activity and personnel, that amorphous and mysterious "administration," which has grown so rapidly over the past century. Furthermore, the growth of this bureaucracy and the procedures which countries adopt for administrative decision making directly affect both the manner in which conflicts are resolved and the costs of conflict resolution. Therefore, for the remainder of this chapter we shall turn our attention to the role of administrative institutions. As before, we shall emphasize American institutions and agencies, since we are most familiar with them.

THE ADMINISTRATIVE PROCESS

Perhaps because "administration" itself tends to be a broadly used term, it is rather difficult to give a precise, meaningful definition for **political administration.** Certainly we know that no piece of legislation is self-executing. Even policies which do not seem to require any special agency or organization still need to be implemented and enforced. Legislation is, of course, law; and laws are useless unless they are enforced. Were they not backed up by sanctions such as court action, fines, and jail terms, their effectiveness would depend solely upon the willingness of individual citizens to obey them. Furthermore, even should all citizens voluntarily agree to obey the law, the manner in which they do so could vary greatly depending upon their interpretation of the particular statute. Thus every government needs courts to interpret the law impartially and to punish those who break it. Every political system also needs administrative officers who will investigate cases where the laws appear to have been broken and indict the violaters.

In short, all societies need an institutional structure to see that the rules and legislation passed by that government are implemented and adhered to. This is the essence of the administrative process: **the implementation and enforcement of governmental decisions.** This process is characteristic both of the bureaucracy and of the judicial system. It is often standard procedure to separate these two in discussion. Yet their tasks are similar. In this country courts are required to interpret legislation and determine where acts are infringements of law. They also are charged with determining whether laws themselves are constitutional or not. They are intimately and continuously involved in questions of interpretation and implementation. Their decisions in many cases determine how laws will be administered and often, as in the case of school desegregation or reapportionment, the court is intimately involved in the implementation phase. For this reason we will not exclude the courts from our discussion.

Yet, if administration is confined to enforcement and implementation, how can we talk about administrative decision making? If administration just applies the law, then is not decision making, which implies discretion and freedom to choose, beyond its realm? The question is legitimate, but it reflects a certain naivete. Rarely is legislation so unambiguously worded that no interpretation is necessary. If administrators are to implement legislation, they must decide what it means, and what types of activity are consonant with it, and what types of activity would be contrary to it. Thus in all administrative acts there is an element of interpretation and decision making. Even the Bill of Rights to the Constitution, which seems to be so unambiguously worded, has been the subject of continual interpretation as to what activities are constitutional and what are not.

For example, the First Amendment to the Constitution reads:

> Congress shall make **no law** respecting an establishment of religion, or prohibiting the free exercise thereof or abridging the freedom of speech, or of the press; or the right of the people peaceably to assemble, and to petition the government for a redress of grievances. [Emphasis mine.]

This is exceptionally clear and seemingly unambiguous language. Yet innumerable laws have been passed and countless judicial opinions have been offered interpreting it. Even if we restrict our attention to the free speech clause, we can understand how seemingly clear statements leave a wide latitude for interpretation. While the Constitution states that there shall be no abridgment of free speech, libel and slander laws generally have not been interpreted as violating this prohibition. The argument is that free speech does not include the right to ruin someone's reputation unjustifiably. Obviously as soon as even one such exception is made, then the limits of free speech become a matter for interpretation, and the clear and unambiguous wording of the First Amendment is subject to debate.

Similarly, consider the first requirement of the amendment: that Congress shall pass no law concerning the establishment or free exercise of religion. Again this seems to call for a clear separation of Church and State. Yet there has been continued controversy concerning the extent to which that prohibition can be applied. There have been numerous cases concerning the constitutionality of prayer in the public schools. Recently, the Supreme Court ruled that such mandatory prayers violate the separation of Church and State, and therefore they are banned.[1]

Similarly, problems have arisen concerning provision of books and other services to students attending parochial schools. In Louisiana, Huey Long campaigned for governor in 1928 on the promise of providing free books for all the school children of the state. Previously the State Board of Education had drawn up a list of books for use in the schools, but the individual families had to buy them for their children. Often the members of the board, in collusion with some publishers, would frequently change the books so that parents could not pass the books on from children to children. Long made use of the issue and extended his promise to students who were also attending private schools, including religious schools. Many challenged the constitutionality of Long's action in implementing his campaign pledge. He maintained that the provision of textbooks in no way could be construed as state aid to religious schools. The books were for the students, not for the schools, and therefore the act would not violate the spirit of church-state separation.[2] Long's argument prevailed and he regarded this measure as an important accomplishment of his administration. The justification was a semantic one which has been used since in many states to circumvent the prohibition of state aid to religious organizations.

The wording of the amendment seems clear, but because each act tends to be interpreted independently, there seems to be much room for clarification and amplification of the original terminology. Some Americans have even questioned the tax exempt status of religious property as being a special privilege which the state has granted to established religions. These exemptions have never been disallowed, but the mere raising of the question indicates the range of interpretation possible in the federal Constitution, and equally as much among the state constitutions.

If the range of constitutional interpretation is so great, one can imagine how broad a range of interpretation exists around the enormously large numbers of legislative bills enacted into law each year. Part of this responsibility for interpretation ultimately rests with the courts.

---

[1] Engle v. Vitale, 370 U.S. 421 (1962); **Abington School District** v. **Schlempp,** 374 U.S. 203 (1963).

[2] T. Harry Williams, **Huey Long,** New York: Knopf, 1969, pp. 273–274.

However, much of the initial interpretation and implementation is the province of the bureaucracy. The latitude given particular administrative units may vary from setting to setting. In some cases legislators will hand down a broad policy directive but provide very little specific detail as to how that policy is to be implemented. In other cases the wording of the bill will be quite specific and there will be little room for interpreting the legislative mandate.

What effect has the expansion of governmental activity resulting from an increasingly complex and technological society had on the bureaucracy? As we suggested earlier, it has led to a large-scale increase in the number of government workers and a correspondingly large increase in the impact which they and their decisions have on the daily lives of citizens. The United States Congress may pass an internal revenue code and make periodic amendments to that code, but the meaning of those regulations and consequently what the individual taxpayer will or will not be allowed to deduct from his taxes is determined by a federal employee in the district office of the Internal Revenue Service. Similarly, everything that a citizen sees and hears on television is the result, to some degree, of decisions made by the members and staff of an administrative agency (the Federal Communications Commission). The FCC licenses stations, sets up operating codes; and, in terms of how well the individual stations have lived up to those codes, decides whether or not to renew their licenses. Today administrative decisions impinge upon and affect the quality and nature of life in countless ways.[3] Indeed, administrative agencies, because of their interpretative powers, do resolve conflict and distribute rewards. They too are agents for conflict resolution. With this in mind, we shall analyze some of the more important characteristics of bureaucracy and administration in the United States today.

THE ADMINISTRATIVE AGENCY

If we are to trace administrative structures resulting from the increased complexity and technological sophistication of American society, we will have to turn all the way back to the period of rapid industrialization which followed the Civil War. The postbellum period was turbulent and at times violent, but it provided many of the characteristics of modern

---

[3] For an interesting account of the rise of American bureaucracy and its impact, see Peter Woll, **American Bureaucracy,** New York: Norton, 1963.

society. This was the era of Carnegie, Rockefeller, Fisk, Gould, Vander-
bilt, and Morgan. Great fortunes were built as the giant combines,
among them United States Steel and Standard Oil, were formed. The
American Federation of Labor was established and became a large and
powerful organization. Unions were gaining strength. It was an era of
bigness and assertion of interests in every sphere of activity. Even in
foreign affairs the United States began to assert itself. The Spanish-
American War, the building of the Panama Canal, the sailing of the
White Fleet, Theodore Roosevelt's mediation in the Russo-Japanese War,
all testify to a change and a "coming of age" in the United States.
Yet along with this growth and the thrust toward bigness there were the
inevitable excesses which generated demands for governmental intervention and action.

Much of the industrial growth brought with it new problems for
the farmer. Railroads often charged the small farmer high prices for
shipping while offering sizable rebates to larger customers. This inevitably placed the small farmer at the mercy of the railroad trusts
and at a competitive disadvantage with large users. Demands swept
the agrarian regions for some sort of governmental regulation of the
railroad. Meanwhile the great accumulation of wealth continued but
was increasingly concentrated in a few hands. Labor and farm riots
were common and demands for cheap money by those who were not
sharing in the wealth increased. In the early 1890s a strong Populist
party called for inflated money and for the free and unlimited coinage
of silver. As the gap between the "haves" and "have nots" widened,
farmers and laborers formed coalitions such as the Populist party and
put ever-greater pressure on the government to act.

At the same time organized labor, just beginning to feel its strength,
made additional demands. Workers sought governmental restraints on
some business practices and called for immigration quotas. The latter
demand stemmed from the fact that immigrant workers provided a
steady stream of cheap labor which was often important in breaking
strikes. If a quota system were introduced, the supply of new workers
would dwindle and wages could be brought up to higher levels. Similarly, industrialists implored government to enact tariff legislation which
would protect their industries from foreign competition. If duties on
foreign products were raised high enough, a domestic market could be
assured and the profitability of industrialization and manufacturing
could be guaranteed. Thus cries for protectionism increased. And even

the consumer was not silent. In the rush of progress, fraud was every-where and quality control was unheard of. This, too, led to demands for prompt and effective political action.[4]

Independent Regulatory Agencies

INTERSTATE COMMERCE COMMISSION. Legislators responded to these demands in various ways. One of their most significant decisions, in terms of its later impact, was that some of the particularly complex and recurring problems, such as the railroads, could best be handled by a new type of specialized administrative machinery. As a result, they instituted the independent regulatory agency. The first of these agencies was the Interstate Commerce Commission (ICC), which was established in 1887 and was designed to regulate the transportation industry, basically the railroads. The commission was composed of eleven members who had seven-year terms. The terms were staggered. The ICC was a unique administrative agency. It was created by the Congress and was required to submit annual reports of its activities to Congress; its members were appointed by the President, but, for the most part, its decisions and policies were not subject to review. While the President appointed the members of the agency, they served for predesignated terms of office and unlike other Presidential appointees they could not be fired except on the basis of criminal misconduct. Be-cause the terms were staggered, at no time would the President be appointing all the members of the commission. Thus, if the President disapproved of their policies once they were in office, there was very little he could do. Furthermore, even though the commissioners were legally responsible to Congress, the nature and complexity of their work guaranteed that for the most part they were relatively autono-mous. The ICC was quick to respond to its mandate and instituted sev-eral rulings which prevented special rates for certain customers, prohibited rebates, and discrimination between haulers. Most reformers applauded the early work of the ICC and the commission became a model for other regulatory agencies which were to follow.

What the legislature had created was a relatively autonomous agency, not subject to popular control, with the authority to legislate and imple-ment policy within its specified area. Furthermore, the commissions enjoy

---

[4] Louis Filler, **Crusaders for American Liberalism**, New York: Harcourt Brace Jovanovich, 1939.

a semijudicial status in that they also function as an appeal board for decisions made by employees of the agency. This is a rather unique combination of powers for any organization.

The Interstate Commerce Commission was and still is concerned with the rates which railroads, buses, and trucks may charge for their services. The ICC's principal criterion in determining these rates is what it considers to be a **fair rate of return on investment** for the company. It necessarily balances the public interest with the fact that the corporations it must regulate are established as profit-making organizations. In order to calculate what a fair return would be, commissioners must calculate such highly technical questions as the proper way to depreciate assets and capital equipment of these carriers, the need for projected capital improvements, the profitability of a given aspect of service, and so forth. The commission is also empowered to award routes, and to determine whether a railroad is justified in discontinuing service on certain runs. This is a wide range of authority and one which substantially affects the life of the average citizen. Thus the ICC determines whether he will have rail transportation and how much he will pay for it, and even, to an extent, the price he will pay for most goods insofar as that price is affected by the rates for rail and truck freight hauling. Yet the average citizen has little control, direct or indirect, over the actions and decisions of the commission. Nevertheless, the blueprint laid out for the ICC has been followed by other governmental agencies.

CIVIL AERONAUTICS BOARD.   As air travel developed, it brought with it many of the same problems that the government had faced with the railroads. Interestingly enough, however, the airlines were not put under the jurisdiction of the ICC. Instead, the government created the Civil Aeronautics Board (CAB) in 1938. This five-member board was empowered with regulatory powers similar to those of the ICC but it had the exclusive responsibility for air traffic. While the CAB was an extension of the principle of administrative specialization, it brought with it certain new problems. Perhaps the most significant one to discuss is that its existence compartmentalized regulatory policy in the field of transportation. Yet this is a field which requires an integrated perspective. Rail, highway, and air transportation cannot be considered as totally separate entities. Action in one area affects the position of other industries. A decision by the ICC to discontinue passenger rail service in several states creates havoc if there is not corresponding action by the

CAB to increase air travel and short-distance flights into areas which have been abandoned by railroads.

Much of our present air traffic congestion and our declining rail passenger service might have been avoided had there been coordinated planning between the agencies regulating these two industries. It might have made sense to forego the development of air transportation on short and heavily traveled runs such as the area between Boston and Washington, and to rely instead on efficient high-speed rail transportation in these areas. Air travel could then be stressed for longer-distance flights. Much of the current congestion in the air corridors of the eastern seaboard stems from the absence of adequate transportation alternatives to the airplane. The willingness of the public to use rail transportation could be noted in the reasonable success which greeted the introduction of the Metroliner, a high-speed train between New York and Washington. Furthermore, the willingness of the ICC to allow railroads to discontinue passenger service in these areas has contributed to this strain. Indeed, the overall results of the lack of planning and coordination has been a severely imbalanced transportation network which only now is beginning to receive government help. The Department of Transportation has been providing underwriting costs and giving grants for the development of high-speed rail transportation. In general, however, the tremendous specialization among the administrative agencies has enabled each commission to bring expertise to its own particular area, but the absence of coordinating mechanisms has made it all too easy for the various agencies to foster uncoordinated and even conflicting policies.

As though the confusion between the ICC and the CAB were not sufficient, there are also several other governmental agencies which are involved in the handling of transportation problems. Perhaps the most important of these is the Department of Transportation. The department was formed in 1967 after Congress, in 1966, passed legislation requested by President Johnson authorizing such an organization. The cabinet-level department was not a particularly powerful agency. The legislation which set up the department left the Secretary with few substantial powers. The bill chiefly established the role of the Secretary as someone who would administer existing programs.[5] The establishment

[5] Congressional Quarterly, **Congress and the Nation**, vol. II, Washington, D.C.: Congressional Quarterly Service, 1969, pp. 232 ff.

of the department represented a recognition that a more coordinated approach to transportation was necessary. However, the regulatory roles of the ICC and CAB were not transferred to the department. They remained as independent agencies whose decisions were beyond the jurisdiction or control of the Secretary of the department. One of the major components of the department is the Federal Aviation Agency. This was an independent agency which became a section of the new department. The FAA has the responsibility for flight controllers, for airport planning and operation, and for setting standards for air traffic safety. The awarding of air routes and the number of carriers that can use those routes, factors which obviously affect air traffic density, are the prerogatives of the CAB. This division of responsibility without the legal means to achieve coordination leads to increasing confusion. Similarly, the ICC has its counterpart in the section of the department dealing with railroads, the Federal Railroad Administration. Yet one may find that at the same time that the department has placed special emphasis on developing high-speed rail systems as an effective alternative to air travel, the ICC has been approving the requests of many railroads in this same area to suspend or curtail passenger service.

A distressing example of the lack of coordinated planning can be seen in the ICC's regulation of commuter rail lines. Over the years the railroads have been seeking to rid themselves of the responsibility for providing rail service from outlying suburban areas into the central cities. They have maintained that this cannot be made a profitable service, and therefore, they should not be expected to continue to bear the cost of subsidizing it. The commission usually has granted reductions in, and in some cases outright suspensions of, service. The result has been, of course, to force thousands of commuters to drive to and from work. This, in turn, has led to demands for better highway facilities and better access roads to the cities. City governments have had to struggle with handling the increased traffic; indeed the failure to integrate rail service into the larger system of metropolitan transportation has created severe congestion, pollution, and noise in the cities. The solution to some of these problems, if a solution exists, can only be found in achieving some degree of coordination among the several agencies and governmental units which determine transportation policies.

Yet even the Department of Transportation, with its subsidiary agencies, does not end the list of fingers thrust into the transportation pie. All requests for mergers among transportation corporations must go through hearings and be approved by the appropriate regulatory agency. Thus the merger of the now bankrupt New York Central and the Pennsylvania Railroad had to be approved by the ICC. Similarly, mergers in the airline industries have needed CAB sanction. The approval of the regulatory commission, however, may not be sufficient in and of itself; it does not indicate that other agencies of the government approve of the merger. Each merger proposal is independently studied by the antitrust division of the Justice Department. Should this division feel that a merger of the lines would be a substantial restriction of competition and thus not be in the national interest, it can threaten to go to court and block the merger. While the division does not have the power to call off a merger, its threat to contest such mergers in federal courts is often sufficient to either block the merger altogether or substantially alter the terms of the proposed agreement.

There is no intrinsic conflict between the antitrust division and the regulatory agencies, but in fact they have somewhat different perspectives on merger activity. The antitrust division tends to be skeptical about mergers. The tone of the division and the rationale behind its founding suggests hesitancy toward all mergers, regardless of the industry in which they are taking place. The ICC and the CAB, on the other hand, are simply concerned with providing better and more efficient transportation and assumes that this, as much as competition, is a goal which the average citizen desires. Thus there have been several clashes in which a merger has been granted approval by the regulatory commission and subsequently challenged in court by the Justice Department.

FEDERAL RESERVE BOARD. Transportation is but one of several instances where administrative specialization leads to conflict and the problems of uncoordinated action. There is a similar split between a cabinet-level department and an independent agency in determining and regulating financial policy. Both the Treasury Department and Federal Reserve Board have considerable influence over the economic policies of the government and, consequently, the economy of the country. The Treasury Department, of course, is responsible for coordinating government expenditures, overseeing the collection of tax revenues, and making recommendations along with the Council of Economic Advisors concerning governmental activity in the economic sphere. The Federal Reserve Board is an autonomous agency, in some respects similar to the

ICC and other regulatory agencies. It was established in 1913 and was an attempt to give some coherence to what had, till then, been a rather chaotic banking system in this country. The Federal Reserve Act divided the country into twelve Federal Reserve districts. Each district has its own Federal Reserve Bank, which acts as a central clearing house for the commercial banks in that region. These Reserve Banks are actually private corporations. All the banks are coordinated by a seven-man Board of Governors of the Federal Reserve System in Washington. This is what is commonly referred to as the Federal Reserve Board. The members of the board are appointed by the President for fourteen-year terms. The powers of the board are quite extensive and exercise a profound influence on the nation's economy. The Federal Reserve Board, among its many powers, has two activities which are most effective: its open market operations and its regulation of the discount rate.

The Open Market Committee consists of five representatives from the twelve regional banks and the seven members of the board. Through the decisions of the committee as to whether it will buy or sell government securities, it has an enormous impact on the amount of money in circulation. By selling securities, especially in large amounts, it can contract the money supply. By buying securities, it can expand the amount of money in circulation.[6] The discount-rate power of the board relates to the fact that this rate determines the costs to member banks in borrowing from the Federal Reserve system. If the board sets the discount rate at a high level, it makes credit tight and can dampen what the board considers to be a too rapid expansion in the economy. By lowering the rate, the board can stimulate the growth of credit and indirectly be a significant factor in expansion of the economy.[7] Within recent years, because of the inflationary pressures in the economy, the Federal Reserve Board has kept the supply of credit limited by imposing a high discount figure. The premise behind such action is that reducing the supply of credit will result in an easing of consumer demand because of the expense of borrowing money to finance purchases. Fewer buyers (less demand) will hopefully lead, in turn, to a stabilization of prices and a leveling off of inflation. In times of recession the lowering of the discount rate increases credit and should encourage businessmen and consumers to spend.

---

[6] Paul A. Samuelson, **Economics,** 7th ed., New York: McGraw-Hill, 1967, p. 301.
[7] Ibid., pp. 302 ff.

This is an oversimplified version of the activities of the Federal Reserve Board, but for our purposes it is sufficient. In general, the board is empowered with several other forms of monetary control. The Treasury Department, through its control of taxation and government spending wields great fiscal powers. In times of inflation the Treasury will try to limit government spending, to limit the amount of money entering the economy, and thereby seek to limit demand which is pushing prices upward. The Treasury and the President may even request tax increases in order to take more money out of circulation. In times of recession, the Treasury may seek to expand government spending to get more money into the economy or it may provide for a tax cut to increase the available supply of money in the economy. While both bodies are concerned with avoiding either inflation or recession, their estimates of the needs of a particular time may vary. The executive branch and the Federal Reserve Board tend to work reasonably closely together; however, there is room for disagreements as to whether the government should be pursuing expansionist or contractionist policies. These clashes have periodically occurred.

Such a disagreement arose in the early 1960s. President Kennedy and his advisers had concluded that the country was in need of strong action to get the economy moving. Many, including John Kenneth Galbraith, maintained that the government's response should be the traditional one of increasing governmental expenditures.[8] Others, led by Walter Heller, felt that the economy would recover more swiftly and completely if the President would recommend and Congress pass a tax cut. Heller's reasoning was that the tax cut would increase the supply of money available for purchase immediately and therefore would affect the economy more quickly than expanded government spending. He won his point and Kennedy recommended the tax cut. This was a victory for what was popularly called at the time the "new economics." Congress was quite slow in responding to the request. The idea that one should deliberately plan a budget deficit to aid the economy was repugnant to many congressmen. It was not until after Kennedy's assassination that the tax cut finally went through. Nevertheless, the President's rationale was that the tax rates should also be considered one of

---

[8] John Kenneth Galbraith, **Ambassador's Journal,** Boston: Houghton Mifflin, 1969, pp. 331, 341–342. Galbraith felt that the tax cut was premature at the time and that if events later made action necessary, increased government spending would be more sensible.

the tools which government could use to foster a healthy economy. In times of distress, taxes should be lowered to free more purchasing power, while in times of inflation the tax base should be raised as a means of reducing consumer demands. Galbraith's argument against this proposition rested in part upon practicality. He maintained that if legislators cut taxes, they would face great political difficulty in raising them again when circumstances warranted. This, of course, is true. What Galbraith did not consider was that governmental programs of increased expenditures are equally difficult to cut back when the times require budget cutting. In other words, both fiscal strategies are not, in practice, as reversible or flexible as their proponents claimed.

Throughout the entire debate many Kennedy advisers pinned much of the blame for the depressed state of the economy on the actions of the Federal Reserve Board. The board had been holding a tight rein on the availability of credit, and this was causing cutbacks in industrial expansion and production. Many conservative economists felt that a tax cut would not stabilize the economy, but because of an unbalanced budget would stimulate inflation. Kennedy and his advisers retorted that at times an unbalanced budget is a necessity. Meanwhile members of the board, including its then chairman, William McChesney Martin, a highly respected figure in financial circles, did not accept the validity of the Kennedy advisers' assessment of the economic situation. During much of this period, while Treasury and Presidential policy was aimed at increasing the supply of money, the board continued its tight money policy. The two agencies of government were pursuing contradictory policies. Yet the only weapon the President had in his arguments was that of persuasion. He could not force any member of the board to resign. Indeed, Martin offered to resign. Because of Martin's standing in the financial community and his long years of service on the board, however, his resignation might have caused Kennedy even greater trouble than his presence on the board did. In any case, there was no mechanism which could force agreement. The Federal Reserve Board was developed to handle specific, and often very complex, aspects of the economy. Yet its autonomous position and limited purview raise the specter of continued conflicts between it and the President and the Treasury.

OTHER INDEPENDENT AGENCIES. Even had we avoided the problem of coordination between the independent regulatory agency and the department, or executive agency at least nominally under the control of the President, we would still see all too many examples of lack of administrative coordination. For example, during the 1960s the Kennedy and Johnson administrations both promised a concerted attack on poverty in the United States. That program took shape under the Johnson administration. Poverty is obviously a multifaceted problem which requires programs in housing, job training, medical care, and education—not to mention an overhaul of the existing social welfare programs. The administrative response to these needs has been both to segment and disperse poverty programs among the several government agencies and to create a new agency, the Office of Economic Opportunity (OEO) which has been given responsibility for certain new programs for the "war on poverty." In addition to the work of the OEO, job training has been placed in the hands of the Department of Labor; most educational and medical programs are under the supervision of the Department of Health, Education and Welfare; housing programs are carried out by the Department of Housing and Urban Development; and aid to small businesses and development of industry in economically depressed areas are programs administered by the Department of Commerce. The inevitable results of this hodgepodge of control and authority have been an absence of coordination, competition among the various agencies for limited funds, and an overall lack of direction among the various segmented efforts. The "war on poverty" has turned into many only vaguely related skirmishes. In part this segmentation is a reflection of an incremental style of decision making. New programs are grafted onto old ones and there is little comprehensive change of structures and programs to meet challenges.

The problems of coordination and complexity loom even greater when we realize that in a federal system such as the United States, much of the dispersion and overlap among agencies that we have seen on the federal level are duplicated in the states. Most states have regulatory agencies similar to the federal ones to handle those aspects of commerce and regulation of utilities which specifically pertain to them. For instance, the American Telephone and Telegraph Company is responsible for approval of its rates on long-distance or interstate telephone calls to the Federal Communications Commission (FCC). The constituent parts of the company, however, notably the local Bell Systems which provide the statewide services, are subject to the regulation of state agencies for their internal rate schedules. All state governments have several such departments which may or may not enjoy autonomy from the governor. Yet even when they are subject to the governor's control, the difficulty of providing coordinated approaches to problems within the state and between the states and the federal government often become awesome in magnitude.

One last, and relatively recent, example of administrative specialization and complexity can be seen in the rise of the public corporation. Public corporations, like so many other specialized agencies, have been formed by the legislature to handle specific and complex problems which are perceived as being impossible to handle through existing government organizations. When Roosevelt decided, during the course of the Depression, to begin an extensive project to control flooding and produce electric power in the Tennessee Valley, a separate and independent government agency was set up. The project had long been a pet scheme of former Senator George Norris of Nebraska. The act was seen as a means of reducing the threat of disastrous and periodic flooding to the area and as a means of providing rural electrification to vast areas at a relatively cheap cost. Because of fears of political influence, it was decided to set up the Tennessee Valley Authority as a public corporation directly removed from political influence. The authority was organized along the lines of a private corporation. The success of the TVA has led to its emulation elsewhere.

Another example of a public authority is the Port of New York Authority, established in 1921. Through the years the states of New York and New Jersey have shared common port problems. The condition of New York Harbor and the ability of the port to handle and move cargo efficiently affects both sides. The establishment of the Port of Authority was an attempt to handle the common problems in a nonpartisan and ostensibly businesslike basis. The legislatures of the two states drew up and signed a compact charging the new agency with renovating and modernizing port facilities and related commerce activities and facilities. The corporation was set up and capitalized through the sale of bonds to investors, the attempt to place the operation of the port on a businesslike basis. The Port of New York Authority is a big business. Its holdings are valued at upward of $2 billion.[9]

The Port of New York Authority has control over the major bridges and tunnels linking New York and New Jersey. It has modernized the port facilities, built a major bus terminal in New York City, and is

---

[9] Duane Lockard, **The Politics of State and Local Government**, 2nd ed., New York: Macmillan, 1969, pp. 491–494.

financing the construction of what will be the world's tallest buildings, the twin towers of the World Trade Center in New York City. Despite this impressive record, several significant criticisms have been leveled against the Port of Authority. Most of them have revolved around the autonomous, and at times imperious, nature of the authority. It has tended to be secretive, has denied governmental bodies access to its books, and at times has appeared more concerned with protecting the interests of its bondholders than in promoting those projects which are. in the general public welfare. For example, the Port of Authority has been very reluctant to take over or tackle some of the problems of the commuter railroads because these tend to be unprofitable enterprises. It was only after pressure was exerted by the state legislatures and challenges from several prominent political figures that the authority agreed to take over the operations of the vital Hudson and Manhattan Tube lines. Having done so, however, it transformed the lines from a rickety and collapsing subway to the modern and efficient Port Authority Trans-Hudson (PATH) system. However, the Port of Authority has been reluctant to take over many of the problems of other commuter railroads into the New York City metropolitan area. Its critics have charged that it is much more concerned with profit-making operations such as bridges and tunnels than it is with solving some other basic problems. However, it must be noted that part of the criticism directed at the Port of Authority exists precisely because the authority has been relatively successful in many of the operations it has undertaken.

Indeed, the Port of Authority, like most of the administrative agencies discussed, has exemplified both the good and bad features of specialization. Such agencies tend to generate groups with specific and professional expertise, but at the same time they may resist and even destroy governmental efforts to coordinate policies and programs. The proliferation of these agencies, who after all compete with each other for scarce resources, at times has hindered as much as helped the resolution of conflict. Yet there are still other implications to the functional specialization and overall decentralization of administration. To these implications we now turn.

SPECIALIZED ADMINISTRATION AND PRIVATE INTERESTS

We have indicated how many of the decisions which affect our daily lives are made in administrative offices. These decisions usually do not reflect spectacular or newsworthy conflicts. Yet these decisions are the result of negotiations, bargains, and coalitions made among decision makers and the persons or organizations who will be affected. What, then, are the effects of administrative specialization likely to be on these decisions? How will administrative agencies respond to the various coalitions and interests which are represented in the decision-making process?

Much of the literature in political science has emphasized that a fragmented or pluralistic decision-making structure allows persons and groups increased access to the political process. Indeed we have seen how the various levels of government multiply the number of points at which persons may raise demands and where decisions may be made. Yet there are certain costs of access to the political process, and these costs may vary from one political body to the next. Certainly it requires more sophistication to be able to locate administrative agencies than it does to put political pressure on elected officials who are much more visible and whose future is, to some degree, dependent upon their political support. Let us investigate the ramifications of the problem of responsiveness.

Some impressive research, done at the Survey Research Center of the University of Michigan, has suggested that group membership tends to be a class-related phenomenon. Upper-class persons are far more likely to belong to organizations, and to more organizations, than lower-class persons.[10] If effectiveness in a decentralized administrative system is a function of organizational sophistication, then even in the United States (which seems to have organizations, associations, and clubs for everything) there will be probably large-scale inequities concerning the degree of access which various strata of society have to governmental decision makers. This inequity will be particularly great in those areas, such as the administrative agencies, where access requires the most organizational sophistication.

If we look back at our discussion of the formation of coalitions (p. 64 ff.), we will remember that one of the primary purposes of coalitions and organizations is to allow those who singly possess only modest means to join together and unite their resources so that collectively they will have the influence they would not have separately. When organizational membership is class-related, however, the amount of

[10] Bernard R. Berelson, Paul F. Lazarsfeld, and William McPhee, **Voting**, Chicago: University of Chicago Press, 1954, pp. 52–53.

equalization which is achieved through organization or coalition forming is bound to be reduced. The implications of specialization on this
process become clear when we look at what has occurred in several
American regulatory agencies. Again, let us emphasize the importance
of these independent agencies. There are about fifty-eight of them, and
they employ some 350,000 people. In sheer volume, if not importance,
of decision making, these agencies perform the great mass of the
legislative work of the government.[11]

Today many of the industries which originally fought so hard against
the formation of the regulatory agencies have made such agencies useful allies. The agencies often serve as a buffer between the public and
the particular industry. In the case of the regulation of public utilities,
this is an important function. The determination of utility rates is always
a controversial problem: The utility company usually feels that its rates
are too low to guarantee a decent rate of return on investment, while
consumers feel that the rates are too high. The regulatory agency, then,
tends to serve as the mediator and to diffuse anger over rate increases.
The complicated procedural patterns of the agencies and their tendency
to have low visibility to the public make them difficult targets for political
reprisal. Indeed this pattern in many ways has decreased the amount
of citizen control over the agencies. Citizens may even begin to feel
that the conflict is utilities plus regulatory agency versus consumers.

In fact, the development of a close relationship between the regulatory agencies and the industries under their control has been described
as part of the normal life cycle of the agency. One political scientist
has noted that

> During old age the working agreement that a commission reaches
> with the regulated interests becomes so fixed that the agency
> has no creative force left to mobilize against the regulated
> groups. Its primary mission is the maintenance of the **status quo**
> in the regulated industry and its own position as recognized
> protector of the industry. The institutionalization of favoritism
> toward dominant groups in the regulated industries is fostered
> by the narrow jurisdiction of the commission. Dealing with only
> one industry or a group of related industries, its vision of the

---

[11] Anthony Lewis, "To Regulate the Regulators," reprinted in Samuel Krislov and
Lloyd D. Musolf (eds.), **The Politics of Regulation,** Boston: Houghton Mifflin, 1964, p. 7.

public interest lacks the breadth and scope that a wider jurisdiction would tend to force upon it.[12]

There are numerous examples of a close relationship between regulatory agencies and the regulated industries. The Civil Aeronautics
Board, shortly after World War II, discouraged the establishment of
coach fares. Representatives of the nonscheduled airlines had suggested
these lower fares but the large carriers protested. The CAB remained
sympathetic to the giants of the industry, and it was not until later that
coach fares were introduced and became standard procedure. Similarly,
after the conclusion of the war, there were attempts to shift all television
to ultrahigh frequencies (UHF) because the UHF band is broader and
would allow a wider array of stations and broadcasting operations.
The opposition of the networks to the cost of the changeover and the
additional competition which would result from it was sufficient to
prevent the FCC from making any decision to shift the frequency bands.

Thus the narrow range of issues with which the agencies are concerned tends to isolate them from other issues of concern. Constant
interaction between the regulatory agency and the regulated industries
has developed a sense of cooperation among the groups and often the
consumer is the outside belligerent. Industries are often the biggest
supporters of maintaining the regulatory commission structure. Not only
have the agencies tended to favor industry but they tend to favor the
established companies over newcomers and innovators.

ADMINISTRATIVE SPECIALIZATION AND DEMOCRATIC RESPONSIVENESS

The creation of functionally distinct and specialized agencies and the
proliferation of administrative units does mean that, by the sheer law
of numbers, there are more organizations from which the individual
citizen or group of citizens can seek redress of grievances. The problem
which arises, however, is that the development of numerous access
points often, although not necessarily, occurs at the expense of coordinating the suggestions and demands which are raised. Without
coordinating mechanisms, demands, instead of being acted upon, may
remain pigeonholed in the particular agency or organization. Or even
if such demands receive favorable action, the results may be far less

---

[12] Marver H. Bernstein, "The Life Cycle of Regulatory Commissions," reprinted in
Samuel Krislov and Lloyd D. Musolf (eds.), **The Politics of Regulation**, Boston: Houghton
Mifflin, pp. 85-86.

than the individual or group expected because of contrary policies or decisions made in other governmental agencies. While a proliferation of agencies may raise people's expectations for achieving quick action, such structures may even slow down the process of achieving meaningful results. Beyond this, as we have seen, specialization may also lead to a very close liaison between the individual administrative agency and its clientele. This tends to narrow the focus of concern of the agency and bring about a system of negotiations which, while perhaps representative of the industries being regulated, may not reflect the range of interests which exist in the country around these issues.

The questions we have raised about administrative decision making are not unique to the United States. All technologically advanced societies suffer from the strains of developing efficient and responsive administrative structures. Many of the criticisms that have been made about the United States have been made in other countries as well. A Norwegian political scientist, Stein Rokkan, raises similar questions about his own country. He notes that the increasingly close liaison between affected groups and governmental decision makers often means that the negotiators, in communicating with each other continuously, tend to lose touch with the country as a whole and to insulate themselves from the demands of the average citizen.[13] To a degree this threatens the democratic character of society. It results in many of the crucial decisions being made not by elected officials but rather by administrators in consultation with those few who have gained access to the administrative structure. A Briton, Samuel Finer, makes similar observations about the policy-making process in Great Britain.[14]

We need not imply that decision makers and powerful industries are conspiring against the public. There is no plot to destroy democratic institutions. Rather, we are simply acknowledging the problems faced by complex democratic societies in developing administrative structures which will provide needed technical expertise and yet minimize the problems of overspecialization and consequent insulation. A bureaucratic system should enable citizens both to raise demands and to be granted action on their demands. The response of the bureaucracy to the demands of the population and the way in which administrators interpret legislative and court decisions comprise a crucial aspect of the

---

[13] Stein Rokkan, "Norway: Numerical Democracy and Corporate Pluralism," in Robert A. Dahl (ed.), **Political Opposition in Western Democracies**, New Haven, Conn.: Yale University Press, 1966, p. 114.

[14] Samuel Finer, **Anonymous Empire**, London: Pall Mall Press, 1958.

political process. They contribute significantly to the degree to which a society responds to and is capable of achieving action on its conflicts. Indeed, the bureaucratic structure may be one of the key factors influencing whether or not people are willing to work within the existing system; citizens will plan their strategies according to what sort of action has gotten results in the past. If decision makers become too isolated, if their decisions create more inequalities and problems instead of less, and the average citizen has no way of reaching them, then people will become increasingly less willing to work within approved channels. This can pose a highly volatile situation and conflicts may erupt in many, and potentially more disruptive, forms.

Although we have stressed some of the disadvantages of administrative specialization and bureaucratic structures, we must remember that all structures impose their costs. Centralization, as we indicated in Chapter 9, poses distinct problems and threats to a democratic society. Decentralization is inefficient and at times may result in many independent structures. Yet decentralization and the multiplicity of agencies can offer greater stimuli for innovation than a strongly centralized system would. Decentralization and fragmentation means that there are multiple agencies performing similar tasks who are in competition with each other for scarce resources. Thus each organization must demonstrate its ability to implement programs and to establish the support it needs in its battle for appropriations. The competitive nature of this process, while perhaps inefficient, does serve as a potential source of flexibility and innovation.

Administrative structures impose costs, no matter what their nature is. The challenge for democratic systems is to develop relatively open administrative structures which will provide multiple points of access, and yet at the same time to be able to integrate and coordinate demands into meaningful programs of action. Administrative agencies must be able to assure specialized professional treatment of problems and yet avoid becoming isolated.[15]

CONCLUSION

We have discussed several of the aspects of legislative and administrative decision making. In both cases, the institutions may not be dealing

---

[15] For a serious and provocative discussion of the problems of administration and democracy, see Grant McConnell, **Private Power and American Democracy,** New York: Knopf, 1966.

with spectacular conflicts daily. Nevertheless, the way that the decision makers respond to minor conflicts will affect their ability to respond to deep-rooted conflict whenever it appears. In Chapter 12 we shall discuss some of the alternatives available to these decision makers as they respond to conflict and seek to prevent it from destroying the political and social institutions of the society.

SUGGESTED READINGS

Blau, Peter M., and W. Richard Scott, **Formal Organizations,** San Francisco: Chandler, 1962.

Cronin, Thomas E., and Sanford D. Greenberg (eds.), **The Presidential Advisory System,** New York: Harper & Row, 1969.

Downs, Anthony, **Inside Bureaucracy,** Boston: Atlantic-Little, Brown, 1967.

Edelman, Murray, **The Symbolic Uses of Politics,** Urbana: University of Illinois Press, 1964.

Finer, Samuel, **Anonymous Empire,** London: Pall Mall Press, 1958.

Kariel, Henry S., **The Decline of American Pluralism,** Stanford, Calif.: Stanford University Press, 1961.

Krislov, Samuel, and Lloyd Musolf (eds.), **The Politics of Regulation,** Boston: Houghton Mifflin, 1964.

LaPalombara, Joseph (ed.), **Bureaucracy and Political Development,** Princeton, N.J.: Princeton University Press, 1963.

McConnell, Grant, **Private Power and American Democracy,** New York: Knopf, 1967.

March, James G., and Herbert A. Simon, **Organizations,** New York: Wiley, 1958.

Peabody, Robert L., and Francis E. Rourke, "Public Bureaucracies," **The Handbook of Organizations,** Skokie, Ill.: Rand McNally, 1965.

Rokkan, Stein, "Norway: Numerical Democracy and Corporate Pluralism," in Robert A. Dahl (ed.), **Political Opposition in Western Democracies,** New Haven, Conn.: Yale University Press, 1966.

Rourke, Francis E., **Bureaucracy, Politics, and Public Policy,** Boston: Atlantic-Little, Brown, 1969.

Sayre, Wallace S., and Herbert Kaufman, **Governing New York City,** New York: Russell Sage Foundation, 1960.

Simon, Herbert A., **Administrative Behavior,** 2nd ed., New York: Macmillan, 1957.

Wildavsky, Aaron, **Dixon-Yates,** New Haven, Conn.: Yale University Press, 1962.

Wildavsky, Aaron, **The Politics of the Budgetary Process,** Boston: Atlantic-Little, Brown, 1964.

Woll, Peter, **American Bureaucracy,** New York: Norton, 1963.

Chapter 12

Responses to Conflict

We have analyzed the nature and dynamics of conflict and the way in which decision makers affect the capacity of a political system to act upon and contain conflicts. Yet we must remember that not all societies are constantly torn by struggles. Indeed, in many societies cooperation and mutual interests may be far more evident than conflict and stress. We have focused on conflict primarily because it is interesting and visible and because it has so many ramifications within the political process. Furthermore, whether to a greater or lesser extent, conflict does exist in all societies. Therefore, in this final chapter we shall consider the ways in which political systems contain conflict and assure the continuity of the political process. In doing so, we shall bring together many of the principles and considerations which we have discussed in previous chapters.

POLITICS AND CONTINUITY: TRANSFERS OF AUTHORITY

The question of the continuity of the political process implies the most basic of all political conflicts, and this is perhaps the most suitable place to begin. If the political system is to be dynamic and continuing, it must allow for the transfer of political authority from one set of rulers to the next. All political systems develop some sort of channels for this transfer of power. In almost any society there are numerous people who desire such authority. Who is to get it? There are several means by which governments have answered this question. Political authority historically has been most commonly transferred by the hereditary principle. Other means have been elections and force.

Each of these channels has been discussed in many political treatises. **Heredity** is the most simple and least likely to be ambiguous. It simply means that upon the death or abdication of the present ruler, his eldest son, daughter, or specified kin accedes to the position of power. States varied in their rules about succession. Some prevented women from inheriting political power.

Elections are a second means of transferring power. By the electoral system candidates must "run," or declare themselves eligible for and interested in the particular office. In accordance with the rules for the given system, those eligible to vote must then select the winner from among all the candidates.

The third means of transferring power, **coercion,** falls into a somewhat different category from the other methods. When power changes hands repeatedly through the use of violence, whether it be through coups, revolutions, or assassinations, we can usually assume that the society has failed to establish well-agreed-upon criteria for the manner in which political authority should be transferred. The more frequently such violent takeovers occur, the greater the instability and the greater the likelihood of some form of force as the basis of rule.

Societies have differed not only in the procedures which they have used to transfer political authority but also in the degree to which those procedures have been accepted. For example, in the 1970 presidential elections in Colombia, supporters of former dictator General Rojas threatened not to accept the results of the elections and to use force as necessary to bring Rojas back to power. The attempt was unsuccessful but it demonstrated that there were segments of the country which were unwilling to abide by the results of the electoral process. Where such feelings are common and acted upon, elections only become a prelude to a battle of force as the means for deciding who shall have political authority. Obviously, providing peaceful methods for the transfer of political authority is not always sufficient to preclude the possibility of violence. The success of peaceful methods depends upon their acceptance by the population. If they are not perceived as legitimate, they may quickly be followed or even replaced by violence. But let us assume that the citizens of a society will accept peaceful methods for transferring political power, what methods does the political system have for peacefully coping with other forms of political conflict?

MODES OF CONFLICT RESOLUTION

As we indicated in Chapter 6, political conflicts ultimately are questions of distribution. They arise and must be dealt with continuously. The nature of the political and institutional setting affects the manner in which societies respond to conflicts and even, in many cases, conditions the types of conflict that they are likely to handle.

Federation

As we have seen time and again, conflicts often arise from the heterogeneous nature of a society. Many countries may include within their borders different nationalities, religions, races, and so forth. As these varying groups interact with each other to reach common distributional decisions, they are likely to have opposing goals which inevitably lead to conflict. A relatively common solution to heterogeneity has been the structuring of a society along federal or confederational lines. A **federation** is a union of relatively autonomous units, each of which maintains some degree of control over certain functions while leaving control over other functions to the central government. In the United States, for example, education generally has been left to the states while national defense is the responsibility of the federal government. In some federations the central government may be limited to relatively few and highly circumscribed functions. In others it may be strong and very few areas will be left to the discretion of the regional units. The United States, Canada, Switzerland, Australia, and (according to its constitution) the Soviet Union are all examples of federal systems.

One of the primary reasons for establishing a federal system is that it offers a means of escaping many potentially divisive issues. In countries which have sharp regional differences among cultures, languages, and races, a federal system can reduce the degree of conflict considerably. It does so by limiting the amount to which these various components of society have to interact with each other. If we assume for the moment that a country is heterogeneous and that the diverse groups are regionally concentrated, we can see some of the advantages of federalism. If these regions are granted autonomy over certain governmental functions, they need not agree with other dissimilar regions as to how these functions should be handled. In essence what federation does is to remove many divisive issues from national control, thus decreasing the possibility that conflict will arise over such issues. The central government concerns itself with problems such as national security, currency regulation, postal service, which are less likely to be highly divisive, at least along regional lines. In this sense, federation can be regarded as an avoidance strategy. It is adopted to provide a system of conflict resolution which will not endanger the existence of the society.

THE SOVIET UNION.   The Soviet Union is, as we noted, a federal system. Throughout Russian history both the czars and the Communists have taken various courses of action concerning the highly heterogeneous population included within the Russian land mass. Soviet territory stretches from Finland to Alaska in the north, and from the Bosporus straits to Manchuria, Korea, and Japan in the south, spanning eastern Europe, Asia Minor, the Middle and Far East. Within the area of some 8.5 million square miles there are many national and ethnic groups. Among the European segment of the population there are four principal nationalities: the Russians, the Byelorussians, the Ukranians, and the Baltic nations of Latvia, Estonia, and Lithuania. Also included in this area are the Georgians and the Armenians. In the Asiatic regions there are Mongolians, Kurds, Indians, Eskimos, and various other nationalities. Religiously the Soviet Union is composed of Russian Orthodox, Catholics, Moslems, and Jews. Under the Communists all religions are discouraged, of course.

It is easy to see why both the size and the heterogeneity of its peoples has always posed problems for Russian leaders. There nearly always have been varying demands for recognition of regional languages and dialects and the normal conflict among groups over their share of resources and government aid. In order to weld this land mass together, the czars often pursued policies of enforced Russification. This policy was based on the assumption that in order to build a unified country it was necessary to suppress regional differences. Therefore, no languages except Russian could be taught in the schools, publications in regional dialects were discouraged, and the Russian Orthodox Church was championed. The czars strove to create one national language and culture which would then help unify this huge territory. They were not always successful. Forced Russification brought with it periodic minority uprisings within the various regions. The individual ethnic groups felt suppressed and highly discontented. Since the Communist Revolution the government has pursued policies vacillating from a willingness to allow great latitude to regional variations and cultures to forced Russification similar to that of the czars. Structurally the Soviets have formed a federal system composed of various republics and autonomous regions. There were significant political reasons for adopting this strategy initially. The Communists were anxious to consolidate their support after the Revolution. They realized that much of the resentment of the non-Russian population was directed at the Czarist policies of Russian supremacy. They therefore employed federalism and autonomy as tactics to gain the support of the various ethnic groups. Their policy of granting autonomy is, of course, restricted by the highly centralized decision-making system, and more often than not regional autonomy has existed only on paper. Nevertheless, the constitutional framework of the Soviet Union is a federal system and is a recognition of the heterogeneous base of the population.

THE AUSTRIAN EMPIRE. Similarly, in the Austrian Empire one of the constant causes of friction was the diversity of ethnic and national groups. Included in the empire were German-speaking groups, Slavs, Hungarians, and various other groups including, in the Tyrolean, Italians. Indeed, the empire became known as the Austro-Hungarian Empire after the nationalist uprisings in which the Hungarians demanded parity with the Austrians. The renaming of the empire involved granting autonomy to the Hungarians in the hope that, by easing the degree to which Hungarians and Austrians had to interact with each other, the empire could thus be preserved. After World War I and the defeat of the empire, however, it was split up and various nationality groups were given their independence.

CANADA. The Canadian confederation[1] is another example of the attempt to use a federal structure to resolve or avoid conflicts among

---

[1] The terms "federation" and "confederation" are used interchangeably, although the latter usually indicates a weaker form of union.

diverse population groups. When Canada achieved its Dominion status (for all practical purposes Dominion status was similar to independence except for the nominal unifying force of the monarchy), it had to devise a system of government which would not exacerbate the hostility between the French- and English-speaking populations. The French Canadians violently opposed the establishment of a strong central government because they knew that they, as the minority group, would quickly have their influence diluted in any formal centralized system. Even the existence of a federal system, however, has not ended the antagonism between French- and English-speaking citizens. The Canadian federation is often strained today and the problem of French separatism and the recurring cry for the secession of Quebec from the federation have been and are significant problems.

THE UNITED STATES.   The Civil War in the United States is another example of a struggle concerning the nature of the federal union. It was a debate over the extent of the federal government's power with respect to the states. This had been a question which was significant in this country since the first days of independence. The first constitution, the Articles of Confederation, had established the country as a very weak union, granting very few powers to the national government. The Constitution changed this and strengthened the powers of the central government considerably. Yet the question still persisted.

The primary question at the time of the Civil War was whether the union, or the federation, was ultimately a voluntary or involuntary association. President Lincoln maintained that, while the United States represented a voluntary federation at the time of its founding, no constituent unit had the right to withdraw from it afterward. Indeed, the Constitution does not mention withdrawal and this omission strengthened Lincoln's argument. The South, however, sought to weaken the nature of the powers of the federal government. Southern spokesmen claimed that the central government had seized too many powers from the states and therefore had broken the covenant of union. The contract either had to be reformulated or voided. The North, of course, rejected this assertion, and the conflict ultimately was resolved through the use of force. The North's conception of one indivisible union was triumphant only because the North was able to muster superior force for its position.

Even today, however, the old battle of federal versus states rights is relevant. As the federal government has extended the scope and magnitude of its activities, there have been continued challenges and debates as to whether these activities are violations of the powers reserved to the states. Since the close of the Civil War, however, the federal government has increased in power and, despite the protests of states rights advocates, the courts have tended to rule that such extensions of power are proper and constitutional.

Although federalism and reserving certain government functions for the states or provinces often does ward off conflict, it can occasionally lead to new and equally perplexing problems. For example, the resources of the state or provincial authority are not so great as those of the federal authorities. As the scope of local activities grows, the burdens which such activities place on local governmental resources must also increase. This has happened in the United States in the field of education. As elementary and secondary education have become universal, local and state governments have had to foot a constantly rising bill for education. In this country the bulk of government resources are raised through the federal income tax. The federal government has first crack at the taxpayers' dollars. The state and local governments are left to finance their operations with the dollars that are left. Obviously the extent of federal taxation limits the taxes which states and localities can levy. With increased demands for better education at all levels and for some provision of tuition-free state and community colleges, the need for funds has continued to rise, sometimes at alarming rates. Local governments have begged the states to assume a greater percentage of the educational burden, and state governments in turn have demanded that the federal government spend an increasing percentage of its tax revenues on education.

In this situation, two attempts to reduce conflict have brought about a conflict of their own. The decentralization of school administration was designed to avoid the problems which would arise from a nationally centralized administration of education which, of necessity, could not take into account local variations and needs. Local control would allow communities to work within a general framework but develop the particular mode of education best suited to local needs. Yet the very act of seeking to reduce the conflicts of centralized administration created the additional problem of inadequate revenues. Consequently state governments, in seeking to reduce the competition among localities for scarce educational revenues, demanded federal aid to education. A second attempt at conflict resolution, that of increasing the amount of available resources, was made. But federal resources are also limited, and so guidelines have been drawn up for the dispersion of federal aid to education. Whether segregated school districts should receive federal monies, and indeed the manner in which one defines segregation, have become problems because of the existence of the federal government in the educational system. Should federal aid be apportioned to the states on the basis of the number of school-age children or by need, and if by need, what criteria should the federal government set for determining need? Should there be aid for higher education and for private as well as public schools? If the federal government controls the purse strings, shouldn't it be able to dictate exactly how the money should be spent and thereby indirectly engage in control of curriculum? Would federal aid and control give the government a big propaganda tool? These and related questions are raised once school funding and the guidelines for educational programs are no longer purely a state or local concern.

Certainly federalism is one valid means of coping, or avoiding the necessity of coping, with many of the distributional conflicts which arise in a heterogeneous society. By granting autonomy to various regions or localities which may be more homogeneous than the larger unit, governments can cut down on the need for interaction among various groups and, therefore, the level of conflict. Federalism is merely a form of administrative decentralization. As such, it offers additional arenas in which citizen grievances can be raised and acted upon. While the problems of coordinated action which exist in a federal system are large, the ability of the system to provide channels for the raising of conflicts and grievances probably does serve to reduce the level of hostility. This is not to imply that federalism is a universal panacea applicable in all situations. Even in those situations where federation makes sense, it may only postpone instead of solve basic conflicts.

Altering the Payoffs

There are additional ways in which a society can cope with its conflicts. Another broad category of response involves the nature of the resources and the payoffs involved in particular conflicts. **Payoffs** are the distributions associated with particular conflicts. They may be in the form of money or status, or they may involve such specific factors as the extension of linguistic parity to the country's second language. As we indicated in Chapter 2, conflict is a function of the stakes involved in a contest and the degree to which the participants view it as a zero sum situation. The higher the stakes and the more closely the situation resembles a zero-sum game, the more intense the conflict will be. Since no resources are infinite, conflicts often tend to develop into situations resembling zero-sum games. Decision makers, by altering the payoffs, may keep a conflict from moving to a zero-sum situation, thereby lowering the intensity of feeling which surrounds it. They can alter the payoffs in either (or both) of two ways. One method is to increase the size of the payoffs by committing additional resources to the resolution of the conflict. The other is to introduce side payments, to offer rewards outside of those involved in the conflict itself. Although these methods will sometimes overlap, we shall consider each of them separately.

Expansion of Resources

When a government is faced with conflicts over the distribution of scarce resources, it often finds that any solution will be greeted hostilely by the losing side or sides. Accordingly, decision makers may try to lessen the costs of losing and may even seek to structure the situation so that all participants are better off than they were when the conflict began. The only way in which this can be done is to add to the resources available for resolving the conflict.

FUNDING EDUCATION. As we mentioned earlier in this chapter, funding education in the United States has posed a great problem for all levels of governments. There is intense competition among school districts for state and federal funds and conflict within school districts as to which programs deserve to be most heavily funded. Private schools as well have begun to increasingly demand some form of government help. In many ways private parochial schools have been particularly hard hit by the need for upgrading their facilities since so much of their operating revenue is dependent on voluntary contributions. Most public school associations have fought any idea of providing state or federal revenues for private schools. They argue that this would remove needed revenues from the public schools. Private schools, on the other hand, maintain that they remove a certain burden from the public school system. If all the children currently enrolled in religious and other private schools were suddenly to enter the public school system, many districts simply could not handle the additional student population.

No matter how tactful the private schools are or how minor their requests, however, state legislatures have always encountered stiff resistance to giving aid to private schools, particularly religious schools. Opponents maintain that such aid would amount to subsidizing religious instruction. They maintain that while parochial schools do relieve some of the crowding in the public schools, to subsidize them would be wrong. They argue that it would be better and more honest if all students went to public schools and the states were forced to face up to their responsibility to provide adequate educational opportunities to all school-age children.

Within the following set of assumptions, let us see how the hostility and level of conflict may rise in such a situation. First, we shall assume that aid to schools represents a fixed percentage of the state budget. Second, we shall assume that in previous years no allocations have been made for aid to parochial schools. Certain legislators are building up heavy pressure for some form of aid to parochial schools, because without it several schools in their districts may be forced to close. This pressure is being countered by the various public education associations, PTAs, teacher organizations, and citizen groups opposed to aid to religious schools. As luck would have it, it is an election year and emotions on the issue are running high. Any aid to parochial schools is perceived of as coming from the revenues previously earmarked for support to the public schools. The pressures being put on legislators who come from districts where there is a relatively well-developed parochial school system and also many people strongly opposed to parochial school aid are enormous. It is the type of situation where no one is likely to be pleased. To grant any aid to parochial schools is to invite the certain wrath of those opposed to such measures and to take on almost the entire public school lobby. To deny aid to parochial schools would be to risk the anger of powerful religious groups and probably all those voters who have children in parochial schools. It may also invite further conflict in the event that such schools, without any state aid, would be forced to close and their students would all be added to the public school enrollment.

In short, our legislators face a serious zero-sum situation. They must find some way to alter the payoffs so as, if not to please everybody, at least to lower the level of hostility. What, if any options are open to them? Their most obvious solution is to raise the percentage of the total budget allocated to education. They can then provide additional revenue for public schools (thus appeasing the public school lobby) and also propose some minor financial assistance to parochial and other private schools. In effect, they are raising the payoffs to all the participants. While the opponents of aid to parochial schools will still be upset over such schools being given any aid, they will be appeased to some extent by the increase in the total support available to public schools. While the supporters of parochial schools may be displeased that the level of support is far from that which they desired, the legislation will at least mark a beginning of state aid to such schools and represent a base from which further commitments can be extracted. The conflict between the antagonists has not been resolved, but the expansion of payoffs for both sides may mute the conflict somewhat.

Increasing the payoffs is always an alternative form of conflict resolution, but it has its obvious costs. If resources were infinite, then one could always expand the resources available in order to mute the conflict. Yet we need only think of the old curmudgeon who does not care about any aid to education, who will fight all increases in governmental expenditures, to understand the possible drawbacks of this strategy. Governmental leaders do not control unlimited resources, and any expansion of payoffs in one area means either a cutback for other sectors of the budget or an increase in taxes. What the alteration of payoffs involves, then, is the problem of setting priorities. The shift of funds from one program to another can always lead to its own set of conflicts. For example, increasing the aid to education may serve to deflect funds from public housing, or may take funds away from highway programs or recreational facilities. Thus, before legislators attempt to solve a conflict through expanding the resources devoted to it, they must carefully consider what the consequences of shifting resources are likely to be.

Side Payments

The applications of side payments to a conflict, on the other hand, does not always involve a reordering of priorities. Political leaders have alternative resources at their disposal which they may apply to the resolution of conflict. For example, the President or Governor presents a budget to the legislature each year. The budget reflects the priorities, the relative importance which the administration has assigned to various services and functions. It is the product of a series of compromises among departments and is itself a response to the demands of various agencies and bureaus for limited funds. When the legislature considers the budget, there again will be diverse demands and conflicts generated concerning the priorities which the budget represents and the various programs in which legislators have a particular interest. The President, of course, desires to have the budget pass in a final form which is closest to his original suggestions. Therefore, he will be hesitant to make compromises on the budget itself. If the budget is changed substantially, he will not be able to allocate resources as he wishes. While it is inevitable that the legislature will make changes, the President will do his best to keep those changes to an absolute minimum. He therefore will seek to build a majority coalition for his budget. In the process, one of the resources he may use is his ability to offer side payments to supporters. He may use the patronage at his disposal as one source of side payments. He can promise jobs for senators and congressmen to make available to their supporters in exchange for the promise from such legislators that they will support the budget. He may win over other legislators by promising to give his support to certain legislation which these individuals strongly want. For instance, he might be able to pick up support by promising some representatives that he would push for gun control legislation or that he will support legislation to revise the immigration quotas. He may promise to campaign for those members of his party who give him support in the legislature. Another form of side payment which a President might bring into the bargaining is the allocation of government services and the placement of government installations. The budget usually includes a certain number of public works projects such as harbor dredging, flood control, model cities aid, government contracts, and so forth. The President can promise legislators that certain of these projects will be done in their districts or states if they will support the budget. This offer of aid is not an unimportant side payment. Such projects provide the voter with tangible evidence that his congressman is working for him. The legislator may be willing to bend a little more to support the budget requests of the President if he knows that he will receive direct political benefit from it.

The use of side payments are a means of achieving support, of building a majority coalition in order to win in a conflict situation. Obviously there is no necessary symmetry in the ability of both sides in a conflict to offer side payments. A President may have a far greater array of side payments at his disposal to form a majority coalition than is true of his opponents. A judicious use of side payments is one way of muting opposition and bringing people over to your side.

Both side payments and the expansion of resources work to modify conflict, to reduce the hostility involved and the potential cost of losing. Yet, there are basic differences between the two means of handling conflict. In expanding resources, one is trying to move away from a constant sum conflict toward a situation in which no one is worse off after the decision is made than he was before. In reality, of course, everybody does not win because the additional resources have come from other areas or programs. But at least, within the confines of the particular conflict, in the process of increasing the payoffs some of the hostility surrounding the conflict may decrease. This approach involves expanding activity and action where there is the greatest degree of feelings and intensity. Governments are constantly involved in such activity: They "put their money where the action is," where there is greatest stress. Since they are dealing with limited resources, decision makers are constantly faced with the problem of reordering priorities, of shifting scarce resources to the most pressing areas. This method assumes that all problems will not rise to the surface at once. Should such a total crisis occur, the capacity of any political system to respond would be threatened. There would be no place from which to draw resources in order to add them to all the programs which needed them. Indeed, this is part of the traditional argument for limited governmental powers. Those who feel that a government should be restricted in its activities note that the more areas in which government is involved, the greater the demands for services, the greater the competition between agencies for scarce funds, and the greater the likelihood of dissatisfaction. If such dissatisfaction continues long enough, the government will not be able to respond to all demands appropriately.

By offering side payments, on the other hand, decision makers can gain support for their programs and placate the opposition by offering them inducements from other areas. In essence they are saying, "I cannot satisfy your demands on this issue, but if you will support me or at least abstain from publicly opposing me, I will help you on other issues." Side payments can be used most successfully with those who are indifferent or at least not very committed to either position on an issue. Yet in offering resources which are external to the dispute itself, the decision maker eventually is still dealing with limited resources. His success in offering side payments hinges upon the amount of external resources which are available and which he is willing to commit on any given issue. Furthermore, as conflicts become more heated and widespread, the number of people who are indifferent decreases, and therefore the likelihood of being able to use side payments as a means of achieving support diminishes accordingly.

Improving Communication Patterns

Another method by which one can avoid the potentially devastating effects of unrestrained conflict is to improve and broaden the pattern of communication. As we indicated in Chapter 7, in any conflict, communication patterns tend to reinforce the opinions of the various combatants. As the conflict becomes more intense and general, communication among hostile and antagonistic parties usually decreases while intragroup communication increases and reinforces the predispositions of combatants. People tend to talk more frequently with those with whom they agree and ever less frequently with their opponents. Gradually each side isolates itself or cuts itself off from alternative and especially adverse sources of information. If such a process continues unabated, polarization of the community or society proceeds at a fairly rapid pace. Political decision makers must therefore concern themselves with preventing such polarization and keeping the lines of communication open. Not to do so is to invite generalized conflict, violence, and possibly even death. From any standpoint such an alternative is undesirable. But what can decision makers do to reverse the process of polarization? Perhaps their chief hope for doing so lies in redirecting and controlling communications so that they reduce rather than heighten the levels of conflict.

THE FORUM. A decision maker's first task, in attempting to reduce conflict, may be to keep the lines of communication open between antagonistic groups. Perhaps he will introduce a forum or some sort of mechanism by which the positions of both sides can be presented. The United Nations is a forum where various nations are able to maintain communication with each other in stressful periods. It is not so much the debate on the floor of the United Nations which may be significant, but rather that in the corridors and in the conference rooms the representatives of various powers are able to talk with each other and prevent conflict from arising out of misunderstanding.

ARBITRATION. In labor disputes where hostilities are mounting,

arbiters are often called in to keep negotiations going and to help bring about a settlement. Union leaders and employers may have been meeting for weeks; and with each new meeting fatigue, tension, and the possibility of the negotiators' making careless or inflammatory remarks have increased. Often such bargaining becomes extremely hostile, and negotiations are broken off. It is usually at this point that arbiters are brought in. Suppose that it was already too late for the arbiter to bring the two sides together for a meeting. He will then talk separately with the two parties, communicating back and forth to each side the position of the other. He seeks to provide a basis for calling joint meetings once again and concluding the negotiations. The arbiter becomes the primary communication link between the two sides and, to the degree to which he is respected by both parties, his presence helps keep communication open and offers the possibility of a negotiated settlement. Indeed, arbitration is predicated on the importance of preventing communication channels from being closed off. The success or failure of any arbiter hangs upon his ability to maintain and sometimes even to reopen lines of communication between antagonistic groups.

THE PANEL. Nevertheless, decision makers may often find other mechanisms more appropriate for keeping communications open between belligerents. For example, a mayor may appoint a panel of distinguished and ostensibly impartial citizens to investigate a conflict and make a report. Such commissions usually provide more than a report. They become a forum where all protagonists can make their opinions known. The commission hearings provide a neutral ground for interaction among parties which would not be possible otherwise. In addition they provide a forum in which the uncommitted may appraise the positions of both sides to a dispute.

Such panels also serve an alternative function, that of legitimizing policy decisions. Often when the government plans a departure from previous policy, it may set up a panel to assess the particular situation and recommend the appropriate forms of action. It may include potential opponents on the panel in the hope that if their support can be gained, opposition or conflict to the policy decision can be reduced.

One example of such behavior can be seen after the conclusion of World War II, when Europe was ravaged and many countries were on the verge of bankruptcy and starvation. President Truman and many of his advisers felt that the United States should provide massive loans and credit to relieve the immediate misery of Europe and aid in the reconstruction of that war-torn continent. Out of this concern was born the Marshall Plan and related legislation.

Proponents of the Marshall Plan feared that there might be great opposition to the program. Economy-minded Republicans in Congress might balk at large outlays of money for foreign purposes. Many Americans were weary of European problems and wished once again to direct their attention inward. Furthermore, the plan involved giving away large amounts of resources when the United States itself was going through the painful transition from a wartime to a peacetime economy and, in fact, when many wartime governmental controls were still in effect. All these factors worked against any extended United States efforts in Europe. In response, Truman sought to quiet his most persistent opponents. Before Secretary of State George Marshall made his famous speech at Harvard on June 5, 1947, President Truman had invited some sympathetic Republican legislators such as Senators Arthur Vandenberg and Tom Connally and Representative Charles Eaton to the White House to be briefed on the administration's plans. Their support was crucial in forming a bipartisan basis of support for the program. Truman convinced the Republican leadership of the House of Representatives (the Republicans were in a majority at the time) to send their own fact-finding committee to Europe to see if the Marshall Plan was justified.

> This eighteen member bipartisan group, whose chairman was the scholarly and dignified Representative Christian A. Herter of Massachusetts . . . sailed on the **Queen Mary** on the last day of August, 1947 and returned a month and a half later. Even such a hard-core isolationist as Chicago's Representative . . . Everett McKinley Dirksen became a practicing convert to the cause of the Marshall Plan as did most of the other members of the group.[2]

The use of one's potential opponents to drum up support for a program is a dangerous but very effective strategy. Similarly, the naming of Paul Hoffman, a prominent industrialist with strong ties in the business and financial communities, to head the recovery program also was a way of reducing potential opposition to the program. Here was no impractical schemer, but rather a hardheaded businessman

---

[2] Cabell Phillips, **The Truman Presidency,** New York: Macmillan, 1966, p. 187.

tackling a difficult but possible and important job. The plan was approved and was regarded as one of the most successful acts of the Truman Presidency.

Redefining the Conflict

Another strategy for resolving conflict involves actually redefining it. As we noted, conflict tends to move from the specific to the general. One means of resolving conflict which threatens to become very severe is to reverse this process and emphasize the specifics, the negotiable aspects of the problem. This is a preliminary and important step before negotiations can actually begin. Being able to redefine the conflict becomes particularly significant in military battles. For example, let us consider a border dispute between two countries. At first there may only be limited skirmishes. As the struggle becomes more involved, however, the original dispute often spreads to a conflict between two types of political systems. The charges multiply and the rhetoric becomes increasingly general and bitter. By this time all-out fighting has broken out, and the possibility for negotiation has decreased.

While two antagonists may be able to negotiate a border dispute, it is far more difficult to bargain about a conflict which has come to include questions of life-style and the virtue of one country as opposed to another. If the conflict is to be settled off the battlefield, both sides will have to redefine the conflict and bring it back to the original boundary dispute and negotiate the points of contention. In the Middle East, the Arab-Israeli dispute might become negotiable if the questions could be resolved to one of drawing meaningful boundary lines. As long as the conflict pits two suspicious and antagonistic communities against each other, resolution seems quite difficult.

In both World Wars, the United States and its allies placed themselves in the situation where unconditional surrender was the only acceptable course of action. Whether such a strategy was correct or not is difficult to assess, since the comparison is always with what might have been. Certainly, the rhetoric of World War I was one of general conflict. The Americans and the Allies were fighting "to make the world safe for democracy." It is hard to think how such a goal allows one to opt for anything but unconditional surrender of one's opponents. How does one negotiate a world safe for democracy?

Similarly, during World War II there was little evidence, at least in the early years of the war, that negotiations with the Nazis would have been productive or, had a settlement been reached, that the Nazis would have stuck to it. In any case, the Atlantic Charter, signed by Churchill and Roosevelt in August, 1941, set out goals for the Allies which precluded anything but the total and unconditional surrender of the Axis powers. The demand for total and unconditional surrender, particularly in the Far East, led to the Yalta Conference in which Russian participation in the war was practically purchased and to the development and use of the atomic bomb on Hiroshima and Nagasaki. One can argue the merits of both decisions. However, they were in many cases the normal extensions of a policy of unconditional surrender.

The ability to redefine conflict, to move from a general, intensified conflict back to the specific points of contention, is not easy, but it often is the only way that a conflict can be peacefully negotiated. In the Korean War, the United States and its allies, under the auspices of a United Nations Security Council resolution, sent troops to help the South Korean government repel the invasion of North Korean troops. The conflict drained the manpower and the resources of all the warring nations. The fighting ranged over South Korea and into North Korea as well, and was protracted and bitter. Indeed, the Korean War, if unchecked, could easily have become the ultimate conflict between Communist and non-Communist forces. When General of the Army Douglas MacArthur recommended to President Truman that he be allowed to pursue North Korean and Chinese Communist troops across the border into China, Truman refused. His refusal, in essence, redefined the conflict. The President maintained that the struggle was not against all Communist systems but rather was a limited response to aggression against the South Koreans by the North Koreans and Chinese Communists. His decision met with great resistence and opposition at home. MacArthur publicly spoke out against Truman's conduct of the war. As a result, Truman relieved MacArthur of his command and this in turn created even greater domestic controversy. Yet, it was probably that decision which allowed for a negotiated cease-fire. While the negotiations did not satisfy either side, and the possibility exists for a renewal of hostilities, it did bring an end to a bloody and costly conflict. Had the war been total, no process of conflict resolution, no negotiation no matter how skillfully handled, would have been successful. It is significant to note that the negotiations did not result in a cease-fire until 1953. Only when conflict is limited and specific in nature can negotiation take place.

LIMITS OF AVOIDANCE STRATEGIES

So far we have been concerned with the various strategies which can be used to moderate conflict. Needless to say, not every attempt to resolve a conflict is successful. As we have discussed, some of the most practical strategies are basically avoidance mechanisms. They are means whereby decision makers can restructure or redefine the problem enough to avoid having to come to grips with it in its totality. Federation can be conceived of in this way. It is based on the assumption that by removing much of the interaction among antagonistic groups, the conflicts will become less pressing, and over time the society will develop the resources to handle them. Better yet, when the patterns of interaction have been changed, the original conflict may diminish or even disappear altogether. For example, many multilingual or multiracial countries, upon gaining their independence, have opted for some sort of federal system. Their hope is that through being loosely bound together in a national state, the various groups over time will create bonds of identity which transcend the original differences. This may or may not be wishful thinking. In Nigeria, federation did not prevent a bloody civil war. Similarly this can be noted in the United States. In Canada antagonism between the French and English populations is still strong. Yet, in the United States, there are signs that some of the regional distinctness is declining. The South still remains somewhat of a separate entity but the rapid pace of industrialization and urbanization makes the differences diminish a bit more each year.

The evidence, therefore, that federation allows time for feelings of national identity to develop is mixed. If, despite federation, conflict still smolders and even flares up, then the alternatives left open to citizens are more limited than ever. The alternatives are forced unification, at the cost of repression or civil war, or allowing dissatisfied groups to secede. Minority groups may feel that if satisfaction is impossible within the federal system, their only alternative is secession. Should the majority group be unwilling to allow such secession (as was the case in the United States), the result may be a tragic and bloody civil war.

There are similar problems involved in the failure of other means of conflict resolution. Consider the use of side payments, the attempt to form a majority coalition on the basis of issues and resources external to the particular conflict. The ability to win here is not determined by negotiation of the issue itself but rather through the application of resources and the introduction of issues external to the central conflict. Such a strategy is often successful, particularly, as we mentioned before, when many potential participants are indifferent to the outcome of the particular conflict. The immediate success or failure of side payments may depend upon whether decision makers have sufficient resources, sufficient side payments to win the support of those currently uncommitted. Yet if this sounds like so much bribery, we need only remember that an alternative way of resolving a conflict is to involve the indifferents by generalizing the conflict. Generalizing, of course, tends to intensify it, to cut off communications between opposing sides, and therefore to decrease the possibility of negotiated settlement. Introducing side payments does not involve these costs.

Nevertheless, side payments are, in essence, an avoidance strategy, and as such bring with them a danger of their own. Remember that, even if the issue is settled, it is not resolved by coming to grips with the problem and the opposition, but relies instead on the addition of external factors. Suppose that a majority coalition has been successfully formed. In the United States, more often than not such a coalition is formed by the agglomeration of minorities.[3] These coalitions of minorities do not pose a problem in and of themselves. Obviously the manner in which such coalitions are formed can be crucial. If on any given issue all groups have an equal chance to become part of the majority coalition, then the resulting coalition is likely to provide for at least limited satisfaction of the demands of the population. As long as the opportunity to participate in coalitions is open, then the problem of majority tyranny is not significant. When side payments lead to the formation of a consistent majority which always excludes certain segments of the population, however, the degree of fairness and of democracy in legislation will inevitably be questioned. Groups which are consistently excluded from participation in a majority coalition may come to feel that their government is unresponsive and incapable of giving any satisfaction or help to them. As those who are excluded from the political process perceive it to be increasingly irrelevant or unwilling to respond to their demands, they will begin to move outside

---

[3] Robert A. Dahl, **A Preface to Democratic Theory,** Chicago: University of Chicago Press, 1956, p. 128.

of accepted channels to seek redress of their grievances. Eventually they may turn to open revolt. Once again we are faced with the question of what happens when all our strategies fall flat, when the process of conflict resolution cannot cope with the strains and demands made on political institutions.

WHEN CONFLICT RESOLUTION BREAKS DOWN

What are the consequences of a political system's inability to resolve conflict peacefully? Obviously as dissatisfaction rises, the probability of violent or antisystem behavior among segments of the population increases. Nevertheless, the responses to such situations vary enormously. Ordinarily either the existing system will be modified drastically and new patterns will emerge or the political elites in power will employ all their coercive resources to reduce opposition and ensure that the present structures are maintained. Most societies can tolerate degrees of conflict and even degrees of violence. However, when the amount of violence reaches a point where the normal procedures of conflict resolution are no longer applicable, change seems inevitable. At the very beginning of the text we indicated that political institutions are established to provide regularity and order among all persons in the society. When violence erupts we know that the system is no longer functioning adequately because segments of the population feel that the existing institutions cannot or will not respond to their needs. Few people can stand great uncertainty and anxiety for long. Yet when the normal political process gives way to violence, the average citizen no longer can order his life with any degree of security. The more violence, the more high-pitched will be the demands for some form of action, either through modification of existing institutions or through repression of those committing violent acts.[4]

In the United States during the Depression many citizens felt that the democratic system no longer was capable of handling their problems and demands. For many of these people fascism represented the way of the future, the only viable means by which a modern technological society could govern itself. For most Americans the Roosevelt administration, despite its many failures, brought with it a renewal of faith in

---

[4] Many have suggested that Nazi Germany and Fascist Italy were precisely such responses to high levels of uncertainty among the population. For a further discussion of this, see William Kornhauser, **The Politics of Mass Society,** New York: Free Press, 1959.

democratic government and in its ability to handle situations of stress.

In France, at the close of World War II, the Fourth Republic was faced with different struggles. France, like other major powers, had numerous colonial territories which were demanding independence. Unlike Britain, which was able to liquidate its colonial empire fairly effectively, the French seemed inadequate to the challenge of letting their colonies go peacefully. On the right, the supporters of General de Gaulle did not participate in the government and had expressed their dismay over its weaknesses. On the left, the republic faced strong Communist opposition. Meanwhile, the pattern of weak coalition governments which had characterized the Third Republic was continued. The French were faced with the problems of decolonization, and the trauma of Indo-China and the humiliation of Dienbienphu accentuated this. On top of all this came the demands for Algerian independence. The inability of the Fourth Republic to decide either to grant Algeria independence or assert dominance there finally led to the demise of the republic and the formation of the present regime, the Fifth Republic. As the crisis over Algeria deepened, most forces turned to Charles de Gaulle, the symbol of French unity during the war, as a man who might be able to unify the country and prevent what seemed like a possible civil war. De Gaulle came to power in 1958 and was finally able to liquidate the French interest in Algeria, but almost at the risk of an army coup against him. In the French case, as in the case of other countries, the instability and chaos which plagued the existing political institutions finally resulted in the breakdown of that system and its replacement. Despite strains, the Fifth Republic has now lasted as long as the Fourth Republic did, and seems, despite problems, capable of continuing.

CONFLICT AND DECISION MAKING: AN OVERVIEW

Throughout this book we have been concerned with conflict and conflict resolution as one of the most significant and interesting aspects of the political process. We have purposely focused our attention on large-scale conflicts. While these may not be typical of the range of conflict which a society must face each day, the ability of a political system to deal with large-scale conflict is perhaps its ultimate test.

Political institutions represent the attempt of civilized man to provide the means for what philosophers might call the just life. It is the job of political systems to provide those rules which allow people to pursue their goals, lead their lives, and plan for the future. As our lives have become increasingly complex, as societies have become more interdependent, there are significant problems which arise from the fact that we may pursue differing life-styles and different goals. Democratic systems face the particular burden of trying to mediate among conflicting interests, of trying to provide for the interests of their citizens and yet insure that their actions in satisfying one segment of the population are not detrimental to others. This is a difficult task and one which can breed conflict.

The resolution of conflict is dependent upon many things. Not the least of which is the character of the political institutions. The way in which a society develops its political institutions conditions its ability to respond to change, its ability to respond to conflict, and the manner of the response. The success of various modes of conflict resolution depends in part upon how much the population desires to remain as an integrated system. The attitudes and predispositions of the population affect whether conflict resolution will be effective and whether it will be peaceful or violent.

With today's complexity and increased interdependence among peoples and societies, the means and channels of peaceful conflict resolution are increasingly challenged. As the potential for conflict rises, so must our capacity to deal with its underlying causes. It is impossible to eradicate all conflict; rather we must understand that an inability to peacefully and sequentially deal with problems means that at some time we may have to come to grips with many problems simultaneously, the magnitude of which may preclude peaceful settlement. Therefore, we must understand both the interaction of factors which cause conflict and the institutional structures which can help us to resolve it. We must be able to distinguish between conflict which is useful and stimulating for the progress of a society and the world and conflict which can only exacerbate tensions and result in violence and bloodshed. This is the challenge of politics and it is with this that the analysis of political institutions and processes should concern itself.

SUGGESTED READINGS

Cooke, Jacob (ed.), **The Federalist**, Cleveland: Meridian Books, 1961.
Dahl, Robert A., **A Preface to Democratic Theory**, Chicago: University of Chicago Press, 1956.

Dawson, R. M., **The Government of Canada**, Toronto: Toronto Press, 1952.

Kornhauser, William, **The Politics of Mass Society**, New York: Free Press, 1959.

MacMahon, A. W. (ed.), **Federalism: Mature and Emergent**, New York: Columbia University Press, 1955.

Riker, William, **Federalism,** Boston: Atlantic-Little, Brown, 1964.

Spanier, John W., **The Truman-MacArthur Controversy and the Korean War**, New York: Norton, 1965.

Tönnies, Ferdinand, **Community and Society**, Charles P. Loomis (trans.), New York: Harper & Row, 1957.

Van Doren, Carl, **The Great Rehearsal**, New York: Viking, 1948.

Name Index

Subject Index

DATE DUE
